RAOUL
'SONNY'
BALCAEN

Published in October 2022

ISBN: 978-1-910505-77-9

Edited by Mark Hughes
Designed by Richard Parsons

Printed and bound in Malta by Gutenberg Press

Published by Evro Publishing
Westrow House, Holwell, Sherborne, Dorset DT9 5LF, UK

www.evropublishing.com

RAOUL 'SONNY' BALCAEN

MY EXCITING TRUE-LIFE STORY IN MOTOR RACING
FROM TOP-FUEL DRAG-RACING PIONEER TO JIM HALL,
REVENTLOW SCARAB, CARROLL SHELBY AND BEYOND

BY RAOUL F. BALCAEN, III
CO-WRITTEN WITH JILL AMADIO AND PETE LYONS

DEDICATION

First, I would like to dedicate this book to Franziska, my loving wife and partner of over two decades. Thanks to her steadfast encouragement, I decided to share my life story of many passions.

Secondly, because it all started with my mad love of motor racing, I would like to acknowledge and honor all the friends who were involved in my early racing career, and who taught me so much not only then, but throughout my life. Their help, genius and insights inspired and influenced my own efforts. Many of them are no longer with us, however their memories will live on. Each one has made their very special contributions and left their thumb print on the evolution of racing. I consider each of them a hero in the world of motorsports, and treasure fond memories of our countless special interactions with each other. Thank you, dear friends:

Ed Iskenderian	Richard "Dick" Reventlow	Mickey Thompson
Ed Donovan	Bruce Kessler	Ken Miles
Tony Nancy	Chuck Daigh	Eddie Meyer
Phil Remington	Harold Daigh	Louis Meyer
Carroll Shelby	Dean Batchelor	Bud Meyer
Jim Hall	Peter Brock	Ed Pink
Robert "Pete"	Larry Shinoda	Ed Winfield
Petersen	Frank McGurk	Bob Toros
Jack Dulin	George Bartell	Nick Arias
Bob Estes	J.C. Agajanian	Vic Edelbrock Sr.
Emil Diedt	Dan Gurney	Vic Edelbrock Jr.
Warren Olson	Skip Hudson	Cal Niday
Pete Clark	Ruth Levy	Sam Hanks
Jim Travers	Joachim Bonnier	Jim Rathmann
Dick Troutman	Phil Hill	Brooks Firestone
Tom Barnes	Richie Ginther	Andy Granatelli
Lance Reventlow	Don Yates	Chuck Pelly

Also, a special thank you to Raoul J. Germain, Jr for his expertise and help with photos

CONTENTS

PART III

PART IV

FOREWORDS

Los Angeles wasn't a global city in the '50s. Residents of its perennial rivals, New York City and San Francisco, dismissed Southern California's huge sprawl of rapidly growing communities as a provincial outpost, rather than a legitimate metropolis. Even its major claim to fame — the slick celebrity machinery of Hollywood — was perceived by its critics as evidence of its lack of seriousness. "Tinseltown," it was called.

But even then, L.A. boasted assets no other American city could match. With its idyllic weather, wide-open spaces and bountiful catalog of natural resources, SoCal had long been a beacon for dreamers and schemers, adventurers and entrepreneurs. The buttoned-down mainstream automobile industry took root in the conservative Midwest. But the anything-goes *racing* industry found a home here in the Southland.

In 1907, motorsports manufacturing colossus Harry Miller set up shop in downtown L.A. to create some of the most advanced racing machines of the time, and a community of racers coalesced around him. Of course, not everybody could afford Miller's jewel-like creations, so resourceful home-builders began upgrading prosaic street cars with clever DIY technology. Before long, they were running their mongrels flat-out on the dry lakes of the Mojave Desert, and the hot rod was born (though the name wouldn't be coined until the next generation).

During the boom that followed World War II, greater Los Angeles emerged as the epicenter of American racing. As the cradle of hot-rod civilization, it also fostered a vast talent pool of self-taught customizers who understood how to make cars go faster. Another element of the region's secret sauce was the presence of the aerospace industry, which created a large cadre of skilled craftsman and a treasure trove of surplus-parts stores filled with cutting-edge components and materials. During the '50s, the sport of drag racing was formalized on the tracks of Southern California. This was where road-racing sports cars featuring American V8 engines were perfected, and when the first American Formula 1 car was built — the Reventlow Scarab, it naturally came out of a shop in Los Angeles.

"It was," says Raoul "Sonny" Balcaen III with characteristic understatement, "a very exciting time."

Sonny ought to know, because he was right there. Born in Los Angeles in 1936, he grew up smack-dab in the middle of all this racing ferment. As a teenager, he successfully raced his own home-built Top Fuel dragster during the formative years of the sport. Later, as a member of the Reventlow team, he was standing in the dyno room when the Scarab Formula 1 engine was fired up for the first time. In between, he was mentored by a who's who of heroes of West Coast road racing, and this experience gave him the know-how to help launch the career of Jim Hall.

I don't want to give the best bits away, so I'll let Sonny recount his remarkable life story in his own inimitable fashion. But the cast of characters you're about to meet includes Pete Petersen, Lance Reventlow, Phil Remington, Carroll Shelby, Leo Goossen, Chuck Daigh, Travers and Coon, Troutman and Barnes. And, of course, Sonny himself, who later went into business with Peter Brock and, after that, founded his own highly successful aftermarket parts company, the Induction Engineering Company.

This book covers both Sonny's fascinating exploits in the racing world and his experience as an entrepreneur. Along the way, he conveys advice about how to succeed in business — and in life, for that matter. Ultimately, this fine memoir is the story of one man. But at the same time, it's also the very personal history of a momentous time and place — a fun read and well worth reading.

Preston Lerner
Motorsports historian, author of the book Scarab

I was initially drawn to the Scarab by two things, its beauty and amazing record as a race car. The Scarab is one of the most beautiful front-engined race cars ever built, and the fact that it continued to win major sports car races for over five seasons is a testament to the thoughtful design and quality construction of the car. I was also fascinated by how Lance Reventlow had, at so young an age, surrounded himself with people like "Sonny" Balcaen who were so exceptional at their craft.

It was only after we began to run the car in vintage races that I fully came to appreciate it as a very special competition vehicle. At racing speed, the Scarab is a delight to drive, very responsive, predictable and secure. It will never turn and bite you unexpectedly. It is a wonderful car in which to go fast. We also learned the extent of the craftsmanship that went into designing and building the Scarab. It reflected the latest European chassis design of the era, but constructed with the quality of an Indy car. Only the Scarab managed to combine the best of both worlds to make it the fastest sports racing car of its era.

Rob Walton
Former Chairman of Walmart, car collector

R aoul writes with the authority of "someone who knows," because he really was there. His stories reflect the free spirit of the times. That's what makes them such enjoyable reading, bringing the reader back to the excitement when white tee shirts and dirty fingernails were status. This book makes you want to get into that time machine!

So take a moment and enjoy reminiscing with Raoul. You'll be glad you did.

Chuck Pelly
Product designer, stylist of first Scarab body

R aoul and I were both 18 when we met at Warren Olson's shop on La Cienega boulevard in Los Angeles. "Sonny" had been hired as a mechanic. I was a parts boy.

All Southern California kids were hot rodders back then, and we also had another 18-year-old, Walon Green. "Wally" joined the team as an all-around helper and to support Warren's wife, Simone, with her work. He went on to be a major writer in the film industry, wining an Academy Award for his documentary, "The Hellstrom Chronicle." Wally Green's first feature film was "The Wild Bunch" for Director Sam Peckinpah.

Also joining our crew was Jack Russell, a mechanic who had just been discharged as a Paratrooper from the Army. Jack went on to be the creator of the movie series "Ocean's Eleven."

So that made three of us four who later went into the movie biz. Sonny took another road to success, and even back then I knew he was different — but I also knew, right away, that we were going to become friends for life!

Bruce Kessler
Filmmaker, Scarab team driver

PROLOGUE
IGNITION

America's first-ever Formula 1 racing engine, a magnificent machine designed and hand-crafted in the USA, barked to life one balmy November day in 1959 near the Pacific shoreline of Southern California. I was there.

In fact, my fingerprint oil was responsible for some of the wisps of smoke we saw curling off the rapidly heating metal. I had helped to build that glistening, bellowing new beauty. It was named the Scarab, and it was going to rule the International Grand Prix world. We were sure of it.

At that moment of mechanical enchantment I'm not sure I was aware of a glamorously pretty young Hollywood movie star standing near me. Well, alright, I was a young man and she was Jill St. John. Of course, I knew she was there.

Nor could I help but see the tall, blond, annoyingly good-looking fellow with her, his face split into a wide grin. You often saw that face in the Hollywood tabloids, because he was an incredibly rich, flamboyant young playboy who couldn't seem to help making news. Beyond that he was a titled European count with a formal name so long you had to turn the page to finish it.

But the takeaway word in there somewhere was Reventlow, and that was the name on our race shop. In what we car racing guys all thought of as real life, Lance Reventlow was one of our drivers, not a pro but one who took a hard, risky craft seriously and was striving to get faster.

We just called him Lance. He was my boss, and Jill was his wife.

The year before, 1958, Reventlow's powerful and beautiful Scarabs had dominated North American sports car racing. Why shouldn't the Formula 1 World Championship fall to him too? It seems to me that the grinning young millionaire was already popping open the bottle of Dom Perignon champagne he had brought along, confident of success.

I hope you can sense the fond smile on my face as I say all that. We racers like to razz each other. In fact I'd been working for Lance for two years, the Reventlows had been kind to me, and we were good friends.

Honest, though, my total focus was on the deafening beast before us. What an exciting occasion — a newborn racing engine inhaling its first whiff of oxygen, savoring its first taste of high-octane gasoline, flexing all its precisely machined rotating and reciprocating muscles and sinews for the first time.

Lance's Reventlow Automobiles Inc. (RAI) was an amazing group of seasoned racing veterans, some of our world's most talented, skillful, brilliant and famous people from all corners of the sport, especially dragsters, Indy cars and the quickly growing sports car scene. By some kind of crazy luck, I had been a member of the team right from the beginning. That was in 1957, when I was 21. I was already a well accomplished race engineer when I came aboard, but my real education was only just beginning.

Every day I had the fortune to be working with — and learning from — the likes of renowned engine designer Leo Goossen, who had created horsepower for immortal Indycar engine makers Miller, Offenhauser and Meyer & Drake; incredible fabricator Phil Remington, who could make literally anything; metalworking artist Emil Diedt, who was hand-forming the F1 car's aluminum body; the great Chuck Daigh, not only our star driver but also an engineer/fabricator/welder/machinist and general miracle maker everywhere in the shop; and Warren Olson, team manager here at Reventlow but also my previous employer, mentor and friend at his own sports car shop up in West Hollywood.

Four other legends worked on our Scarabs. First were car-building partners Dick Troutman and Tom Barnes. They had polished their fabrication talents with famed Indycar pioneer Frank Kurtis (father of the low-profile "Roadster" concept that won the 500 in 1953 and 1954, ending the more upright "dirt car" era), and recently had launched their own business with a clever and successful sports car. Chuck Daigh had been their winning driver.

In addition, engine masters Jim Travers and Frank Coon, who combined their names to create the brand TRACO, were literally next door to RAI. Travers and Coon had built much of Scarab's desmo F1 engine, and the dyno we were using actually stood in their shop.

All of us racers were happy — if sometimes noisy — neighbors there in Culver City's magical "Thunder Alley," aka West Jefferson Boulevard, not far from Los Angeles International Airport.

For all the other guys around that dyno that day, this first run of a new powerplant must have been old hat. Or maybe they were like me, trying to act like it wasn't the thrill of a lifetime.

Having come from drag racing, where I built and drove my own cars, I knew my way around hot-rodded passenger car engines. But here was one that never saw an assembly line. It had been designed on blank paper purely for open-wheel competition at the highest level. How imposing it looked, bristling with what I thought of as exotic, advanced technologies like twin overhead camshafts and desmodromic valves.

It looked bigger than it was, I thought. Inside, its cylinder displacement was a lot smaller than commonplace pushrod motors that I'd grown up with — a mere 150 cubic inches, per the 2.5-liter maximum required by Formula 1 regulations at the time, compared to my own dragster's unrestricted 302. But there was no denying what a gorgeous little motor it was. An exquisitely crafted work of handmade art.

One that suddenly burst awake like a sleeping bear. As we stood around it, maybe with some of us trying to resist the primal impulse to run away, it started firing angry bursts of exhaust roar into a duct that vented the fumes up through the ceiling. A hose spewed hot cooling water out across Traco's shop floor into the alley. The vibrating thing was bolted securely to stout steel rails on the floor, but as it revved up you could feel all that horsepower penned inside working up a nervous frenzy to stampede.

I didn't know what a Formula 1 engine should sound like, but frankly, I expected it to be louder. Under the exhaust sound we could hear all the rotating and reciprocating mechanical elements hard at work. Kind of noisily, I thought. And the sound didn't seem quite right.

Because of my years of drag strip experience I knew that the more air you get into an engine the more performance you achieve. As you work with dragsters, you start being able to tell how they're performing by their sound. Listening to the Scarab straining against the resistance of the test bed, it seemed to me that the intake ports could have been larger. I thought the oil galleys looked a little constricted, too.

I kept all this to myself, of course. I may have been the young kid on the block, but I had been around that block long enough to know that opinions of juniors are seldom welcome!

That shining memory is from a time long ago, way back in the middle of the last century. But I keep seeing it in my mind. I have to assume it was a seminal moment that would help shape and guide my life — a life filled with equally memorable occasions and, to be honest, achievements of which I am darned proud.

My early years were impelled by a passion for racing. I was a pioneer driver and builder in drag racing and other motorsports. I gained expertise in making engines put out more power, including inventing and manufacturing the necessary special parts. At various times I have been an engineer for legendary racers Carroll Shelby, Jim Hall and Bruce Kessler, among others.

Always an entrepreneur, I started up and was CEO of my own successful company, IECO, to manufacture equipment to transform a Plain-Jane ordinary car into a hot GT. I parlayed my business experience into consulting for other automotive companies, including Shelby's. I have an MBA degree in Economics.

Beyond that I was an avid pilot and plane owner. And I love motorcycles. I am an Oenologist — which means an expert in the science of making wines. Also I count myself a dedicated gourmet, as fine dining is all part of fine wine appreciation.

"The Gearhead Gourmet," a friend calls me. I like it!

Those are all different things, but I feel that I was able to be successful at them because I applied the same hard-driving enthusiasm that I had for racing, way back at the beginning.

For me it really was the Golden Age of racing, and I was right in the thick of it, helping to make it happen. In return, racing made me who I am.

PART I

CHAPTER 1
MY OWN
BEGINNINGS

When I was young I was known as Sonny, for the logical reason that I was named after my father, Raoul. His name was also his father's, which of course makes me Raoul Balcaen, III.

Other than that faint, false aroma of aristocracy, I think I'm a pretty normal, everyday guy.

Both those names have roots in what is now Belgium. Our surname, which we pronounce with the accent on the second syllable, "Bal-KAIN," has been known for centuries in the university city of Ghent.

Although it's located inland, halfway between the North Sea coastline and Brussels, Ghent has long been a busy seaport, thanks to extensive networks of canals linking up with natural rivers. Plundered by Vikings, conquered by Rome, then a prosperous market town in the Middle Ages, Ghent is most notable in American history as the site for the signing of the Treaty of Ghent, the 1814 agreement that ended the War of 1812 between the United States and Great Britain.

Three years later, in 1817, King William I of the Netherlands (Belgium was not yet an independent nation back then) founded *Universiteit Gent*, the oldest institution of higher learning in the city.

The earliest records of my ancestors date back to 1684 with a Joannes Balcaen. Several generations later we find my grandfather, Raoul Gregorius Francis Sylvanius Balcaen number I. His story began in 1879.

Grandpa Raoul was a graduate mechanical engineer, one of very few in Belgium in those days. His skills attracted the attention of an American railroad businessman, who was seeking highly qualified engineers for his company. He recruited Belgium's *Monsieur* Balcaen and brought him and his wife, Rachel (*née* Verlot), to America as immigrants. We're not precisely sure of the year, but think it was in the 1902-1905 timeframe. The couple settled in Rochester, New York.

That's where my father was born in 1911 and given his father's full name.

Raoul the second was the youngest of five children. First was my future uncle Louis, who may have been born in Belgium but who would grow up to be an engineer with Eastman Kodak company there in Rochester. Next came two sisters, Rachel and Marie, and then a second son. My uncle Paul became a tool and die maker. He was two years older than my father, Raoul.

My grandfather's new employer was the Buffalo, Rochester and Pittsburgh Railway. It was quite a well-established, sprawling system, built to transport coal as well as passengers, and apparently it included urban tram lines. Mr. Balcaen's keen engineering mind went to work inventing and developing automatic switching systems for train tracks and turntables, along with other products. His equipment was brilliant stuff, and it was patented. But the patents were retained and owned by the company that employed him.

That happened again to him later, when he helped set up the new Rochester Carburetor Company. All the patents he earned were held by the bosses rather than the inventor. My grandfather never saw a nickel of royalties. That little fact seems to have lodged deeply into my own brain.

Whether that played any role in what came next I can't say, but the primary motivator was a doctor's advice. He told my grandmother Rachel to get out of the Upstate NY winters and find a warmer, dryer climate.

Her third son, my father, was the first to go to Los Angeles. I'm not sure if he was sent on a scouting expedition for the family, or just came on his own. Maybe a little of both, because he was an adventurer, an explorer, and a teenager. He wanted to see what was happening.

That would have been 1929 or a little before, because that's the year that old news reports say the German passenger airship *Graf Zeppelin* visited Los Angeles. I remember my dad telling me that he walked many miles out from the city of Los Angeles to the airport to see it. That was Mines Field, which was just a little airstrip then, but now it's Los Angeles International, one of the biggest and busiest in the world.

Dad loved aviation, so I'm glad he got to see what at the time was a modern engineering marvel. Eight years later the Zeppelin's sister ship, *Hindenberg*, tragically exploded at Lakehurst, New Jersey, costing many lives. The disaster ended use of such hydrogen-filled behemoths.

Sometime in the early '30s his parents followed him across the country. Raoul the Ist carried on in the railway industry for a time, doing engineering work all across the area for Pacific Electric. Their vast urban transit system featured the famous "Red Cars," beloved then and lamented now. The Balcaens settled on Bixle Street, which lies on the western flank of downtown L.A.

Then he redirected his engineering genius from railways to airways and joined Douglas Aircraft, which in those days was on the airport at Santa Monica. Not far down the Pacific Ocean coastline from there he bought a nice home in Playa Del Rey.

PDR, as it's known for short, was a glorious beachside community back then. It was difficult to get to by road, which kept it quiet and secluded. It had many notable residents whose homes were beautiful, many of them Spanish colonial like my grandfather's.

Behind his garage Engineer Balcaen set up a small shop filled with machine tools, most of which he constructed himself. What a place of wonders it was to me as little boy. I loved hanging out there with my Grandpa, watching him working his mechanical magic.

I appeared on the scene on May 12th, 1936. I'm told that makes me a Taurus, the same as Ferruccio Lamborghini, who used the image of a bull to represent his exotic Italian supercars. I don't know if astrology has any bearing on who I turned out to be. It's more likely that a bigger influence was the fact that I happen to have been born in Hollywood — which was a nice place back then, let me hasten to say! Here's how that came about.

My father shared my grandfather's keen interest in machinery and cars, but his big passion was airplanes. So instead of following his dad into engineering, mine joined the California Air National Guard, where he learned to fly. He went on to West Point to become an Army officer, but imperfect eyesight dashed his dream of being an Army Air Corps pilot. He stayed on regardless, and served as a logistics officer in Europe during World War II and several years after. He was a military man through-and-through.

But he had many other interests. He loved driving cars, riding horseback, skiing, anything involving speed. He pursued his love of flying and eventually became a plane owner.

Why did he take up residence in Hollywood, my future birthplace? It might have had something to do with a girl. My future mother had moved out from the East to be with her sisters, who were pursuing careers in the movies. Just how she and my dad met isn't in my memory any longer, if it ever was, but I presume he was already living in town, because he was working for a business mogul named Arthur Letts, Jr.

Mr. Letts was the son of the man who founded both the Broadway and the Bullock's department stores, still landmarks in Los Angeles. Before he died in 1923 Arthur Letts Sr. was developing a former ranch on the West Side into what became Holmby Hills, Westwood and the UCLA university campus.

His heirs continued those projects, along with running the family retail businesses. In 1928 my father's boss moved into his own lavish new residence on the grounds of the Los Angeles Country Club. "The grandest estate in Holmby Hills," that house was called. Today we know it as The Playboy Mansion.

Purely by coincidence, my wife and I now live quite near there.

I can't say just what my father did for his boss, but I'm sure he was given plenty to do. Obviously Mr. Letts had a lot going on in some very high circles of Hollywood and Los Angeles city society. Maybe that's how my dad met my future mom, through her connection with the movie industry.

Janet Lucia Nicol was born in New Jersey. My mother's paternal grandfather Nicol had moved to the US from Scotland, while on her mother's side, her grandfather Winklhofer came from Austria. Both men made themselves wealthy in America.

Mr. Winklhofer was an immigrant who fought in the American Civil War. The story goes that he was barely off the boat before being handed a rifle and told, "Here, young man. Fight for the North and you're an instant citizen." Which he did and proudly became an American. A clever inventor and also a successful businessman, he manufactured button snaps for shoes in Newark, New Jersey, and also operated a chain of variety stores.

My mother's Scottish grandfather, Douglas Nicol, became prosperous in the maritime business, and was an original investor in the Lipton Tea Co.

That investment tied into his keen interest in yacht racing. As Commodore of one of the yacht clubs in the New York-New Jersey area, Mr. Nicol was involved with the periodic America's Cup match races, which were hosted by the New York Yacht Club.

That no doubt brought him together with his fellow Scot, Sir Thomas Lipton. The famous head of Lipton Tea was a five-time challenger for the America's Cup with his own sailing yacht, *Shamrock*, and four of those important regattas took place off New York City. Sometime in that period, 1899 through 1920, the two became good friends — mind you, history says that Sir Thomas was friendly with everybody.

My mother's father, James Douglas Nicol, was a car man like me. He had an Auburn Boat-Tail Speedster, a very sporty luxury automobile of the day, and I remember riding in it with him. I have a fainter memory about his owning a car dealership or distributorship, possibly for Franklin, that fine old American make distinguished by its nicely engineered air-cooled engines.

Even more interesting to me, my grandfather James Nicol was something of a car racer. I cannot establish that he was a driver, but family lore says he fielded a car in the Vanderbilt Cup races. That was the first major international automotive event in America, a series founded in 1904 to run over dirt roads on Long Island, New York. Its first winner was American George Heath aboard a French Panhard. We can find no record of anyone named Nicol connected with any of the competitors, either that year or later.

But that doesn't mean he wasn't, because the Nicol family had tangible proof of its connection to racing: a victory trophy from the Indianapolis Motor Speedway. It was for one of several endurance events held at the brand-new track before the first 500 Miles race. That happened in 1911, so "our" trophy would be from either 1909 or 1910.

I remember seeing that memento at my mother's family home. The trophy was an imposing thing with a figure of a winged Mercury on top. Unfortunately, I can't remember what the inscription said!

Back to the Vanderbilt Cup for a moment. The race moved Out West in 1914, running that first year in Santa Monica, up the beach from where we later settled. The great Ralph DePalma came in first there, perched high aboard one of the best racing cars of the era, a big, burly, technically highly advanced Mercedes. He called his "the Grey Ghost." The following year de Palma won the Indy 500.

All that was well before our time, of course, but my mother, Janet, found pleasure in driving as much as my father Raoul did, and thus the enjoyment and love of automobiles was an ingrained family tradition of at least three generations. I was just thinking, we Balcaens were involved with the four great revolutions in powered transportation: sail boats, railroads, automobiles, and airplanes.

Some of the brightest, happiest memories of my childhood are of my grandfather's workshop, and being there with him and my father, we three Raouls together, working on cars. That's how I learned about engines, which held special fascination for me. I was often able to diagnose a problem in a running engine by its sound alone.

Dad nicknamed me "Sonny," and I helped him rebuild a 1936 Pontiac engine. I learned how to use every tool and gauge in his tool box. I knew when he needed to be handed the dial indicators, the valve spring compressor, or the compression gauge. I never took my eyes off the meticulous work he was doing on the engine, and my mechanical genes, inherited from my Belgian immigrant grandfather and my American-born father, kicked in with a vengeance. I vowed to build my own racecar one day.

World War II broke out in 1939, and as it raged across Europe it affected us in America with rationing. That included gasoline, which became difficult to find. No new automobiles were being built, and new parts were in short supply, so most items that wore out had to be refurbished, not replaced. Tires were mostly recaps because there was little rubber available.

My own memories of that time include the sight of barrage balloons floating overhead. When the Japanese bombed Pearl Harbor in 1941, forcing the United States into the war, we went into emergency production of military aircraft and equipment. There was a real fear of enemy air attacks against the multitude of factories and other facilities sprawling across Los Angeles.

My dad was a First Lieutenant in the U.S. Army. Assigned to the Signal Corps, Fifth Army, he was posted to North Africa for the invasion of Italy that took place in September 1943.

One of Dad's wartime actions resulted in his being awarded the Soldier's Medal for heroism. The Allied Forces had attained a foothold on the Italian Boot, and Dad was stationed in Naples. There the Signal Corps stored many of its supplies in a cave, and suddenly the interior erupted in violent explosions and fires. When things seemed safe again, a fellow officer of father's went in to inspect the supplies. That's when another explosion ripped through the cave and trapped the man inside.

Here is the official description of the event on the citation accompanying my father's Soldier's Medal:

> The President of the United States of America, authorized by Act of Congress, July 2, 1926, takes pleasure in presenting the Soldier's Medal to First Lieutenant (Signal Corps) Raoul G. Balcaen (ASN: 0-1633462), United States Army, for heroism on 26 December 1943, at Naples, Italy. After Several fires and explosions at the Fontinella Caves, Naples, had placed considerable Signal Supplies in jeopardy, an additional violent explosion occurred. In the face of the fact that there was considerable danger of the cave collapsing and that visibility inside was impossible because of dust caused by the explosion, First Lieutenant Balcaen disregarded the extreme personal danger involved and entered the cave to determine the well being of a fellow officer who was making an inspection of prior damage to the cave. First Lieutenant Balcaen found this officer slightly dazed and headed in the opposite direction from the entrance. By his courageous action and utter selflessness, First Lieutenant Balcaen maintained the highest traditions of the military service.

The medal was presented on January 16, 1946, at Headquarters, Mediterranean Theater of Operations, by General Mark Clark, leader of the Fifth Army. Clark was the youngest four-star general in World War II, and deputy to General Dwight D. Eisenhower, the future President of the US. Dad was one of General Clark's aides in the Italian Campaign.

He rose up through the ranks, being promoted to Captain and later to Major.

Before he left for Europe, Dad had moved his family to my grandparents' house in Playa Del Rey. There were four of us children, my younger brother and two sisters.

I was thrilled, of course, because Grandpa's machine shop was filled with the kind of equipment that young boys love to be around. My grandfather designed and built machines and tools to shape, cut, mill and handle several other different functions.

That shop became my playroom. From the age of six I'd sit quietly on a chair and watch him work with lathes, drill presses and other tools. It was the most exciting time of the day for me, sharing a hobby that was already seeding and nurturing a full-blown desire to do what Grandpa was doing — innovate.

Both my grandparents spoke English accented by the French they grew up using in Belgium. They were also fluent in several other languages, but I suppose the French connection is why, when Grandpa worked at his machine tools, he wore one of the blue smocks you see mechanics wearing over in France and Belgium. Noticing that I hardly ever left his side in the garage, my grandma Rachel made me a miniature duplicate smock sized for my six-year-old frame. I wore it with great pride.

CHAPTER 2
INTERLUDE IN ITALY

At war's end officers' families were permitted to travel to Europe. In 1946, the year I turned 10, my mother, two sisters, brother and I joined Dad in Naples.

The U.S. Army had requisitioned several houses and apartment buildings to house the military, although tenants paid the rent on them. With my father's high rank we were fortunate to occupy an extremely large apartment one floor beneath the penthouse in a palatial, Mussolini-era building in town.

I remember the beautiful parquetry flooring that graced the rooms, and the elaborate furnishings and wall coverings. There was a magnificent grand piano on which I took lessons. Before the Italian music teacher arrived Mother would spread Chanel Number 5 perfume under my nose, because at times the tutor tended to smell of garlic!

On some weekends Dad took me to his office. It was something worth seeing. There in Caserta outside Naples was an incredible 18th-century Royal Palace built to rival its French counterpart, Versailles. The ancestral home of the Bourbon-Two Sicilies dynasty, when Spain controlled the region, it is a UNESCO World Heritage site today. Now completely restored, it is absolutely splendid, well worth a visit. But I tell of the years after World War II, when the US and British armies had taken over the sprawling — but still sumptuous — palace and set up a command center. Going there with Dad was a special occasion, and I'd dress up for it in my miniature army uniform, which my mother asked a local tailor to make for me.

Among Dad's duties were logistics, finance and strategic planning, and I'd peek at the data, which fascinated me. The office was filled with teletype machines, basically automatic typewriters that made a massive racket when they were all going at the same time. Teletype was their primary means of communication, bringing in all the Army's critical intelligence the same as computers do today — but a whole lot quieter!

My father was a serious history buff, and he showed me the statistical analyses that generals used before going into battle, with possible moves and their potential consequences. Information was gathered about everything on both sides: numbers of troops, tanks, artillery, aircraft and so on, and where they were positioned, and how they were supplied. It was all analyzed by teams of people doing everything by hand, without computers of course.

I was tremendously impressed. I took it all in, learning how wars were fought, supplied, managed, and maintained. I am sure this part of my education enhanced my skills when I became an engineer, a racecar builder, a business owner, and much later in life an economist.

Naples was not the fascinating place back then that it is today. There was tremendous war damage to homes, buildings, bridges and other infrastructure. The port city suffered heavy bombing by both Germany and the Allies, leaving the harbor in ruins and devastating much of the city center. It was sad to see the flattened landscape.

Happily, one of Naples' neo-classical structures, the Teatro di San Carlo, was only slightly damaged. That's where I first learned to love opera.

I guess my mother was right when she once remarked that I was "extremely precocious."

By the age of eleven my urge to be an entrepreneur, which had always been at the back of my mind, came forward and I started up two small businesses in Naples. The first was when I saw an opportunity in money exchange.

The U.S. Government paid its foreign-based military with a form of currency called "scrip." The Italian lira was worth less than scrip, and the British pound in those days was the universal world currency. Its worth then was about two and a half dollars. Seeing a differential in arbitrage, I traded with some of the Italians on the streets, exchanging the scrip for liras. I made a profit of approximately $5! It was a quick and easy way to make a buck, and it became a good little business for me.

Another business of mine was shining shoes. I used to enjoy polishing and buffing my dad's Army shoes, determined his should be the shiniest. He received many compliments for them. When he told fellow officers living in our building who did the work, I found myself polishing several other pairs of shoes at a very nice rate of pay.

Another activity that I was partial to was odd, I imagine, for a young boy. I have always liked to be in the thick of things, usually quietly listening and learning about whatever was going on. Often the most interesting times were when my father invited foreign officers from Allied armies to formal dinner parties at our house. Among the guests were Brits, Italians, and some Yugoslav partisan fighters who had served with Marshall Tito during the war. One of these soldiers was a woman, a colonel, I believe, a very attractive, elegant lady who wore short pants and high knee-socks. She was very impressive!

Although we employed a full-time maid and a cook, and for formal occasions supplemented them with extra catering and serving staff, I wanted to be one of the waiters at those dinners.

I had observed the etiquette of serving, and participated at these exclusive evenings by draping a napkin over my arm and becoming one of the wait staff, albeit a rather little one. I took the task very seriously, mastering the correct protocols, noticing whom to serve first and from which side to place a plate. I didn't do any serving, but I cleared the dishes as quietly and as carefully as I could, while listening with curiosity to the conversation around the table.

Overhearing people from other lands and cultures as they exchanged views and news gave me quite an education about the world.

I also enjoyed listening in to adult discussions when we went to the British Officers Club and the American Officers Club. Knowledge I gathered then would serve me later in life.

In many ways, our Italian sojourn meant that our family was lucky. We lived better in Europe at that time than we would have in the United States, which was still under rationing. We shopped at the U.S. military's Post Exchange, the PX, and ordered clothes from the Sears, Roebuck catalog. We bought imported gasoline.

One downside: We rarely had fresh vegetables, because of the probability of undulant fever and other infectious diseases.

CHAPTER 2

I was a student at a British school in Vomero, Naples. Located high on a hill, it faced south with a stunning view of the Bay of Naples and Mount Vesuvius, the volcano so famous for burying the ancient city of Pompeii. Many years later I went back to Naples to see that school, as well as our old home at Via Giosuè Carducci, no. 42. I was happy to see both still standing and well kept.

We stayed in Italy for almost three years, traveling around the war-torn country in Dad's Jeep whenever he had leave. Our Jeep was different to most because of its seats and coachwork. The British Army drove luxurious lorries, what we'd call the Rolls-Royce of trucks. Compared to our six-cylinder Dodge-powered trucks, their transports were equipped with beautifully crafted leather seats, similar to the Bavarian bull hides that the British luxury automakers used. When one of Dad's British friends found the seats still intact in a bombed-out lorry scheduled for the scrap heap, he gave the seats to my father. Thus my parents rode very comfortably, while my brother and I sat on the numbing metal side carriers. Our sisters occupied the U.S. Army-provided hard-pack canvas seats in the rear.

On weekends we'd visit the Isle of Capri, where we stayed at a former sanatorium that was turned into the Grand Hotel Quisisana. It was not too far from the ancient castle of the Roman emperor Tiberius, who was known to throw adversaries from Capri's cliffs.

We spent time in Rome, too, and toured the Vatican. One of Dad's hobbies was art history and his knowledge was extensive. He'd point out places of interest during our time in Rome. When he took us to see Michelangelo's sculpture, La Pieta, I asked why one of the toes and part of a forefoot were eroded. He told me that so many people had touched or kissed them over the ages that some of the marble had been worn away. We also went down to the burial crypt below St. Peter's, and up into the echo-producing dome.

Actually we were photographed on top of St. Peter's, which is not permitted these days.

Many of Rome's grandiose buildings were blackened by time. Today, those buildings are gleaming again. On our travels we would pass crashed warplanes with their nose in the ground, tanks with their tracks blown off, and several hastily posted signs warning of minefields. They were grim reminders of the terrible havoc that war wreaks, and those

ABOVE *Raoul Balcaen, Jr., my father, as a young pilot in the California National Guard, about to get into the observation seat of a Stearman biplane to photograph construction progress on the new Hoover Dam. That puts the occasion somewhere in the 1931–36 timeframe.*

RIGHT *Raoul and Janet Balcaen, my parents, with Dad's brother, Paul Balcaen, and Mom's sister, Beatrice Nicol. The year is 1935, the year before I was born, but I have no further information about this picture.*

LEFT *Dad held the rank of First Lieutenant in the U.S. Army when he and two other officers viewed a Roman ruin in Oran, Algeria, during World War II shortly before the invasion of Italy. My father was very much a Roman scholar, as he had read every volume of English historian Edward Gibbons'* massive The History of the Decline and Fall of the Roman Empire.

ABOVE *A photo taken shortly before my father's retirement from the U.S. Army. Now Colonel Raoul G. Balcaen, Jr., he was a true and dedicated American soldier. Standing next to him is my stepmother, Toni Balcaen, with a group of other officers.*

LEFT My grandfather, Raoul G.S. Balcaen, Sr., as he was photographed just before he left Belgium in 1900 to do engineering work on railroads in northern New York. He was the only member of our branch of the Balcaen family to come to America, as the rest remained in Europe.

RIGHT My grandmother, Rachel Verlot Balcaen, posed for this picture before she came to America with my grandfather. She was often homesick, and took the children back to Belgium for their summer vacations as often as possible.

LEFT My father had become Captain Balcaen when Rome, Italy, was finally liberated from German forces. Here he is on the balcony of the captured German headquarters, which still displays a Nazi flag.

RIGHT Dad, Mom and us four kids atop St. Peter's Basilica in Vatican City, Rome, 1946. They don't let you up there these days. That's me at the left, with my younger siblings Joan, Norman and Barbara.

ABOVE The beautiful Bay of Naples in the south of Italy. That's Mount Vesuvius at the far end of the bay. I spent several years of my childhood in this fascinating area.

ABOVE All-American slugger. Back in Playa Del Rey, California, I was a pretty regular American boy — until the day Mom ignited my passion for cars and speed.

RIGHT *The newspaper clipping that made me "famous" — even though they spelled my name wrongly! I'm third from left, between big Frank Startup, the usual driver for our team, and his partner Ed Donovan. Both were great mentors to me.*

MEMORIES - FOR ED DONOVAN, Frank Starrtup and Sonny Balcane. Shows their 1st rail 4-cyl - Fargo - Ford. Speed 129mph, 1956 winner at the old Saugus, California drags. (Photo submitted by Charley)

ABOVE *The Donovan-Startup rail shows how primitive the early days of drag racing were. These cars seemed very fast back in the day, but evolution over time has been truly amazing. Notice how high drivers used to sit, perched above the rear axle. The engine, a nitro-fueled four-cylinder Ford, produced a lot of horsepower. I also got to drive it, my first experience in a real dragster. I was so startled by the power that my shoe came off the gas. Frank laughed and called me "Balloon Foot."*

ABOVE *My friends Frank and Ed in their little raceshop, standing proudly behind a new streamlined dragster they built. It was very innovative, with its Ford engine (equipped with a Riley four-port head and Winfield cam and carbs) laying on its side for a lower hood line. Sadly, it never saw the light of day. But Ed Donovan went on to great fame, founding a company to engineer and manufacture highly successful racing components, especially engines. His aluminum-block Chrysler Hemi 417 was the forerunner to every Top Fuel V8 racing today.*

RIGHT *Ed Donovan's love of four-cylinder torque reached its peak in 1963, when he replaced his production-based Ford with this made-for-racing Offenhauser Indycar engine. Then he bolted on extra performance with a GMC 671 supercharger. Displacing 320 cubic inches (instead of the usual 270) thanks to a longer-stroke crankshaft, it attained 183 mph in just over eight*

seconds on the quarter-mile Pomona dragstrip. Driver Frank Startup, wearing a fireproof safety mask here, said the car had so much "off-the-line" torque that it would set the tires smoking throughout the quarter mile! We never knew how powerful it was, except it was more than dynamometers of the day could handle. All we could do was calculate it must be between 800 and 1000 hp. Whatever, it was the World's Fastest Four!

images have never left me.

The piece de resistance of our travels was a winter vacation at a ski resort at the village of Engelberg in Switzerland. When we got to the lodge I thought I'd died and gone to Heaven. Italy was lovely but war-torn, while Switzerland, which had remained neutral during the war, was pristine, shining, and perfect.

At the start of our trip Mom and my siblings went by train to Milan, but Dad and I drove the Jeep up there. When my father decided to do something he wanted to do it right away, so we kept driving from Naples all through the night. In the midst of the Liri Valley, some distance south of Rome, we were driving in darkness but there was a full moon. Nevertheless, we somehow went off the road and ended up stuck in a culvert.

I fell out on the right-hand side — there were no seatbelts in those days — and looked around. I was in instant shock. All I could see was a huge field of white crosses!

It was the Monte Cassino war cemetery with more than 1,000 graves of Polish soldiers who died during a battle at the Benedictine abbey. It was an eerie, scary, incredible sight and one I can still see in my mind's eye. I feel that this incident, surviving an accident and rolling out of the jeep on its side in a culvert, and immediately being confronted by stark evidence of so much tragic death, was important in terms of determining my life's values. The whole Italian period was a very poignant part of my life.

Dad managed to set the Jeep back onto its four wheels and we drove on into Rome. He always liked the good life, and I found myself in a hotel that was the most magnificent I'd ever seen, the Excelsior. Built in 1906, it became the temporary war headquarters for General Mark Clark when the U.S. Army entered Rome in 1944. It was once owned by the Aga Khan, who famously was married to Rita Hayworth. The Italian movie "La Dolce Vita" was filmed at the hotel.

As was the custom, my father took my shoes and his and set them outside the door of our bedroom before we retired. In the morning I was amazed to see them cleaned and polished.

After meeting up with the rest of the family in Milan we traveled the rest of the way on a train with a steam engine. Going through the St. Gotthard Pass, a tunnel through the Alps that connects northern and southern Switzerland, was an adventure. When we came out into the sunshine there was snow everywhere, a beautiful sight.

We children had been longing to get to the other end so that we could have some ice cream. We weren't allowed gelato in Italy because of the fear of sickness. We had no milk in Naples either, only the powdered version from the PX.

Shortly after we arrived in Switzerland a U.S. Army colonel, or perhaps he was a general, fell down on the ski slopes and broke his leg. Luckily, Dad and I were close by to help him get down the steep hill. It was the first time I'd skied down a toboggan run, sheer ice with a narrow wall on each side. One hell of an experience! Then we took the man to a Lucerne hospital.

After that, we went shopping. Dad always looked at shops that sold watches. This particular day a watch shop was next to a sports car dealership. Their featured car was a sleek Italian roadster, a 1946 Cisitalia. I thought it was amazing, and learned there was a Cisitalia sports racing version, too, bearing the name Mille Miglia, the legendary 1000-mile race around Italy. That was probably my first exposure to a real Italian sports car. It was unforgettable.

Dad was enthralled with it too, although when we got back to the States he bought a standard, big Chrysler Town & Country, which was popular then.

Our family left Italy, along with most of the Allied Forces, because of the Communist uprising that was enveloping the country. We were given fairly short notice to leave, and after three years in Italy and visiting so many other countries, we had acquired quite a few souvenirs, furniture, and what-nots, to say the least. Fortunately, the U.S. Army packed us all up and crated everything including cars to the seaport of Livorno, where we boarded a Liberty ship.

One of a class of cargo and troop-carrying ships that were mass-produced during the war, a Liberty could carry 500 troops. We had to board ours while it was anchored offshore in the Mediterranean Sea, another exciting adventure for me. We reached it in a small boat, then transferred up to the big ship. The entire procedure was fascinating, and I watched every moment as families were taken on board.

My mother and sisters had a minor state room, although nowhere near anything you'd call luxury. My brother and I slept with the troops in bunk beds that were tiered five deep. The six-day voyage took us through the Straits of Gibraltar and then out into the Atlantic Ocean.

At one point during the crossing there was a fierce storm, causing our ship to heave as deep waves crashed over the bow. Some of the G.I. war brides, traveling with their new husbands, leaned over the rails suffering from sea-sickness. Swabbing the decks became a daily chore after such storms. For a change, I was happy to not to want to be a part of this activity!

Finally we reached New York Harbor, when everyone rushed on deck to gaze in awe and cheer when the Statue of Liberty came into view. Lady Liberty is a sight that has evoked deep feelings for millions of people, whether they were coming to America for the first time or, as in the case of the troops and the Balcaen family in particular, returning to a beloved country that was like no other.

I wondered what new adventures awaited me. One thing for sure, I was anxious to get back to grandfather's machine shop. This time around I wanted to be tinkering with a car of my own, while figuring out new entrepreneurial avenues. Luckily, neither took me long.

CHAPTER 3
A PASSION
IS BORN

My passion for speed hit hard when I was about 13. Our family moved back to Playa Del Rey in 1948. Not long after, and not far away, I witnessed my first hot rod race.

Dad was staying on in the Army as a career officer, so he was promptly stationed in Ogden, Utah. Mom and the rest of us settled back into my grandfather's Playa Del Rey home, where we'd been at the beginning of the war. My grandmother had passed away, so Grandpa probably was glad of our company.

His house was on Trask Avenue, a short residential street that runs parallel to the beach but inland a short way at the top of the hill, with nice views of the sparkling blue Pacific Ocean. I mention this because I want to paint the picture of an almost idyllic place to be a teenager back then.

PDR, as it's called for short, was a beautiful little community at that time. There were good roads and many big lots with walled estates. One of them, the biggest property in the neighborhood, was the home of celebrated film and TV character actor Charles Bickford. John and Elaine Bond, who published *Road & Track* magazine, lived around the corner. Another house belonged to the daughter of a great Shakespearean actor named Charles Middleton — although he was better known to us as "Ming the Merciless" in the old Flash Gordon movies! His daughter was my mother's friend, so Mom was always over there.

From PDR my mother often drove us to a movie theater up in Culver City. That was a center of filmmaking, with several big production studios but also theaters, restaurants and so on. It was only about five miles away up Culver Boulevard. This was a wide road that cut almost dead straight through land that was still undeveloped, so it was kind of dark and quiet along there. That's important to my story.

One evening on our way home from the movies we were stopped by a young guy holding up traffic. We could see lights, lots of people standing around, and cars parked all over the place.

"Ma'am," the young fellow asked politely, "would you be kind enough to wait a few minutes? We're having a little bit of a speed contest here and we don't want anyone to get hurt."

Mother agreed to wait and we watched along with hordes of other people, many of them cheering and excited about this "little speed contest." What we now call a street race was as dangerous and illegal then as it is today, but it was attracting lots of people and lots of loud, wild-looking cars.

Remember, I'd just been living in war-ravaged southern Italy. If people there had a vehicle at all, it would be small and cheap and slow. What was happening in California was much, much more interesting. Especially what I saw going on that night on Culver Blvd.

The drivers seemed to be just kids, teenagers. Not rich kids, either, but regular kids with older vehicles. America didn't manufacture any private cars during the early '40s, due to the war. Most of the cars I noticed that night were Fords, both coupes and roadsters, particularly from two popular model years, 1929 and 1932.

I also soon noticed that a lot of the cars had home-made body alterations, especially by removing the fenders, so the wheels were out in the open air. A lot of guys left the hoods off, too, so they could display elaborately souped up engines that were gorgeous to a gear head like me. Some owners went as far as "chopping" the tops, cutting out several inches of the original height and welding it back together to lower the silhouette. That made for a dramatic, ferocious new look, like racecars.

And a lot of the bodies — what remained of them — were painted in vivid, almost wild colors with flames and everything else. The big, famous color of the '50s was called "Burple," kind of a purple-red. Candy Apple came later.

They looked cool. Hot rods, these exciting vehicles were called. I was riveted.

Pairs of them would line up waiting for their turn to start. Then they smoked away down the center line at what looked like incredible velocity. The engine sound seemed overwhelming. Almost painfully loud, but enjoyable to my ears, like rock music I suppose.

Hearing those thunderous engines and feeling their vibration, smelling the burning tires, understanding the huge horsepower that was produced, and seeing what I knew were hopped-up Ford Flathead V8s streak along a strip of city street at over 100 miles an hour made my young heart beat about as fast.

But what was that strange whistling sound? I later learned it came from the vertical steel grilles in front of the radiator on 1932 Fords, which was one of the most common makes and models for a hot rod. A unique sound!

As they went roaring by it was like a scene from the later movie, "Fast and Furious." I couldn't take my eyes off the spectacle unfolding before me. The atmosphere was electric. It fired up my imagination. I couldn't think of anything that could surpass being behind the wheel of one of those hot rods and taking part in the flat-out, unsanctioned contests.

Watching that street race that night in 1948 was the most exciting moment of my life. I was spellbound, smitten, hooked. From that moment on I itched to have a racecar of my own, to figure out where I could improve its performance, and to go blow the doors off competitors.

A few months later we were playing horseshoes in our back garden and I got hit with one, splitting my head open. Mother rushed me to the Santa Monica hospital. As he was stitching me up the doctor asked, "What do you want to be when you grow up?"

"A racecar driver."

"Oh? Then I'm not stitching *you* up!"

I can't say if he was just joking, but if he hoped to dissuade me from my career choice it didn't work.

Apparently my mother didn't see it the same way, because she used to take me to the Midget auto races at Gilmore Stadium. I remember smelling castor oil there for the first time. It was called bean oil, because it came from the castor bean tree. It had a high viscosity, so it could stand up in racing engines, like the Offy 105s in the Midgets. The bean oil would seep into the combustion chambers, and burn along with the Methanol/Nitro fuel mix they used, resulting in a unique odor.

When I first caught a whiff of it I began to ask questions. Seeing my interest, my mother bought me a Thimble Drome midget toy car. It was about ten inches in length, made of die cast iron, and powered by a model aircraft engine. I'd buy a special fuel for it. I loved that smell and I'm sure that my sensitive nose later helped me when I became a wine expert able to pinpoint the various grapes and their flavors.

Thanks to my curiosity about the Thimble Drome I sought out and met the gentleman who designed the toys. The company, Ohlssen and Rice, was in Long Beach, where you could buy a pint of the fuel that included a mixture of nitromethane. They had gallons of the stuff and no one else knew where to get it easily back then. That was going to come in handy later.

So was something my father taught me: he never took a no for an answer. He was still in Utah when the racing thing began for me. One time when we were up there visiting him he arranged for me to see a famous Bonneville Land Speed racer and his car — Ab Jenkins and the "Mormon Meteor."

Dad was an officer of course, and he was used to giving orders, so he called a former mayor of Salt Lake City and said, my son's in town and he would love to come over there and see the Mormon Meteor.

Well, that former mayor was Ab Jenkins! So we went over and saw the streamlined, bright yellow Mormon Meteor.

"Never take no for an answer." Words to live by.

Also I had my first glimpse of the very interesting, nicely made new Porsche sports cars from Germany while visiting my father. A couple of his buddies at his base had brand-new ones.

A little later he was reassigned to Sacramento, in Northern California. He had his own plane by that time, and he'd fly down to pick me up. It was an Aeronca, a little high-wing tail-dragger with tandem seating. I sat in the front with him behind me, giving me my first flying lessons.

I was 14 then, I think, which was too young to get a pilot's license. But I did so a few years later, about 1959-1960. I bought a plane of my own, too, a 4-seat Cessna 172.

But I'm getting ahead of my car racing story.

I soon discovered a community of young Southern Californians with a passion for racing that matched mine. Hot rodding was developing into a culture all its own. Maybe even something of a religion.

Our bible was a magazine devoted to the sport called — what else — *Hot Rod*. From Petersen Publishing, the first issue had come out in 1948. Its first editor was Wally Parks, who later founded the National Hot Rod Association (NHRA), the biggest motorsports sanctioning organization in the world. Wally was a wonderful guy. I feel honored that in years to come we became good friends.

Hot Rod magazine was full of fascinating articles about drag racing, reports of event results and new record speeds, the street machine scene, the right ways to hop up a car and build a racing engine, stories full of fascinating photos about the latest project vehicles from a rapidly growing list of masterful craftsmen... my 13-year-old self was enchanted.

There were copies of the magazine at the local Boys' Club, where I'd sit for hours and read them from cover to cover, devouring every article.

After studying illustrations of engines and their parts in the magazine, I used a couple of the ideas to modify my mother's 1946 Chevy. Its engine was the company's famous inline six-cylinder, which dated all the way back to 1929, when people nicknamed it the "Stovebolt." It was a strong and reliable powerplant for literally millions of General Motors vehicles.

I fell in love with that Chevy 6. If anybody asked me why, I might have said it had a more advanced design, it was technically superior.

The reality was, I liked it because it wasn't a Ford! I wanted something different. Even way back then there was a tremendous rivalry between fans of the two brands, and I considered myself a Chevy man through and through.

The work I did on Mom's stock Chevy 6 was the beginning of my career as an engine builder and aftermarket performance entrepreneur. Putting together all the knowledge I was gleaning from Hot Rod Magazine, I got some key hop-up parts and installed them to heat up Mom's engine. A new intake manifold with three carburetors, plus a new camshaft to open the valves wider, really brought that engine to life. I was only 15, but Mom let me take her hot new car out street racing a few times.

Well, I'm sure she would have if I'd asked her!

What an adventure, driving down to Culver Boulevard and along to "our strip," where my new buddies were lighting up the night. I quickly learned that, if drag racing looks super-simple, it isn't! Sure, all you're doing is trying to accelerate in a straight line over a short distance... but it's a hard thing to pull off fast enough to get there first.

For younger people today, maybe I should make sure they realize that back in my teenage years it wasn't just a matter of mashing the accelerator pedal and leaving the car to do all the work. In the '50s we didn't have automatic transmissions, not many of us anyway, and nobody could even imagine electronic driveline controls taking everything out of the driver's hands.

To learn to drive back then, there was no way around mastering age-old skills like operating a friction clutch with your left foot, simultaneously modulating engine performance with your right foot, and coordinating both those operations while changing gears with your right hand. There was a technique to it.

It wasn't that complicated with a car like my mother's Chevy. These were big, bulbous, heavy passenger cars and the horsepower wasn't exactly neck-snapping. But if you wanted to beat the other guy, and I sure did, you still had to make the most of what you had.

If you released the clutch too abruptly the tires would slip, maybe spin a little. You want to avoid smoking the tires, because you're wasting time. And you had to be able to get it through the gears quickly, but with aplomb, so you didn't miss a shift. Those days we only had three-speed gearboxes, and my Mom's car had a column shift, what they called "three on the tree." That was an unusual motion to master.

Ideally you want to "speed shift" as fast as you can but without missing the shift, and do it at exactly the right engine rpm, to get the best acceleration. Our old passenger cars didn't have engine tachometers to signal just when to shift, we had to rely on our ears. At the same instant you shifted, you had to pop the clutch in and out. Maybe you'd ease off the throttle a bit, to keep from over-revving the engine. We didn't have computerized power train controls.

Boiling it down to the basics, you learned to watch the flagman and then just work the throttle and clutch properly, and go like hell 'til you hit the finish line. It proved you had more power than the next guy.

It took time and lots of practice to get everything right, or as right as you can. It's that perpetual challenge of doing it better that makes racing so fascinating and so much fun. Especially when you start getting some wins, as I began to do!

My Chevrolet's main competition were Flathead Ford coupes, or Buicks with that fine straight-eight, overhead-valve engine. There were lots of big Buicks in those days. But I got so I could hold my own against them.

When I started on the streets there wasn't much formality about it. You'd get together at one of your favorite places, a remote stretch where development hadn't arrived yet. What we were doing was illegal, of course, but since there were hardly any homes and very little traffic, and it was night time, unless somebody called to complain the police usually didn't come out there.

We would scout out places all over the L.A. area to do this. There was still a lot of undeveloped land back then. In my area we had Vista del Mar, the dead straight beach road down from PDR past LAX. That was usually deserted in those days.

Heading east, out beyond the general area where Jack Northrop was building military aircraft at what is now Hawthorne airport, it was still mostly farm fields and we could find good places. Or we'd go up to the flats of the San Fernando valley to race. Hard to believe now that all those areas used to be dark and deserted.

If it was a new spot for us, we'd establish a starting point and somebody would drive a quarter mile or so out to mark a finish point. Then we'd line up two-by-two. A guy with a flag would signal when to go. The racing was as straightforward as it gets: first car to the far end wins. No timing clocks or anything, not for us then.

These casual events were at the beginning of the sport in those days. There was nothing organized, it was all patched together each time with whoever showed up.

All that seems like a long time ago. I want to say that I have long since matured, just as the world has, and I came to understand that we should not have been doing those dangerous activities on the public road. That's why it was illegal. But it did happen, history can't be erased, and street racing in my early years was an important part of my life.

Until, finally, mother put her foot down and took back her car. I'm not sure she really loved what I'd done to her engine as much as I did.

Drag racing evolved from there, of course, and everything about it changed. Later on, when I started driving dragsters professionally, it was an altogether different job. More power, more speed, more complexity, more cost, more risk.

That's why I say "thank God for Bob Petersen and Wally Parks," because as the publisher and editor of *Hot Rod* magazine they could see this incredible groundswell of enthusiasm building, and also see the need for sanctioned speed events to get the racing off the highway. The public who wanted to watch had to be protected, and so did the competitors. We all went through scrutinizing to check our vehicles and our equipment for safety, and the race promoters had ambulances there on standby.

I'll come back to all this later, when we get to the story of my Top Fuel "digger."

So keen was I to be part of the racing community that I started figuring out a plan to buy my own car and set it up. Maybe I would even build one from scratch. I was confident I could do it. All I needed was the finances. It was a dream that I knew would come true with the kind of determination I felt whenever I set my mind to achieving a goal.

It was real horses that opened the window of opportunity to have my own horsepower. Not far from our house in Playa Del Rey was a ranch and riding school covering several acres of what was open land in those days. Now it's densely populated Loyola Village next door to LAX airport. Oh well.

I went over to the ranch to learn how to ride, and came to love horses. The ranch was owned by Don Benchoff. He was a real smart guy from Iowa who became a mentor to me in various ways, although he was often real cranky.

But Don offered me the chance to become a ranch hand, and I was delighted to set to work cleaning out the stables and taking 20 or more people out on guided tours and moonlight rides. I loved those opportunities to be with the horses.

One of my fellow ranch hands, Burt, was a veteran of the 1898 Spanish-American War, which lasted only a few months before Spain surrendered to the United States. Burt, a brawny fellow, had been one of "Teddy's Rough Riders," a famous volunteer cavalry group headed up by the future U.S. President Theodore Roosevelt.

I used to kid him because of the saddle he put on his big old mare. It was his old McClellan cavalry saddle with leather side skirts and wooden stirrups, standard U.S. Army issue since 1879 and still in service into the 1940s. Trooper Burt was quite an impressive sight when he rode around in his Rough Riders blues uniform and distinctive cowboy hat.

I really admired him and he became another mentor to me, teaching me a lot, especially about the history of our country. I became an avid scholar of history throughout my life.

But back to my main story line. Often I rode the horses past a particular gas station, and one day I stopped and went in to ask for a job. As we talked I soon realized that the owner knew almost nothing about cars. He said I seemed to know what I was doing, and so he hired me! I had landed a paying job at something like 50 cents an hour.

My job was pumping gas. That was back in the day when having someone fill up your tank included getting your windshield cleaned and your oil and tires checked, all for 25 cents per gallon.

While I was doing that, it seemed to me there was an opportunity for my boss to add a few extra services to the lube jobs he offered. I suggested that we also do repairs and tune-ups. I would handle the work and get paid for it, the gas station owner would profit from selling the auto parts, and we'd have a nice business going.

I also had a bicycle repair business for the neighbors' kids, running it out of our garage at home. So the entrepreneurial enterprise that had sprouted in Italy was flowering nicely in California.

Pretty soon I was elated to find that I had so many jobs I could drop out of high school and fatten up my savings account even more. I was only in the ninth grade, but I was totally bored with school.

Here again I ought to point out that I do not recommend this to other young people. What worked for me would not work for everybody. I have actively counseled the son of a good friend to not emulate me. He took the advice, stayed in school and got a fine education that greatly enriched his life.

My father was disappointed that I left, of course. His wish was for me to go to West Point and be a career officer like him. But I wasn't really fond of military life, because I grew up on Army bases. Being a child of World War II and living in Europe during the aftermath, seeing all the destruction in Italy, really gave me a feeling that this is not the way things needed to go.

My father would look at things very practically; he wasn't emotional about any of it. His view was, there's a job to do here and this is what has to be done. His real expertise was logistics and finance and strategic thinking. I never wanted to do that.

I'd learned several valuable lessons from my dad, including a strict work ethic, but his path was not mine. My heart was set on building cars and going racing. That single focus filled my mind 24/7.

PART II

CHAPTER 4
GONE RACIN'

Losing "my" racecar when Mom took her Chevy away didn't mean I lost my desire to be a racer. If anything, it strengthened my determination. Working industriously at the gas station to make it happen, I saw my savings increase by the day.

A day came when I had enough cash to buy my own first car. I found an old '36 Ford coupe for a hundred bucks. It had that chopped top we all liked, and it already had grey primer, so I could have gone ahead and made a real hot rod out of it. But it was a Ford. It had that Flathead (side-valve) engine. I left it alone and didn't keep it very long before I switched to an overhead-valve '38 Chevrolet sedan. Hey, a Chevy man is a Chevy man.

Not long after that I sold the '38 for a '37 Chevy that I liked better. That one I heated up a little and kept for a while. You might laugh when I tell you I bought it from an old lady in Pasadena, like the song. True story. She was a retired schoolteacher. Nice lady.

I guess enough time has gone by so I can confess that, back when I was street racing my mother's car, I was driving without a license. I was too young. The driving age in California was 16 (and still is) and I wasn't there yet. But as of May 12th, 1952, I was legal at long last. The world was mine.

In the evenings I liked to gather with my buddies at a drive-in called Scrivner's. It wasn't far from PDR, an easy shot about six miles straight out Manchester into Inglewood, across from the big cemetery there. It's the same area where the big new football stadium is now.

If you remember the movie "American Graffiti" you've got the picture. Scrivner's was one of the chains of car-centric, flashy fast-food restaurants that were springing up all across SoCal and beyond. Typically they were marked by a giant pylon to catch your eye and draw you in to a comparatively unremarkable little building underneath. That was the kitchen, mainly, there wasn't much room inside for dining. But the parking lot was big. We were there for the parking lot.

Sure, everybody knows about drive-in culture now, but think how novel it was for us back in the early '50s. It perfectly suited our teenage love of something new, of a place we could feel was our own, of somewhere we could show off our flashy rides.

We'd pull in around the drive-in and cute carhops on roller skates brought our orders to the driver's side window. We'd spend hours there, soaking in rock 'n roll music, munching on burgers and fries and swilling root beer floats or something, checking out hot rods (and maybe a girl or two) and swapping stories.

Mostly it was a gabfest. Everybody's car was different and interesting, and everybody else wanted to discuss them. We'd rehash races we'd just run or watched. We'd "bench-race" about engines and builders and drivers, and share racing gossip. Maybe somebody would tell a tall tale or two.

I'd mostly talk about engines, because they were my favorite specialty. I knew engines top to bottom and inside-out, and had strong opinions about their performance.

You could hear the hotter mills making a sound we called "loping," sort of a rolling, irregular beat. It was because of the trick racing camshafts they had. It frees up the engine to rev faster to make more power, but at some cost in low-speed smoothness.

I had put one in my mother's car, and I guess that's one of the modifications that she didn't much enjoy.

I learned so much by hanging out there at Scrivner's, where I met a lot of people who helped me and who would remain lifelong friends. Two important ones were Ed Donovan, pioneering race engine builder extraordinaire, and his business partner Frank Startup, who drove their successful dragster. When they showed up one night at the drive-in we became good friends.

They were about eight years older than me, and were very, very influential for me. I was like a mascot to them. They were both really solid people for a young guy to be around, and Donovan became a mentor.

Really, I think of Eddie Donovan as my great guru. I'll have more to say about him in another chapter.

One night Eddie blew me away when he said I was too good a mechanic to be working in a gas station. He told me I could get a much better job. He said he had a friend, Bud Hand, who worked at a place called Rabuzzi Motors in Culver City. Rabuzzi imported Jaguars, MGs and Austin-Healeys, and to service all of them Bud needed a helper. Ed said I should go over.

Never one to let a stroke of luck like this slide by, I went to see Bud at Rabuzzi's. Thanks, I am sure, to Donovan's good words I was instantly hired as an assistant mechanic. I must have been 16 or 17.

Bud Hand was one of the sweetest guys I have ever met. He had suffered from polio and wore an iron leg brace, but he moved around like you'd never believe. He had kind of a difficult time getting into the MGs, and sometimes he had to use his hand to push on his knee to operate the clutch, but he could down-shift with the best. He was a well-known driver of MGs and MG Specials, especially, on road-race courses around the area, such as Paramount Ranch, Pomona and Santa Barbara.

Bud told me I should start accumulating some tools by saving some money each week. I knew that professional tools were essential, and so when the Snap-On truck would come by once a week, I'd buy a tool of the week. I accumulated a solid collection.

Life was great. I had landed a dream job where I could bring my creative skills to the fore, and I was kept busy all day. So I was glad I hadn't hesitated to drop out of school and buy the tools!

I was paid a split commission until one day Bud told me, "You're really good. You could do this work yourself. I'm going to tell Rabuzzi that you are a fully-fledged mechanic and should get the full commission." So I started making a good living working on what we then called foreign cars. That's how I got familiar with sports cars.

But at that stage my passion was still drag racing, and about that time is when I finally built myself a dragster.

Looking back, those were really lucky days for me. The time was right to be a young drag racer. Hot rodding was just getting started, it was developing rapidly, and what began as impromptu street competition was becoming more organized and safer.

The first dedicated drag strip opened in 1950 in Santa Ana, where the great C.J. "Pappy" Hart obtained the use of what is now called John Wayne airport. It wasn't so big and busy back then. Hart's enterprise put in place the infrastructure and procedures to control crowds, inspect the cars, and respond to accidents and injuries. Of course it also became possible to make some money back. This is an expensive sport.

In 1951 Wally Parks left the editor's chair at *Hot Rod* magazine, and worked with publisher Bob Petersen to set up the National Hot Rod Association (NHRA). One of Wally's first priorities was what he called the Safety Safari, a nationwide initiative to reach youth and to guide the new sport in the proper directions.

As the racing became more serious, so did the racers. Guys started adding nitromethane into the fuel, which really boosts the horsepower. When they ran up the strip you could smell the Nitro along with the burning rubber. I couldn't get enough of it, just like thousands and thousands of new fans.

Most of the hot rodders in those days were also doing high-speed runs on the flat, dry lake bed at El Mirage, up in the desert north of L.A., and then they'd come down to short-distance drag races on Sunday. The cars were dual-purpose that way. When they came down from the desert they always had "lake dust" on them, kind of a white powder, and I was totally impressed.

I was 17 years old in 1953 when the nearly bare chassis of one of these "Lakes cars" became available, and I had saved up enough money to buy it. My intention was to convert it to a Top Fuel dragster, so I tore it apart and rebuilt literally everything. I did almost all the work myself, in my time off from regular jobs, pouring my heart and soul into it.

Doing it yourself means you can do it your way, and I took full advantage of that freedom. My choice of engine was unusual for the time, a GMC truck six-cylinder. Most guys were using V8s, but as I kept on developing my six it started making ungodly amounts of horsepower.

The car was very light, too, thanks partly to my using mostly magnesium to build the body, instead of the aluminum that was more commonplace. *Drag Racing News* made my car famous by nicknaming it the "Bantamweight Bomb."

I was not only the builder, I was the driver too, and I was very successful. That car won me a lot of drag racing trophies all over Southern California. At 17 years old I became probably the youngest, keenest and most competitive drag racer in California and certainly in our community. I was more reticent than most of the guys, but in my heart there was sheer bliss. At my core I felt a fierce desire to devote the rest of my life to racing.

I continued to be dedicated to my hobby during the '50s, working on my dragster to make it state of the art. When I was satisfied I had done everything I could to improve my Top Fuel dragster's performance, I set to shining everything up and the car was dazzling inside and out. A labor of love and passion.

The hands-on practical experience taught me mechanical skills as I went, while reading manuals and doing the math along with the work made an engineer of me.

There's a lot more I want to say about my dragster, and I'll tell the whole story in a special chapter later on.

My day job at Rabuzzi's got better when, a few weeks after Bud Hand got me promoted, he came and said, "Sonny, I've given in my notice. You can take over from me. I know you can do it."

I was still very young to take Bud's place, but my love for the job must have been evident to Mr. Rabuzzi. Fortunately, he agreed to my promotion and I willingly took on the responsibility at the age of 18, grateful for his faith in my innate abilities.

My workload increased because I was still building my own racecar over at our home garage at night. I'd rush from one place to the next one with just as much eagerness to arrive at one job as at the other. I could barely believe my luck. I really have no idea how I packed it all in.

When I look back I realize that any young person who has that same spirit and is risk-taking enough to recognize an opportunity can go ahead and get involved in what they love to do. It's easy to dream about getting into racing either as a driver or both, but unless you look for a way to move forward, and much of it is luck as I was fortunate enough to have, it is doubtful if your dream will become reality.

Bud took a leap of faith. He looked for the way forward because he did indeed quit the agency and opened up his own shop. I admired him for that.

Prior to Bud leaving he introduced me to a friend who occasionally dropped in to chat and share what was going on. The man's name was Warren Olson and he would have a massive and powerful effect on my life.

But not for a while yet. I'm not really sure why I left Rabuzzi's, because I had a good position there and was doing a good job. Maybe I was missing Bud, or maybe I was getting bored with servicing sports cars. In any case, I was ready to go when an offer came along to be service manager at the Hudson Hornet dealership on Wilshire in Santa Monica.

More responsibility, more money, and more interesting cars. Or so I must have thought. That was the period when "the Fabulous Hudson Hornet" was dominating NASCAR stock car racing — powered by an inline-six engine.

But if I anticipated working on racecars powered by my favorite type of engine, I would have been a little deflated to find myself preparing entries for the Mobil Gas Economy Run.

I must have shared this with Ed Donovan, because within a month he introduced me to a famous Indy mechanic named Pete Clark. He had been Rex Mays' builder and mechanic, and all the rest of us in the infant days of drag racing looked up at Indy people. In our estimation they always built the beautiful stuff. It was always thought-out and there was some funding behind it. We kind of took our marching orders from Indy.

Pete ran a GMC truck agency, Novotny Motors on La Cienega, and of course I was really hot for that engine and GMC parts and stuff. So I went to work for Pete on GMC trucks and Cadillacs at Novotny's. Right up until the day in 1955 when Warren Olson walked into the shop. It wasn't by chance, he was looking for me.

He said, "I'd really like you to come to work for me. I know a lot about Porsches and I can help you learn about them. Are you interested?"

Was I interested? Was I ever! So that was the bit of luck that changed everything.

CHAPTER 5
TURNING PRO

I went to work for Warren Olson bursting with eagerness. I knew he was a top-notch racing mechanic, particularly on sports cars. In the early '50s he worked for some of the best-known California racers, such as Ernie McAfee and John von Neumann.

This would be my first job where I was paid to be involved in motor racing. I was now a professional racer.

Warren Olson could give the impression of being little austere, but he was of Norwegian descent and Scandinavians don't have a reputation for excitability. And he sure knew his business. I like the way author Preston Lerner described him in his book *Scarab*: "Dignified and unmistakably competent, with ample experience dealing with difficult people and thorny situations..." I guess I wasn't "difficult," because Warren always treated me fine.

He and his wife Simone had a race preparation and general service business for high-end foreign cars like Porsches and Ferraris and other exotics. When I came on board they were on La Cienega Boulevard in Beverly Hills, on a stretch known as "Restaurant Row." It was across the street from a well-known gathering spot named "Tail o' the Cock." But Olson's first shop was a little small, so we soon moved a short distance away to a new, larger building at 631 North Robertson in West Hollywood, right on the border with Beverly Hills.

Just off Santa Monica Blvd., between the Sunset Strip in one direction and Rodeo Drive at Wilshire Blvd. in the other, it was an ideal location to take care of Hollywood-type cars, the expensive, flashy models that actors and other people in and around show business drove.

Kind of a head-turning place for a young guy. Olson's client list was sort of a Hollywood Who's Who. You'd be working on something and in would walk somebody famous. I took care of cars belonging to Mary Pickford and William Holden, among others.

That's where I first met Bruce Kessler and Lance Reventlow, who were to become good and important friends. From a wealthy family, Bruce was racing his mother's XK120 Jaguar and other cars, and Warren was taking care of them. One day Bruce came in with his boyhood buddy Lance Reventlow and Lance's girlfriend at the time, Natalie Wood. Another head turner for sure.

It just seemed natural to mingle a little with these celebrities, most people were so friendly. There was a sort of core group that welcomed me, such as actor James Brolin, actor-singers Gary Crosby (son of Bing Crosby) and Ricky Nelson, and singer-songwriter Jimmy Boyd, who wrote "I Saw Mommy Kissing Santa Claus." A special thrill was meeting ballet dancer and actress Yvonne Craig, who played Batgirl in the '60s television series, "Batman."

Not that I did a lot of dating. For one thing, I was spending all the money I earned on my drag racer. But anyway, ladies didn't notice mechanics. At races the drivers were surrounded by female fans flirting and taking photos with them, while we crew members were getting down and dirty working on the engines and the cars. Women rarely looked our way and never asked for crew or mechanics' autographs. Why should they? We were not the glamorous side of racing!

To my great delight, in Warren's shop I was working not only on Porsches and Ferraris, but also on Jaguars and Maseratis and Mercedes-Benzes. The cherry on the top was when Olson imported the Cooper racecars from England. When Warren signed up as Cooper's distributor in Los Angeles, we became a nucleus that was starting to move out of the passenger car business to something different. It was a head-spinning time to be part of it all, to be part of history, and I soaked it all up like a sponge.

Warren had been trained on Porsches by Germans from the factory who worked for Johnny von Neumann, the importer for Porsches and Ferraris. Johnny also drove them in races, and founded the California Sports Car Club with fellow sports car racer Roger Barlow.

Von Neumann came from humble beginnings as an immigrant from Austria. It's said that he added the "von" to his name to inflate his prestige with Americans. He began his rise by selling Volkswagen cars in a garage behind a small gas station.

Neumann reminded me of William Harley, founder of Harley Davidson, who designed a small engine. At first he added it to a bicycle, which was a failure, then a motorcycle, which was global success. Henry Ford, too, climbed the mountain to success, taking nothing and turning it into something. Those are the American ideals of entrepreneurial spirit, and "von" Neumann was a great example of that, I thought.

Being exposed to all of these concepts, thanks initially to Ed Donovan and Frank Startup, and having a basic propensity for exchanging ideas with wonderful people, I realize now even more than ever that I worked with men of genius. Plus, it didn't hurt my self-esteem when Donovan said to me sometime in the '70s, when he and I were both established in business: "Sonny, you have done more in 30 years of your life than most people do in a lifetime."

Every day I worked with Warren Olson he passed his knowledge of Mercedes-Benz and Porsche machinery along to me. The more I learned about them the more I developed a respect for German engineering.

We never sat around on our hands waiting for work, there was always plenty available. At Warren's shop I received 50 percent of the labor on particular jobs, so the quicker I could get them completed the faster I could move on to the next engine.

One of my most enjoyable projects was when one of my drag racing friends took a Porsche engine apart and couldn't figure out how to get it back together. It was all in bits and pieces. We called this "an engine in a basket." It was an easy task for me, as by then I knew those engines intimately.

One of my most complex and satisfying projects was restoring an old Bugatti for Lance Reventlow. He had purchased a 1937 Bugatti Type 57 Stelvio convertible, right-hand drive, from a medical doctor in Beverly Hills. When we examined the car we both realized it was in need of major repairs and substantial refurbishing. The car had been driven in Europe during the war years, before coming to the U.S.

Despite my tender age of 19, I suggested to Lance that I could do it, and got the job among all my other work responsibilities at Warren's shop, and in addition to my drag racing activities.

I completely dismantled the complex French machine down to the last nut and bolt, including the frame rails. Then I proceeded to completely rebuild the chassis, then the engine, gearbox and differential, the braking system, shock absorbers and suspension, literally everything on the car. There was not one single piece untouched. We even recreated a completely new wiring harness to match the original.

The body was being finished separately by a friend of mine in French blue color. I was very fortunate to have Andre Lerdet, a gifted Swiss wood and antique restorer, redo the entire dashboard and steering wheel. One of my hot rod friends owned an instrument repair business and he restored all the gauges.

Bugatti's engine was a straight eight-cylinder with double overhead camshafts. The cylinder block was integral with the complete head, all one piece without seams. This made it very similar to the American Offenhauser ("Offy") racing engine used at Indy, so I had Offy manufacturer Meyer & Drake Engineering rebore the cylinders for new oversized pistons. Those I was able to obtain from the Bugatti factory, which was still in business in those days in Mulhouse, France. They were able to service all the components that I needed to rebuild the engine to factory original, all in one convenient spot.

We corresponded in French, which came from growing up with my Belgian grandfather.

After completion of the chassis work in early 1957, but with body and coachwork still to be installed, *Road & Track* magazine pictured the chassis that way on the cover of its October 1957 issue.

That came about because one of the fans who liked to hang out with us, a Formula 3 racer named Russ Kelly, was also a journalist and photographer. He got *R&T's* publishers, fellow car enthusiasts John and Elaine Bond, to come over to look at the Bugatti project. I had already met them too, because of their living near my family home in Playa Del Rey. The Bonds were so enthralled with the quality of the restoration that they decided to have Russ make a formal portrait of it. He brought a huge roll of bright red background paper with him, which is called scrim in show biz, and set up the shoot right at Warren's shop.

Seeing that gorgeous chassis gleaming on that spectacular scarlet magazine cover was a pretty prideful moment for me. And it wasn't the last time one of Reventlow's cars would appear on the front of *Road & Track*.

Once I had finished installing the coachwork a couple of years later, complete with new top, I was happy to see that Lance enjoyed driving the Bugatti around Beverly Hills. It wasn't looked upon as a restored car, but rather felt like a brand new one.

However, I guess I should confess that I committed some American errors with the pure-blooded European machine. All those nuts and bolts that I removed from the chassis were unique, because Bugatti specially-made every single one to their own designs right in their factory. So I didn't simply swap them out for new ones.

But the hot-rodder in me couldn't resist improving them by sending them all out to be cadmium-plated. Also, I had the bumpers and some of the axle parts chromed. Doing those things were egregious sins to Bugatti people, I found out. They preferred restorations to absolutely "pur sang" (pure-blooded, ie. thoroughbred) perfectly factory-original condition. But that car did sparkle.

Sometimes before and after shop hours I took on outside jobs, like building special Chevy racing engines. In fact the Small Block V8 was getting to be my new favorite Chevy, the moneymaker for me. I did that work in the garage at my mother's house.

I remember installing a Chevy engine into a Ferrari, which is sacrilege, but people did it rather than pay through the nose for a replacement from Italy. The thing went fast as hell, and one time when we were testing at Willow Springs I went off the track, so obviously there were problems. But then the guy didn't want to pay me, so I stopped work on it.

My test-driving people's racecars was commonplace. When I'd done something, I wanted to make sure it was all working properly. But I never, ever had any desire to be a sports car racer. My Top Fuel dragster was way faster and more exciting, in my mind at least.

Workdays at Warren's wasn't all work all the time. We managed to squeeze in a little fun. One day Reventlow and Kessler brought me a couple of new Go Karts they'd bought and asked what I could do for them. I managed to get more speed and power out of the little 2-stroke motors, and made an exhaust system so they would sound powerful as well. We raced them up and down the streets in West Hollywood, along Robertson Boulevard and Melrose. The switchboard in the local sheriff's office would light up with complaints. But this was just a sideline, a lot of fun and lots of laughs.

Warren Olson was amazingly generous with his time and talent. There were some issues with my dragster that I was uncertain about, and he told me to bring it in. So I put it on my trailer, whose tires were just about bald, and went over to his shop. He helped me engineer a new seat mounting structure so that I could sit behind the axle, instead of above it. I also had to move the whole engine back in the chassis, to get more weight on the rear for better traction. What a challenge!

Then there was the challenge of moving into middle management.

The Olsons were getting so busy with racing, they left me running the shop. I was good at it, it turned out. I was able to make a success of it as far as making money and controlling everything. I had several European mechanics working under me.

Lance Reventlow and Bruce Kessler had been close friends ever since they were schoolboys. One day Lance came into the shop and said he really liked what Warren was doing for Bruce, and that he wanted us to start working on his cars too. He had several different kinds, Cooper, Maserati, Porsche, Ferrari — he could afford anything he wanted.

When Lance bought a Mercedes 300 SL, the famous Gullwing coupe with the doors that open upwards, it wasn't just any old run-of-the-mill German supercar. He special-ordered a rare competition model from the factory store on Sunset Boulevard. Its whole body was specially made in light aluminum, instead of the regular steel. It had magnesium wheels and more magnesium throughout the car.

We didn't get to do too much work on it, because the factory store had a German mechanic who they wanted to work on the car. So we would go to the races to change the tires, manage the pits and so forth. We used to run at Torrey Pines and Santa Barbara, places like that.

I also prepared and raced several of Lance's other cars of the time, before he formed the Scarab team, such as his Cooper 1100 sports car, Cooper Formula 2, and his 2-liter Maserati. We raced these locally, in and around Southern California, before Lance and Warren Olson went to England. I didn't go along on that trip.

Lance had been reasonably successful in American club racing, but on the other side of the Atlantic he was racing against the English. He came back and said to me, "Any bloody little English farm boy can blow me off!" The farmer may have been Jimmy Clark, one of the all-time great race drivers who was in fact Scottish and a sheep farmer, but anyway Lance just got a real good lesson in life.

Next thing, Lance Reventlow said he wanted to build an all-American racecar. Just like that my life changed again.

CHAPTER 6
LANCE REVENTLOW

Let me sketch a picture of the real Lance Reventlow, as I saw him anyway. One day he sent his Rolls-Royce car to LAX airport to pick up a new houseguest, a gentleman from Europe that he'd never met.

Quite an important gentleman, a German aristocrat in fact, a descendant of nobility whose full name was Wolfgang Alexander Albert Eduard Maximilian Reichsgraf Berghe von Trips. The "Graf" part meant he was a Count. Thankfully his friends could just call him "Taffy."

Von Trips was tall and slender, had the chiseled good looks you see in idealized portraits of European royalty, was extremely well educated and of course beautifully, impeccably mannered. On top of that he was a prominent Grand Prix racing driver. As a fully fledged member of the Ferrari factory racing team, he had earned distinction in both sports cars and Formula 1.

Why was he visiting a prominent Hollywood Playboy? Well, family connections, maybe. Lance happened to be a "Graf" too.

The chauffeur-driven Rolls duly picked up the distinguished guest at LAX and conveyed him back to the Reventlow homestead in Beverly Hills. Lance's friend Bruce Kessler had gone along, to chat pleasantly and make von Trips feel welcome.

The chauffeur pulled smoothly into the drive, parked the elegant car with precision before the grand entrance, got out, turned his back, and strode away into the house.

Leaving Lance's guest's luggage untouched.

Red-faced with anger, Graf von Trips briskly followed into the salon in time to see the chauffeur plop himself down comfortably on one of the velvet sofas, take off his cap, and fling it carelessly onto a nearby matching chair.

Appalled, insulted, enraged, von Trips began fuming at the man's arrogant, rude, disgraceful behavior. Timing it perfectly, the "chauffeur" stood back up, held out his hand with a big grin and said, "Hi, I'm Lance Reventlow!"

Ah yes, Lance Reventlow. One of the biggest characters I've ever met in racing or anywhere else. Knowing him was not only one of the most interesting experiences of my life, but our friendship led to a series of lucky opportunities for my career

Despite not being of noble lineage myself, I too was a guest in Lance's home, and many times. Really, I was just a mechanic for Lance, working on cars like a Cooper 1100, a 2.0-liter Maserati, and a Mercedes-Benz 300 SL. Yet after work he'd often invite me up to Beverly Hills for one of his many parties. I didn't look like a mechanic then, because by nature I try to always be clean and properly dressed.

Lance tried hard to be a Regular Guy. I guess I would too, if I was the only child and heir of one of the richest women in the world. Even back in the '50s that meant very, very rich. Obscene wealth isn't necessarily a good thing. I think one of the most revealing things Lance ever said was to a newspaper writer, who had asked why he wanted to be a race driver and build his own racecars.

"I want to prove I can do more than inherit money."

Although Hollywood handsome and often called "Golden Boy," Lance did not come from a happy family. His mother was Barbara Woolworth Hutton, heiress to the fortunes of the F. W. Woolworth retailing empire and financier E.F. Hutton. She was good looking, and spent her limitless inheritance ostentatiously, so she was attractive fodder for the tabloid press. "Poor Little Rich Girl," is how the papers enjoyed referring to her with their characteristic tact and empathy. Her mother committed suicide. Her father ignored her. Isolated behind walls of money, what chance did she have of normal human relationships?

Lance's father was a Danish Count, whose entire Gatling Gun of a name was Kurt Heinrich Eberhard Erdmann Georg von Haugwitz-

Hardenberg-Reventlow. Reventlow senior was Ms. Hutton's second husband, and he didn't last much longer than the first. She had also married and divorced movie star Cary Grant before Lance was old enough to catch racing fever from husband no. 4.

Prince Igor Troubetzkoy was a French aristocrat of Russian descent, an athlete in both cycling and skiing, and an early Ferrari enthusiast. In 1947 he bought three of the very first Prancing Horses ever made, and in one of them he partnered driver Clemente Biondetti to take victory in the incredibly tough Targa Florio road race through the mountains of Sicily.

That was 1948. Lance was 12, and the excitement of his step-dad's lifestyle made him a fan of European racing. In his teens Lance bought several exotic cars and drove some of them in competition. He was only modestly successful. Lance was a damn good driver, I thought, but a little hard on the equipment compared to some.

In those days, sports car racing was a gentleman's sport and Lance fit the ticket as compared to hot rodding and drag racing, which were my passions. Most of the sports car drivers in his crowd were a sophisticated group in Beverly Hills and Hollywood.

My world was a little different. I grew up watching and then racing older sedans that we all souped up ourselves. When I got involved with sports cars it was to make a living, working on them during the day, then spending all my earnings building my own dragster at night.

You might not think Lance and I would have much in common, but we got along great. We were only a couple of months apart in age, maybe that was part of it. And we were both crazy for racing, that would have counted for more.

I found myself swept up in his social life, and Lance knew everyone in Hollywood. I'd go along to hang out with his friends at places like the Luau restaurant on Rodeo Drive, which was owned by Lana Turner's husband, Steve Crane. Among the frequent diners were Ronnie Burns, the actor son of George Burns and Gracie Allen; the son of champion boxer Max Baer, actor Max Baer, Jr. who was in the Beverly Hillbillies TV show; and singer-songwriter Grace Slick, from Jefferson Airplane. They all seemed to accept me as a friend and contemporary.

One of the girls I particularly liked, although we were not dating, was named Celeste. She raised horses and I'd go riding with her. Her father was from Missouri, and started a Rent-a-Car company long before Hertz. Celeste's brother was David Shane, a good friend of Bob Petersen who started *Hot Rod* magazine, and whom I would meet later. David was a hunter, like Bob.

Bruce Kessler was usually around, too, and he often got together with Ronnie Burns, who caught racing fever. Ronnie bought a Formula Junior car, a Lotus which was considered a Formula 1 training car. But one time Ronnie let Bruce run the little open-wheeler at Riverside, where he was badly injured when the car flipped over going through the series of swerves known as the Esses, much to Ronnie's dismay and angst.

I soon met Lance's manservant, Dudley Walker. A typical Brit, elegant and charming, he had been batman to a flying officer in the Royal Air Force during World War I. Dudley was in Cary Grant's employ when Lance's mother, Barbara Hutton, sent him to work for Lance, probably to watch over him.

Dudley loved automobiles and often came to the races with Lance. He always kept his car polished to perfection, really spiffy. He enjoyed talking about cars. I liked talking to him about what would be considered mundane matters, but I was curious about his duties at the house, about laying out Lance's clothes, about making sure the cook prepared special meals when guests were expected.

Dudley was very distinguished-looking, and perfectly groomed with well-coiffed gray hair. He almost invariably dressed in coat and tie.

In fact, Dudley could have passed for a duke or an earl. He had, indeed, worked for an aristocrat, a British portrait painter, and accompanied him to the States in the late '30s when his boss had a commission to paint a celebrity in New York.

I well remember that Dudley didn't put up with fools, and would tell them to "bugger off" if they annoyed his employer or him. Lance was very fond of him, and vice-versa.

Years later, when I had my own company, Dudley and I often met for lunch. He'd teach me about wines, particularly French Bordeaux. I put the knowledge to good use later on as an oenologist, and as a member of the Los Angeles chapter of the Commanderie de Bordeaux. I became the person in charge of our wine cellar, the *sommelier*, so to speak. I strove to perform my duties in a manner to reflect credit on my mentor, Dudley Walker.

Bruce Kessler's friendship with Lance began when they met at boarding school in Arizona, where both had been sent to treat asthma. They shared an interest in sports as well as cars, and became inseparable. Bruce was into boxing, and looked pretty tough. "People thought I was Lance's bodyguard," he says.

Bruce was not born to wealth like Lance, but his parents had built their own affluence so the two young men could afford to pursue their passion for racing. They spent a season together racing in Europe.

Returning to the States in 1955, 19-year-olds Lance and Bruce were living a celebrity-filled life in Hollywood. Lance married a starlet, Jill St. John, and the couple lived in Beverly Hills in a magnificent home on top of a hill with a 360-degree view. The Reventlows gave many parties that I attended.

Lance also became friends with fellow racer James Dean, who was starting a meteoric rise playing the role of a teenage rebel on the silver screen.

He wasn't really acting. That fall, on September 30th, 1955, Lance and Bruce Kessler would be the last to talk to Dean while having a rest stop together at Blackwell's Corner, a crossroads in the farm fields of the Central Valley about 150 miles north of Beverly Hills. They were all on their way to a road race in northern California near Monterey, Lance driving his Mercedes-Benz SL Gullwing coupe and the 24-year-old Dean driving with his mechanic, Rolf Wütherich, in his new Porsche 550 Spyder. "Little Bastard" was the name he had painted on his small, lightweight, very fast open-cockpit racecar.

After lunch they arranged to meet again for dinner, but Dean was soon stopped for speeding. After resuming his drive, barely 30 miles from the lunch stop he died in a high-speed, head-on crash approaching a blip on the map called Cholame. The mechanic somehow survived, as did the oncoming driver. A melancholy shrine to James Dean was put up near the spot and remains there to this day.

Lance and Bruce went ahead with their racing plans.

Lance was mechanically adept and knowledgeable about cars and engines, and at one point he took Kessler to the Lister racing car works in England. Listers were big sports racers that were dominating such racing in Great Britain. They normally carried six-cylinder, twin-cam Jaguar XK engines — Le Mans-winning engines — but Lance was thinking of buying a Lister and fitting it with a more powerful Chevy V8 (as other Yanks were).

What he saw in the Lister shop changed his mind. As he examined the car in detail, he found more and more things about the British chassis to criticize. It seems that voices were raised and arms began waving between Brian Lister and Lance. Finally, Lance walked away.

Outside, he declared to Bruce Kessler that in his opinion the Lister was a piece of crap and that he, Lance Reventlow, could build a better car! Bruce agreed. The two drivers came home, their heads filled with exciting plans to build an all-American sports racer.

CHAPTER 7
THE SCARAB

S uppose you set out to manufacture your own automobile. You get to name it, so what brand moniker would you come up with?

Many people simply write in their own surnames, like Ferrari, Ford or Porsche. Colin Chapman chose a flower, Lotus. Many brands are acronyms for corporations, such as ALFA, BMW, GMC. If yours will be a performance car, how about something evoking the world of predators, like Jaguar or Eagle? Carroll Shelby called his a Cobra; fair enough.

Lance Reventlow branded his new car a Scarab.

Sounds nice, doesn't it. Something different, mystical, almost regal. To the ancient Egyptians, there were religious connotations having to do with immortality. A topic you could safely bring up to keep an erudite conversation going over a formal dinner table.

But Lance meant it mischievously. I imagine him growing up enduring stuffy formal dinner parties with the haughtiest crowned heads of Europe, personages educated in the most prestigious of universities and forever making sure you knew it. How boring for a boy, especially a free-wheeling American boy. Maybe that's why he liked to let his inner prankster loose.

Scarabs are dung beetles. They are born in and feed on, well, biological waste. Clearly this connotation appealed to Lance's boyish mind, and on seeing his cars, it seems obvious he had noticed that many varieties of Scarab beetle are a nice shimmery metallic blue. I can almost hear him stifling laughter.

It was 1957 and Lance Reventlow was 21 when, back home from his unsuccessful attempt to take European racing by storm, he set to work on an American racing car of his own. He invited Bruce Kessler, Warren Olson and others to join him in forming Reventlow Automobiles, Inc., or RAI.

Since everybody was already established at Warren's Sports Car Service on North Robertson, that's where the Scarab project began. Work on chassis 1 began right away, but Olson's existing customers had to be serviced as well. He could spare only three garage bays of the eight total in his service shop. Obviously, manufacturing a new brand of racing car required more space, more equipment, and more people, so RAI was going to need its own HQ.

No problem. Lance's funds seemed unlimited (or so it was thought, but in fact the purse strings were firmly in his mother's hands) so, bursting with confidence, he, best buddy Bruce and his new general manager Warren Olson set about making it all happen.

First up, the key to success would be assembling the right personnel. So the new team reached out to the most talented racecar craftsmen available in Los Angeles. Because they would need to know what the end product was to be, high on the list had to be someone to design the car.

KEN MILES

In fact the creation of any racing machine is a collaborative and evolutionary process, so the Scarabs were shaped by many hands. But the starting points were laid out by an auto and motorcycle mechanic, racecar builder and highly successful driver from the industrial English Midlands named Ken Miles.

The story goes that Miles tried to run away from home and go to America as a young teenager sometime in the '30s. He got stopped then, but rebelled again at the age of 15, leaving school to apprentice himself to automaker Wolseley. The deal included education at a technical school, and Ken got a good education there to judge by the skills he showed later.

When World War II broke into everybody's life he served in a British Army tank unit during the 1944 invasion of Normandy. Postwar he raced a wide variety of older cars in England until he finally achieved his lifelong ambition to move to America in 1952. He was 34.

In Los Angeles he became service manager for the local MG distributor, and set about making his own MG-based racing Specials. His first was good, his second was exceptional. Known as "The Flying Shingle" because of its noticeably low, wide stance, it featured a "space frame" chassis made of numerous steel tubes welded into a rigid but lightweight truss structure. This construction principle was well established in aircraft, but it was leading edge technology in racing at the time.

The Shingle's stiff frame, low weight and low build gave good handling around turns as well as high speeds on straights, and Miles was a superb driver, well able to get the best out of his creation. He won victory after victory in SCCA club competition, making both Ken and car famous in sports car circles.

Then he did it all again, putting together another special out of a small, rear-engined Cooper powered by a Porsche engine and transmission. Ken didn't pioneer this idea, Seattle-area VW dealer Pete Lovely had already done it, but both their "Poopers" were fast and successful. Miles racked up a lot of wins in 1958.

I have to say, this old drag racer feels kinship with fellows like that. Road racers use the name "specials" for such ingenious combinations of different car parts, but the idea is exactly the same with our "hot rods." We're brothers.

Miles became a highly respected and well-liked leader of the Cal Club sports car group, and a good writer of technical articles for enthusiast magazines. He also designed racetracks.

Ken was gregarious, but did have a feisty side. He was a battler with a short fuse. People who jokingly referred to the Brit as "Teddy Teabagger" risked his wrath. Fellow racers called him "Side Bite." In circuit racing that term refers to how well a tire grips the road through corners, but it served as well to describe Miles' characteristic way of firing pithy English-accented comments out of the side of his lean jaw.

Warren Olson went to him and said, "Ken, I want you to design our new Scarab."

CHUCK DAIGH

The main mover and shaker behind the development of the Scarab, Chuck Daigh was a tough Irishman from Long Beach, California. He had been a paratrooper in the war, when he jumped into enemy territory during the Allied invasion of Sicily in 1943. Surviving that, he went into car racing and by the early '50s he was one of the top drivers in America.

Chuck always said that he was a mechanic first and foremost, and that showed in his driving. He could pinpoint a problem with a machine, and adjust his driving technique to keep it going. It was the same ability we saw in Phil Hill, America's first-ever Formula 1 champion and winner of many long, grueling endurance races like Le Mans. Both men had an innate mechanical sense for what was wrong and how to deal with it, although Phil didn't usually get his hands greasy like Chuck.

They had some good battles on track, and one of the most memorable was at Riverside in 1958. Phil was a contracted Ferrari man, and he was in one of John von Neumann's that day. Chuck was driving our lead Scarab. That was one of the greatest sports car races ever seen in America... but I won't spoil the story here. Look for Riverside 1958 — the first "Times Grand Prix" — to come up later on.

When I first met Chuck Daigh at Warren Olson's facility in West Hollywood, he already had a reputation as a winner, thanks to a car called the Troutman-Barnes Special. Built in 1954 by two other future members of the Scarab team, it was a workmanlike open two-seater with a smoothly egg-shaped aluminum body over a multi-tubular steel chassis. At first the engine was a Flathead Ford V8, but that later was replaced with the newer OHV product used in Ford's Thunderbird.

Ken Miles raced the T&B Spl. as well as Chuck Daigh, but it was Chuck who drove it through 1957 and scored numerous strong finishes at West Coast road courses like Santa Barbara, Paramount Ranch, Palm Springs and Riverside Raceway.

An impressive record for any car, but especially when it was the first product of their own from two guys who came out of the shop of a famous Indycar constructor.

TROUTMAN & BARNES

Dick Troutman and Tom Barnes had been fabricators for Frank Kurtis, the chassis building genius whose Kurtis Kraft Engineering literally transformed Indycar and oval-track track racing in the early '50s. Kurtis pioneered Indy's "Roadster" design, where the Offy engine was steeply inclined to one side, thus offsetting the driveline (gearbox and prop shaft) so the driver could sit lower. The roadster configuration quickly became "the" Indy car standard.

Kurtis also produced burly, sturdy two-seaters for the sports cars crowd. Possibly that's why Troutman and Barnes started itching to build a racing sports car of their own. They did so on their own time, actually constructing their own T&B Special in Troutman's home garage.

Resolute spirits, creative minds, gifted hands, practical experience, on-track success... pedigree enough for Warren Olson to snap them both up for the Scarab project, along with their driver Daigh. Actually, at the beginning of the Scarab project Chuck was more of the chief mechanic, and he personally built the car's first Chevy racing engine.

Chuck's brother Harold Daigh also came aboard for a while. Both were old hot rodders and expert mechanics, and Harold became the crew chief on Lance's Scarab no. 16. Chuck took the same role on the no. 5 car, the one he was driving, so was his own crew chief!

Harold had been a major in the U.S. Marine Corps in Korea, a fighter pilot who flew both P51 Mustangs and the newer F86 Saber jets. After joining Reventlow Automobiles Harold often flew company missions in Lance's airplane, a twin-engine Cessna. I have a story to tell about that too, later on.

TRAVERS AND COON (TRACO)
Chevrolet was now making the hot new American engine, the Small Block V8 seen in Corvettes as well as many, many winning racecars. It was the obvious choice for the new Scarab. RAI's jack-of-all-trades Chuck Daigh built the first one, but more were needed. To Warren Olson, the obvious choice to build Scarab's Chevys was the partnership of Jim Travers and Frank Coon.

Travers and Coon ("Tra-Co") were known as "The Rich Kids" because they had worked with millionaire Indy team owner Howard Keck. The head of California's Superior Oil Company, which his father had started, Keck lavished money on his race team, providing more and better parts than most of the other team owners. His own Kurtis Roadster won the Indy 500 twice with Billy Vukovich sitting behind Travers and Coon Offenhauser engines. Following the popular "Vuky's" tragic death there in 1955 Keck folded his racing team, so Travers and Coon set up their own business, Traco.

Their "Rich Kids'" nickname was occasionally misquoted as "whiz kids," although that actually applied to a group of smart young executives at Ford Motor Company. But Traco's "kids" were indeed young *Wunderkind* geniuses. Although they specialized in building Offies for Indycars and Midgets, they had plenty of magic left over to make Chevrolets really roar in Scarab's road racing sports cars.

Conveniently, their shop in Culver City was literally next door to the one RAI soon moved into! They played roles in the Scarab story from first to last.

The experience Travers and Coon gained with Reventlow and the results they achieved expanded their business exponentially. Traco Chevys would be the top choice of many other teams far into the future.

There were others at RAI who I'll write about farther along, but here at the initial stage of the project is the place to mention an extremely creative young industrial designer and car enthusiast named Chuck Pelly. Maybe styling has nothing to do with a racecars's performance, but looks do matter to all of us.

Lance wanted his Scarabs to be beautiful, so he asked someone to recruit a student from the famous Art Center College of Design in Pasadena. Bruce Kessler told me an anecdote about it: "I said, okay, Lance, I'll go and see if anybody wants to work with us. The principal I talked to obviously thought I was out of my mind when I explained my mission, but he called the art students together. They all frowned at me when I asked if anyone was interested in designing a racecar. They all looked at each other and were saying the same thing, 'Who let this guy in here?' Finally, in the back a hand slowly went up. That was Chuck Pelly, who went on to become one of the world's most famous automotive designers!"

Young Art Center student Pelly designed a body so beautiful that it forever cemented Scarab's place in the hearts of enthusiasts.

To be fair and tell the whole story, Pelly's first body lines evolved over time, partly due to running experience and, honestly, to suit personal tastes. Emil Diedt and others formed and reformed the malleable aluminum, in particular the nose shape. The original radiator opening was bigger than turned out to be necessary, so Emil "skinnied it down" to be more streamlined, and it must be said to look better.

Similarly, others on the team also had a hand in their areas of the car. Construction was racing forward faster than the designer could produce drawings, so Ken Miles' original chassis layout was further developed by Warren Olson and Chuck Daigh, among others.

My interest in this project was unbounded. In a funny way it was almost personal with me, because it was truly an American machine: its roots had grown in many other nations.

A transplanted Englishman had designed its space frame, the car's basic skeleton. I saw it as really an enlargement of Ken Miles's own"Flying Shingle" Special, but rather than that car's little four-cylinder MG engine the Scarab was built for the bigger, heavier, much more powerful Chevrolet V8.

In the same way, every other component and system of the complex machine was being designed and constructed by individuals who, like Ken Miles, had roots in other nations and cultures, but who themselves were Americans.

So was the car they were building. The Scarab was European in concept, but American in reality. Almost every component of it was technology that we were building right here in the United States. Not British technology. Not French, nor German, nor Italian. That came straight from Lance. His car had to be All-American.

Alright, maybe it was missing some Belgian-American heritage. But my time was coming.

Almost as soon as Warren's shop completed the first Scarab, which was the single left-hand-drive car that Lance would race as number 16 (and which would figure prominently in my own future), RAI moved to another facility spacious enough to build two more cars.

Only one thing wrong with that — they left me behind!

CHAPTER 8
REVENTLOW AUTOMOBILES, INC.

Why Culver City, of all places? Wasn't that just an obscure little cluster of movie studios, the so-called "Heart of Screenland?" Yes, but a lot more was going on in that growing community near the airport and the ocean.

Earlier I described how my passion for car racing began on a particular stretch of Culver Blvd., the thoroughfare that led from our home in Playa Del Rey to the movie theaters up in the larger town. But I left out a few other interesting facts about the area.

Not many people today remember that Culver City was once an important center for auto racing.

Back in 1924, a steeply banked oval speedway made of timber was constructed near the intersection of Culver and Overland. Newspapers said a crowd some 70,000 strong went to the opening events just before Christmas that year, and the track went on to host national championship AAA Indycar races for three years. In qualifying for one in 1927, Frank Lockhart set a world speed record of 144 mph aboard a supercharged 91 cubic inch Miller. That was an astounding velocity back then, one that the Indianapolis Motor Speedway couldn't match until 1956.

But land values were rising rapidly, while wooden tracks tended to deteriorate at a similar pace. Later in 1927 the speedway was demolished to make room for houses.

So West Side L.A. race fans had to go elsewhere for a couple of decades, but by the time World War II was over a dirt-surfaced "bull ring" was hosting Midget races at Lincoln and Washington, where a dog racing track had been. The car track stayed in operation until 1954, when the property was repurposed for a Douglas aircraft plant.

Today historians have to find the local Costco superstore to know where the old dirt track was. As for the preceding board track, its site is now a Culver City park. When we Balcaens went to the movies we were practically on the spot.

I don't think I knew about those old racetracks when I was that young, but I like to think there was something in the air I breathed!

A lot of other guys must have been affected too, because when the tracks were active a performance industry formed around them. Many of the products made in Culver City won races across the entire nation, even at Indianapolis. When the local tracks went away the local racing businesses saw no reason to go with them, and so a lot of what Reventlow Automobiles needed in the way of car building and engine tuning expertise could be found in one convenient spot.

Scarab's new home was at 11930 West Jefferson Blvd. For those not familiar with the Los Angeles area, it's just north of LAX airport on the lower terrain, where the yacht harbor Marina Del Rey is today. Jefferson extends inland from near my boyhood home, Playa Del Rey, branching off of Culver Blvd. to run right by the spot where famous aviator and movie maker Howard Hughes used to have his own airfield and aircraft factory. A little farther along the boulevard passes under today's multi-level junction of the Marina Freeway with the massive San Diego Freeway, aka Interstate 405.

The area has changed a lot since the '50s, of course, but Reventlow's old headquarters building is still there. You can find it a little back on West Jefferson from the freeways toward the ocean on the south side of a four-lane street lined with both homes and businesses.

Why am I going into such detail about some old auto workshop? Because West Jefferson is a hallowed place to racers. Right next door to Lance's rented space is where engine building geniuses Jim Travers and Frank Coon already had their Traco Engineering HQ. Mere minutes away was a host of machine shops and magnesium casting foundries and other specialist businesses that RAI could rely on for quick, expert service. One of great importance was Halibrand, famous throughout American racing for their Quick Change rear axle gears and also their light, strong cast wheels.

Scarab wasn't part of the scene for very long, but West Jefferson remained a racing hotbed for decades. It gained such fame that, some time after we were gone, everybody started calling it "Thunder Alley."

The brick walls of the Reventlow and Traco shops literally touched each other. The buildings weren't identical, RAI's was a little bigger, but neither was what anyone in racing today would call spacious. A bit narrow, not much longer and with only one level, both seem cramped and dark to our eyes now. But somehow magic happened there.

Scarab crewmen quickly outfitted their new place with the best equipment money could buy, including machine tools, a metal-working shop and appropriate welding gear. Warren Olson had lured Dick Troutman and Tom Barnes to be the chassis builders, and a large, dead level steel table was made so that they could ensure their measurements were precise. Scarab space frame chassis were made of lengths of steel tubing joined at many angles, and it was vital that everything be clamped into proper place before welding so the structure came out perfectly straight.

Although I didn't work there at the beginning, when I finally rejoined the team I was amused to observe that, although we had top-notch equipment, the most accurate way to check and set the chassis balance on its four wheels was to use four everyday animal feed scales, one under each hand-made Halibrand magnesium wheel. If one or another weight was different than it should be, we made adjustments to the springs and shock absorbers until the corner-to-corner balance was just right.

One time we had a Scarab up on the scales when Chuck Daigh joked, "Maybe we should lighten it up a bit on that side because Lance might bring his wallet!"

When I think back to those days I realize we worked with practically nothing, compared with the engineering and fabricating capabilities they have today. We designed and built the parts, tested them, and won races with them, all pretty much by hand.

Today, in the 21st century, there is a wealth of materials, data, technology, and machinery available. Computers run everything with a precision we couldn't even dream of in the '50s. Just about everything a race mechanic needs is at his disposal. You can buy complete parts ready to bolt into place, no creative modifications required. It is so much easier to build a racecar or a hot rod now. In those days we designed and built from scratch. It was a do-it-yourself world.

We worked our tails off day and night. We were always, always working. This was a serious time, not one for playing.

B ut wait... Last you heard, I wasn't moving to the new shop along with the Reventlow team.

Well, I wanted to, and desperately! In fact, absurdly, with my youthful hubris I wanted to be the head guy. I'd always wanted to be a crew chief, to be in charge and satisfy my entrepreneurial independence. Realistically, of course, I knew I wasn't capable of it at that stage, but that didn't stop me hoping for it.

Unfortunately for my hopes, it seemed that I was such a good manager and mechanic that Warren wanted me to stay behind to manage his West Hollywood shop. He was needed in Culver City to head up the Scarab project for Lance.

I'll be honest, it was a disappointment at first. With the fierce passion I had for racing I'd have chosen the Scarab race team without a moment's hesitation.

Sure, I knew it's not all fun. Campaigning a racecar is a lot of work, and the work can go on through all hours of the day and night. It's physically exhausting. You get tired mentally, too. There's a lot of planning that goes into it, not to mention the pressure. Not only is the deadline absolute, so is the necessity to build the safest, fastest, most reliable racing machine possible. Literally, people's lives hang on the integrity of your work. So does your employer's success.

Nevertheless, racing competitively, doing the job so perfectly that you give yourself a realistic chance of winning, is the most satisfying and exciting thing I could imagine doing in life.

But although I did manage to go to some of the Scarab track testing, before they were ready to race, most days I was stuck in the same old retail shop up near Beverly Hills working on the same old ordinary movie star cars.

Well, ok, I'm selling it short. Olson's job offer was a good one. It put me in charge of the Ferraris, Maseratis, Porsches, Jaguars, and other exotic foreign cars that came in for service and repairs. I was still eager to work on and learn all about them. They were the epitome of power and performance from German, Italian and British makers. I poured myself into every minute I spent with them.

At the same time I directed a group of European mechanics working on them. That would further my ambitions about developing management skills. I'd realized I had some talent in that area thanks to working with Simone Olson. She was the brains behind her husband Warren's shop. Warren never really wanted to bother with management or any of that stuff, but Simone was a UCLA grad. She was a smart lady, and she really ran the organization. I happen to have the same kind of gift that she did for management, and I learned a lot from her.

It suited my entrepreneurial bent. I can say it in hindsight, but I really knew where I was going and what I wanted to do at a young age. I knew my motivations were there, and I knew what to do.

My restoration of Lance's Bugatti was still ongoing at the time, but was turning out so nicely that it brought me a flood of new freelance customers coming out of the woodwork.

One of them thought I'd work on the restoration of his Bugatti for nothing, because I was a young guy and could further my skills. I had enough sense to turn him down.

That sort of thing happened a few times, including with the owner of a Ferrari who told me after I'd done the work on his car that he couldn't pay me. He said the stock market was down and he didn't want to dip into his capital!

I knew my youthful appearance belied my expertise, but dealing with people like that quickly made me a student of human behavior. Later on, when I went to university I took many business classes that included the people side of it.

So running Warren's shop taught me a lot about controlling and running an important business, picking up the best way to handle customers and employees. I was only in my early twenties, yet I felt like a seasoned entrepreneur. Warren was nice enough to tell me I was making a success of my golden opportunity.

Besides, I was still racing my GMC dragster regularly, with relative success in the Top Fuel class — the fastest class.

And my story has a happy ending. One day I would find myself down in Culver City working on Scarab racecars after all.

But first I went to Texas.

CHAPTER 9
WITH JIM HALL

O ne of my favorite all-time heroes is the extraordinary racecar engineer, designer and champion driver Jim Hall from Texas. His name holds a special place in racing history both as a driver and a car builder, and more than a special place in my heart.

His most famous legacy is the brilliantly innovative racing cars he made and named Chaparrals for the famous "Road Runner" birds of the South West. With his great friend and partner Hap Sharp and a small team of master mechanics — plus some undercover help by Chevrolet engineers, who weren't supposed to be racing! — Jim drove his own Chaparral to the 1964 National championship of the Sports Car Club of America.

In following seasons Chaparrals scored victories in Florida's 1965 12-hour endurance race at Sebring, the 1966 Canadian-American Challenge Cup Series ("Can-Am") and the same year's 1000-kilometer race over the tortuous Nurburgring in Germany. In 1967 the team won another long-distance race in Europe, at Brands Hatch in England. All that led to Chaparral's historic Indy 500 victory in 1980.

Chaparrals introduced several advanced technologies, the most significant being in aerodynamics. The 1966 Can-Am car astonished the racing world with a driver-adjustable "flipper" wing mounted directly on the rear wheel hubs. This arrangement forced aerodynamic loads straight into the tires to improve their hold on the road. It was an innovation that would reshape racing cars worldwide — until the principle was outlawed.

The same fate awaited Chaparral's 1970 Can-Am car, which had an elaborate system of extractor fans and articulated skirts to generate "ground effect" under the vehicle. Put another way, the car became a giant, self-powered suction-cup pushing the rubber down. The fan principle was promptly banned, but ground effects generated by the shape of the car itself are still the key factor in most racecar designs to this day. Chaparral's 1980 Indy winner introduced that design to American racing.

But all that still lay in the future when I first met Jim....

As best as I can reconstruct the timeline, I probably got to know the quiet, studious, very talented young man from Texas during 1957 at our local California tracks, maybe Hourglass Field in San Diego. Jim Hall was driving a sweet little 2.0-liter Maserati there, and I would have been all over it with interest and admiration and loads of questions.

The next step was thanks to Carroll Shelby. It wasn't unusual for famous drivers and other gearheads to walk into Warren's shop, shoot the breeze and look around at the work going on with customers' cars. One morning in 1957 I was working on a Cooper when Shelby stopped by and came over to see me.

I already knew Carroll, thanks to a race driver named Ruth Levy. I used to take care of her Porsche in the shop, and I made it really go quickly. So Ruthie and I were good friends, and of course she knew her fellow driver Shelby — who was the hottest thing in sports car racing then, the 1956 national champion.

I don't know if Ruthie had raved about my work, or maybe Jim Hall sent him to find me. Anyway, Shelby had a job offer.

The year before he had parlayed his fame by opening a dealership in Dallas called Carroll Shelby Sport Cars Inc. He was a partner with Dick Hall, older brother of Jim. But because Shelby was frequently off racing in Europe, Dick suggested that his brother come in to help out.

Jim was available, because after graduating that spring from Cal Tech in California with a degree in mechanical engineering, the job waiting for him at Chevrolet in Michigan was cut.

The job Dick Hall needed his brother to do was to stand-in for Carroll Shelby, who had been demonstrating the performance of the cars they sold by racing them in front of prospective customers. As a marketing plan it was brilliant, but not every dealership had a driver who could handle the role.

Jim Hall could, though. He'd been racing for years, ever since he turned 18 and started college. The cars he had raced included a big Cadillac-engined English Allard, not an easy machine to master. Hall himself owned a Chevy Corvette and half of the Shelby-Hall dealership's Ferrari 750 Monza, a top-of-the-line 3.0-liter sports racer of the day. Jim was also campaigning the dealership's 2.0 Maserati, meaning he had two feisty Italian stallions to deal with.

Would I, Carroll wondered, be interested in going to work for him and Jim as his race engineer? My job would be prepping, setting up and otherwise looking after the dealership's stable of racecars, plus a Lotus that was coming.

I just leapt at the chance, because I wasn't going to be part of the Scarab racing program. While the other guys were getting the all-new sports car built and ready to race in 1958, Warren wanted me to stay out of that and focus on running what to me what was his pedestrian retail business.

I was good at that job, I was getting valuable experience at business management, including directing a group of European mechanics working there.

But I was still a young racer at heart. And I had that burning ambition to be a crew chief. The opportunity to go back to the tracks with Jim Hall was too good to pass up.

He and I were only a few months apart on age. Carroll was a little older, but both were tall, handsome, lanky Texans, and both spoke with distinctive Texas accents. Jim could be taciturn in his behavior, but we got along great.

So I packed up my tools and belongings and made the long drive to Dallas. Out behind the "Sport Car" dealership there was a row of service garages, and that's where I set up and got to work.

It was a lot of work. I'd have to repair any damage to the cars and tune up the engines and check everything over, trailer them to the tracks, be chief mechanic and pit crew there, then head back to the shop and do it all over again for the next race.

After the perfect climate of Southern California the weather in the Lone Star State was not wonderful, with extremes ranging from very hot and humid to very cold. But recognizing the great honor of being

Jim Hall's chief race engineer, and knowing that I would still make occasional trips back to Los Angeles when necessary, made it seem worthwhile.

Late that year Shelby had a lead on a Lotus 11, the very streamlined little sports car that Colin Chapman had designed and which was dominating the small-bore sports car classes around the world. This 11 was a special one, with a bigger Coventry Climax engine than the usual 1.1 liters that Lotus put in that model. This would be a 1.5, with twin overhead camshafts rather than the usual single-stick design.

Shelby decided that Jim was going to buy this trick car and go out there and try to beat the Porsche 550s. So Jim handed over the keys to his Chrysler 300C and sent me off towing an empty trailer to Idlewild airport in New York, now called Kennedy airport. That was a long drive, but I love driving and that big, luxurious 300C made it pure pleasure. At the airport I loaded up the sleek little Lotus and headed straight down to the port of Miami and put it on a barge to Nassau, way out in the Bahamas.

It was the first weekend in December, 1957, when Jim first raced the Lotus, right out of the box. I didn't have any time at all to go through the little English car before Jim took it out for its maiden run at Nassau.

Typical of the era, the sports car course there was laid out on an airport, Oakes Field. Jim managed to get in several laps during practice and we made adjustments as well as we could in the pit. Jim took a fourth place in one of his races, but dropped out of the other with damage. Stirling Moss was the winner and we placed 36th of 51 entries.

While cleaning the car and getting it ready for the next outing, I decided to go the extra mile and rebuild the whole car. I spent a lot of time on the little four-cylinder engine, tuning it up and getting it running really nicely. Later on I also had the car repainted by specialist auto racing artists, with striping by Von Dutch of hot-rodding fame. I really seriously maintained that little car.

In the middle of January, 1958, we were back in Miami for another airport race, where the Lotus gave the same results as in Nassau. That's what race records say, anyway. Frankly, neither Jim nor I have any memories of that one at all.

However, I do recall going go to Havana the following month for the Grand Prix of Cuba, a sports car race through the city streets. Jim wasn't entered there, but my friend Bruce Kessler was racing a Ferrari there, so I just went on my own. And I made the local paper!

No, not because I was involved in the famous Fangio kidnapping incident. But I'll tell the whole story a little later, in the Bruce Kessler chapter.

In March it was back to Jim Hall's Lotus and another airport event, this time at Phoenix, Arizona. This was a race I will always remember vividly. It was my biggest thrill with the problematic little car — right up until it turned into my worst disappointment.

Jim and his Lotus 11 were racing neck and neck against Jack McAfee's Porsche 550, which had dominated that season in the 1500-cc class. The two were locked tight together as they sped by the pits and we saw the Lotus zip right past the Porsche. It was the last lap. Who would come back into sight first?

Suddenly there was a massive roar from all sides! My buddies lifted me onto their shoulders. I already knew it was MY car, Jim's Lotus-Climax, that the entire crowd was rooting for! And yes, I was right! Here was Jim streaking down the straight toward the checkered flag!

That's when Colin Chapman's super-light space frame chassis suddenly broke where it held the differential housing in the rear, sending our Lotus careening out of the race. Jim was very lucky not to get badly hurt.

Talk about luck. Ours turned right around the very next weekend on yet another airfield at Mansfield, Louisiana. (Not to be confused with the town of the same name in another state that anchors what is now Mid-Ohio road-race course. The place I'm talking about is now called De Soto Parish airport, a former auxiliary base to Barksdale AFB near Shreveport. We used a lot of airports in those days, before there were many purpose-built road courses.) Jim ran two races at that Mansfield event and wound up with a third place and then a win.

Not in the Lotus, though. He had gone back to his Maserati, clearly a more solid racecar than the little English Lotus. We only ran the 11 one more time, in April at Palm Springs Airport. It did finish that race, in fifth place. But the Lotus venture was a lot of work for not a lot of payoff. We never did beat the Porsche.

Between Mansfield and Palm Springs I did another side-job for my friend Ruth Levy and Denise McCluggage, who were co-driving a Fiat Abarth Zagato at Sebring, Florida. Rather than bore anybody with one more race story, let me share a more colorful anecdote about me.

Kessler was there too, driving a Ferrari for Luigi Chinetti. Both "our" cars were entered in the GT class. As Bruce wrote it up:

> I was staying in a real dumpy house that had been rented for me because all the hotel rooms had been booked up. Sonny, who was hauling [his] car on his trailer, told me on the phone he had nowhere to stay, so I invited him to share my place. In the middle of the night I was sitting in the living room when I heard him come screaming through the door. He slammed it closed, hit the light switch, plunging the room into darkness. Then Sonny just sat on the sofa, kind of quiet.
>
> I hadn't heard the trailer pull in. It makes a special grating sound, so I asked him where it was, because all I heard was a car coming up the driveway. Sonny said he left the trailer somewhere else.
>
> Turns out he'd met a girl whose father owned an orange grove. Sonny was parked among the orange trees making out with her when her father came along in a tow truck, shone a flashlight at Sonny, and pointed a gun at him.
>
> "Jesus Christ, what did you do?" I asked Sonny. He replied that he jammed on the ignition, threw the car into gear, and took off. I asked him about the girl who was in the car with him. He said he slowed down after a mile or so, leaned over to the passenger door, opened it, and rolled her out!

Bruce! No, I completely deny it! I didn't "push" the young lady, I just politely tapped her on the shoulder and suggested our date was over. What's more, her father didn't point a gun at me. It's just that I could see he had one.

Another interesting episode: one day when I was working at Carroll Shelby Sport Cars, Shelby asked me to take a ride with him. He had invested in some oil wells and wanted to go check on them. I remember that he was wearing his alligator skin loafers. Carroll was always well-groomed in those days, a hot shot, and liked to be fashionably dressed.

We hopped into his brand new, right-hand drive Rolls-Royce Silver Cloud, one of the marques his agency sold, and drove out of town. When I say drove I mean Carroll's idea of driving a passenger car was as if he was on a racetrack and all alone.

It was the ride of my life! For some of the way we were on small roads and at times almost off-road. He drove the socks off that thing. A Rolls can really handle well, but they tended to sway in those days and I thought we were going to tip over! I was on edge the whole time.

It took us about two hours to reach the oil wells, where Shelby chatted with the oil workers. I'm sure they were used to seeing oil barons drive up in Rolls-Royces and Bentleys. Then I had to be Carroll Shelby's passenger again for another two hours all the way back to Dallas.

All during this time I was getting more and more tired of living in Dallas. As a California boy I was fed up with the Texas weather. More importantly, the area didn't have the fabrication specialists I was used to relying on back home, experts who had learned their trade in the aerospace industry and founded one of the world's greatest auto racing centers.

Plus, I missed all the military surplus stores in Los Angeles where I could buy stuff that I wanted to use in my racecars. I used to feed on the surplus stores for all kinds of handy things. Need fuel lines? Aircraft fuel lines are great. Want to easily take off your body panels to work on the car? Aircraft use these wonderful Dzus fasteners. Oil coolers too, and so forth. I had been trained and educated in mining surplus stores by Pete Clark and Eddie Donovan, but there was literally nothing like that in Texas.

Also, drag racing was still in my blood. I wanted to bench race with my buddies and smell the Nitro and blast my digger down a dragstrip, but it was sitting in L.A. 1500 miles away.

Carroll Shelby was pleased with my work for his star driver, Jim Hall, and was not pleased about my longings for home. But he could see I was stressed. So he came to me one day and said, "Don't you need a vacation in California?"

He added that he had a brand-new car that I could drive back there. A beautiful, luxurious 1958 Impala.

Hey, what a great boss!

The car came with a catch. I would actually be ferrying it out there for Shelby, and I would be delivering it to a friend of his. She was a movie starlet named Jan that Carroll had been going with, and the stunning new car was a little gift.

Shelby was still married then, but… well, OK, he's my boss. So when I get to L.A. I phone the lady and arrange to meet her. I drive up and there she is with another guy. Who she introduces to me as her husband.

Race car drivers… pretty women… Hollywood… what can I say.

As for Shelby's take on this little incident, it seems that my small act resonated with him, because author Rinsey Mills mentioned it in his authorized biography of Shelby. In fact, I felt honored to be included four other times in the book.

However, a little vacation trip didn't satisfy me. Jim Hall came to my aid. He was getting a new racecar, which was going to need a lot of work (I'll explain in a minute), and he backed me up when I said that Los Angeles would be a better place to do the work than Dallas.

Finally it was agreed that I could relocate to L.A., and keep working on Jim's cars there. I had been towing them all over the country anyway. Where the long drives started from didn't matter as much as the quality of the preparation I could do in California. Let alone my state of mind as I did the work.

So I packed up all my stuff, loaded a trailer with Jim's Lotus, and drove it all back home to Los Angeles. I found a suitable workshop in Culver City, and Jim paid the rent. Then I bought Jim a nice new Chevy pickup.

The spiffy new Raoul "Sonny" Balcaen World Headquarters (I say it tongue in cheek, friends) was behind a gas station off of Venice Blvd. where it crosses Robertson. It was near my friend Jimmy Nairn, a great machinist, and not far away from the Buick agency owned by Bill Murphy, who was a well-known racer with his Buick-powered Kurtis sports car.

How far from Reventlow Automobiles? Maybe four miles. No distance at all, and I'm sure I stopped by from time to time.

But I was still Jim Hall's man, and he was still competing in races all over the country. He'd call me in Los Angeles ahead of time and tell me where the car had to be, and I'd make it even if it took all-night driving bouts clear to the east coast.

I always made it a point to get to the track early so I could get in a few practice laps myself. Great fun! The car rarely needed tweaking after I arrived, as I'd checked it thoroughly before putting it on the trailer. When Jim showed up the car was ready for him to step in and go.

My turns around the track were joyful, but I still had no desire to become a circuit race driver. I wanted to focus on the technology and involvement from a mechanical point of view.

Besides the races there was that other project he had me doing for him, a new car from England.

Like several other American drivers, including Lance Reventlow, Jim Hall's partner Carroll Shelby got interested in a big-bore sports racer from England made by Brian Lister's company. Lister was having a lot of success in Europe with six-cylinder English Jaguar engines, but we Yanks were dropping in Chevrolet's new V8. We were finding that it lent itself very well to being modified to make a lot more horsepower.

Carroll came up with the idea to import a Lister and make the same upgrade for Jim to drive. I was excited to be chosen for the job.

When the Lister was delivered to me in Los Angeles, it was little more than a chassis with a body. It lacked an engine, a gearbox, and just about everything else. Some of what did come from the factory didn't look quite right to me, so I rebuilt a lot of chassis components. Also I had the car painted in the same nice blue that we used for Jim's Lotus. Blue was his preferred color in those days.

While I was at it I also painted the Chevy pickup to match the team theme. I'm a hot rodder, I like to make things look pretty.

But the main job was building and installing the Lister's Chevy engine. I already had the blueprint in my head for what I wanted to do, but I got my drag racing friend Frank McGurk to help me. He was kind of a semi-sponsor of mine with the GMC six in my dragster. He knew a lot about those engines, he even wrote a book about how to rework them, and when Chevy's V8 came on the market in 1955 he started making speed equipment for them as well.

So with his parts and his know-how backing me up it was pretty straightforward to build a nice Small Block. I bored the cylinders out by an eighth of an inch for a little more displacement, and spent much time working over the cylinder heads to increase the airflow. Stewart Hilborn supplied the fuel injection for it. I ran it on McGurk's dyno and we got 330 horsepower out of it, which was pretty good at the time.

When I fitted the American cast iron V8 into the steel tube English chassis I was creating what to me was a Hot Rod. Brits might call it a Special, or maybe a Hybrid. Whatever you want to call it, the car looked beautiful, and you can imagine how gratified I felt when Jim told me that I had done a great job. He said, "You used your head" in making it ready to race.

To finish that job, I took the new machine out to Willow Springs, where I test-drove it to make sure everything was right before handing it over to my driver.

But I wouldn't be going along with the Lister to the races. Time had come for both Jim and I to move in different directions.

Aside from my work with Jim Hall, there was a personal project that obsessed me. I was no longer racing my dragster, because I had no spare time and a good offer came along for the engine (details to come in another chapter). But that didn't stop me trying to build a sports car of my own design. Work had gone as far as welding up the chassis frame, and I had a Chrysler Hemi V8 that I meant to drop into it.

But trying to do all of the above was getting to me. I've always been a hard worker, I like to go full throttle at everything, but never letting off the gas can overheat your engine. I remember Jim remarking that occasionally I would get belligerent!

He very kindly excused it, because he knew I was overwhelmed and exhausted with everything I had taken on. Yet he was aware that I never failed to give him my most meticulous attention, and he told me so. When there was something to be done, whatever I was involved in, I just went ahead and did it. I often got less than two or three hours' sleep. No wonder I occasionally got a bit testy!

For his part, Jim was losing interest, as he said, in running his shops in two different places. He wanted to consolidate everything back in Texas. He loved to fly the Lone Star flag in the pits, and all that stuff. He's very patriotic.

But if he was taking his cars back to Dallas, it was time for me to turn the page. I'm pleased to say that our parting was perfectly amicable, and Jim and I are still good friends to this day. He's given me generous help with this book.

Later that year, 1958, I did get to see him race the Lister-Chevy. Jim's first time out with it was the annual Santa Barbara airport races that August. The car performed well, but dropped out of both the preliminary and the main event when dirt particles blocked up the fuel injection.

I saw this happen, but from another team's pit. My old buddies at Reventlow had welcomed me back and made me Crew Chief on the Scarab that Bruce Kessler was going to drive. This was chassis no. 003, into which I installed an Offenhauser engine. We were at Santa Barbara too, trying it out.

But busy as I was with RAI, I found time to go see Jim and have a look at the car I'd built for him. I have to say, I wish the fuel filter that I'd originally installed hadn't been removed for some reason.

Jim Hall's Lister continued along the same lines through the rest of the year, but once all the new-car gremlins were finally gone, success did come. The following season, 1959, Jim scored a couple of wins back in Kansas and Texas. Then he moved on to a different car, just as I had.

I want to stress that working for Jim Hall was a truly great several months of my life, a very educational period with a lot of good experiences.

When I look back, I remember that both of us were so young then, in our early twenties, but we were fearless and kept charging. We both knew our business and we discussed every step of the work we did. Jim might have been a little hesitant when I first started working on his racecars, but he told me that he soon realized I was capable of it.

Years later, after we had both retired, Jim remembered how we learned from each other, swapping ideas and trying out options, he with expertise learned from his engineering books and I with years of hands-on experience.

Jim was kind enough one time to tell me that he learned quite a bit from observing how I took care of cars, both in the shop and at the track. Coming from a trained professional engineer, his opinion made me feel especially proud.

CHAPTER 10
RETURN TO REVENTLOW

Parting with Jim Hall in mid-1958 didn't mean I was out of work. By now I was well-recognized as a race engineer, engine builder and racing mechanic on sports cars, and most people in drag racing knew me from the winning Top Fueler dragster that I built and drove.

But Hall was no longer paying rent on "my" shop, and since I wasn't a drag racer anymore — there just wasn't any time for it — I had sold the leftover chassis of my old digger.

So it would have been hard to say "no" when Jim Travers of Traco Engineering asked me to come back to the Scarab sports car team.

"Crabby," as we called him, was also a racing buddy, and of course the engine shop he ran with his partner Frank Coon was right next door to Reventlow on West Jefferson. The two businesses were pretty much joined at the hip at that point.

The year before, I had watched the first Scarab sports racer go together at Warren Olson's shop in West Hollywood. Now Warren was in charge of Lance Reventlow's own place in Culver City, where the other two cars were made.

I couldn't resist. I arrived too late to be involved in building them, but I worked on all three, both in the shop and at the races for the rest of the season.

Reventlow was already a winning team when I first punched in at Culver City. That's right, everybody had to punch a time clock that Simone Olson had installed. Thanks to her and Warren, RAI was a properly organized, well-run operation set up for success. I pay attention to things like that.

Of the Scarab trio, chassis 001 was a left-hand-drive two-seater which Lance himself raced wearing his "lucky" number 16. Lessons learned from that prototype resulted in several improvements to cars 002 and 003, so they were called "Mark II" models. The pair wore numbers 5 and 3 for Chuck and Bruce respectively.

Let's leave out all the juicy technical details here, but one primary change was to seat Chuck Daigh and Bruce Kessler on the right-hand sides of the two-seat cockpits, English-style. Of course, that meant they had to shift with their left hands, but that's not hard to get used to.

The two cars had the same chassis, but at first they carried different engines. Instead of another Chevy, Kessler's no. 3 would be a test bed for an Offenhauser Indy-type powerplant to be installed as an experiment.

Chevy's Small Block V8 was still new, having been launched only three years earlier in 1955, but most people running any kind of racing in America were choosing it over older, less efficient, heavier Detroit powerplants.

Unfortunately for Lance's long-range ambitions, even this "small" Chevy was now too big for international sports prototype racing, including the all-important Le Mans 24-hour event. New 1958 regulations in Europe limited fast sports car engine displacement to no more than 3.0 liters, or 183 cubic inches. America's 335-inch/5.5-liter Chevys were nearly twice that size.

Don't even suggest simply substituting a 3.0 Ferrari or Maserati or other established European brand of engine. The fiercely patriotic young man we worked for demanded an American powerplant.

I can't say just when during this sports car process Lance started thinking about also breaking into Formula 1. No doubt his close friend Bruce Kessler came back from his abortive experience in Monaco full of stories and ideas.

At that time F1 engines were limited to 2.5 liters, close enough for one basic design to be adapted for both F1 and the only slightly larger international sports cars. So why shouldn't RAI tackle both?

Unfortunately, the only existing American-made possibility was the Meyer-Drake Offenhauser Indy car engine manufactured in Los Angeles.

I say unfortunately because the "Offy" was not designed for road racing. During the '30s, when Fred Offenhauser and his right-hand man Harry Miller developed their engine, the market was oval track racing, period. Their highly specialized, beautifully made, very strong four-cylinder twin-cam became the weapon of choice for everything from quarter-mile dirt "bull rings" near towns all over the USA to the 2½-mile paved speedway in Indianapolis.

In 1958 the Offy was still dominating the Indy 500, and there were no signs its long reign would end.

But it just didn't work for road racing, as Briggs Cunningham's team had just recently discovered. It was right for Reventlow Automobiles to investigate the situation themselves, though, especially since they had Offy specialists Travers and Coon right next door. So Scarab no. 3 had a 3-liter version of the Offy installed for testing. The job included an air inlet scoop on the hood, making the third car easy to distinguish by eye.

The new car was ready in time for Bruce to drive in August at the Santa Barbara airport. I heard later that the team told him the car had never been fired up or run, so obviously it had not turned a lap of testing. Oh, and it didn't have much horsepower. That information didn't seem to bother Bruce, so they hauled the car north to Santa Barbara for him.

"The first day I ended up winning my class by just dumb luck," remembered Bruce, "after someone spun out. The next day the car almost vibrated itself apart when I ran it!"

As I said earlier, I was also at Santa Barbara that weekend, where Jim Hall was doing his own first race with the Lister-Chevy I had built for him. Unfortunately, we had a crash that weekend. But later in the year Jim would start winning races with the Lister, and continued doing so in 1959.

Although the Offy-powered Scarab won the Santa Barbara preliminary race, it was more by luck than speed. In the main event it practically shook itself apart. Cunningham had been right, the Offy just wasn't going to work for sports car racing.

It wasn't only that our cars weren't built to withstand the vibration inherent in "four-banger" engines. Running on gasoline instead of the Methanol it was designed to use, it lacked the strong low-end torque so valuable when accelerating out of turns, it was short of top-end horsepower needed on straights, and the driver complained of sluggish response to his throttle pedal.

Plus, the thing was much heavier than a Chevy V8. Scarabs always understeered around the corners, and the extra weight on the front tires made it worse.

Back at the shop, RAI yanked out the Offy, plugged in one of their regular Chevys and Bruce took it out to test. He said it had so much more power, he almost killed himself!

As explained earlier, the first time I saw the car in the Offy configuration, which turned out to be the only time it raced, was when Bruce turned up at the same Santa Barbara race where I was with Jim Hall and the Chevy-engined Lister that I had built for him. Of course, racing was free and friendly in those days, we all worked out in the open and everybody was welcome to come by everybody else's pit area to see what they were up to. It's very different today, very different!

By the time I went back to work for Scarab, the third car had a Chevy V8 like the others. It made me very proud when this car was assigned to me to be prepared for races. It was my responsibility all through the process to make sure everything on Bruce's no. 3 was handled correctly and completed on time.

It's hard to describe how happy I was. I'd been asked to rejoin the Reventlow team at last, and now I was crew chief on "my own car."

Sometimes I also worked on the other two Scarabs, as well as going to races and working in the pits. At the same time I had to finish restoring Lance's Bugatti. After I joined Jim Hall the year before there was nobody at Olson's shop who knew how to proceed on the old French classic, so they brought it down to RAI and stored it away in a shed on the lot alongside. I'd work on the Bugatti out there when I had spare time — ha-hah. My plate was well and truly full.

My Scarab duties included going along for test sessions at local tracks like Riverside and Willow Springs. I'll never forget one day at Willow, way out in the empty nowhere north of L.A. (those deserted roads would have made a great place to go street racing with our hot rods!), when Chuck Daigh treated me to some hot laps in his passenger seat.

"The Fastest Road in the West" that track is called. My inner drag racer might have been skeptical of that claim, until we were blasting around Turn 9. That's a very long, very fast right-hand sweeper with a nasty hook right at the end, before it shoots you out onto the pit straight.

There I am, sitting to the left of Chuck on the outside of this right-hand turn, no steering wheel in front me and hardly any wind protection either. I can't say which is louder, the air howling by my ears or the exhaust roar from the side-pipe under my hip. We're probably doing something like 130, and Chuck has the thing sliding and skittering, dancing on the brink of control like great drivers love to do.

That's when I feel the front tires break loose.

Off into the desert we sailed, bouncing along and throwing up sand, finally coming to a stop half buried in the stuff. I don't mind admitting it was a frightening experience.

For one of us, that is. I looked over at Chuck. He looked back and said calmly: "Pushes the front end a little bit, doesn't it?"

That season of 1958 was the "Year of the Scarab," as author Preston Lerner put it in his book on the team. Reventlow Automobiles Inc. enjoyed almost total dominance of sports car racing across the USA. Lance himself scored RAI's first victory in May, when Traco horsepower helped his no. 16 defeat great driver Richie Ginther's Ferrari around the Santa Barbara airport course.

In August Chuck in car no. 5 took his debut victory on another airport outside Reno, Nevada. Wins kept coming as the team toured the East, New York, Connecticut and Illinois, winning again and again — which meant defeating Briggs Cunningham's strong stable of Lister-Jaguars.

All of which set the stage for Riverside in October, where our Chuck Daigh raced Phil Hill's Ferrari in one of the greatest back-and-forth, high-speed duels ever seen.

The Italian car finally faded in the heat of the California day. The American machine went all the way to the checkered flag. Terrific stuff, and the publicity was worldwide. People say that this exiting race is what put Riverside on the map.

Not everybody knew that we scraped through by the skin of our teeth. A spur gear had broken in the quick-change unit behind the transmission. At any moment it could have broken another cog, seized up solid and put us out.

We were supposed to run all three Scarabs that day, but Lance crashed his no. 16 in practice, so he "asked" to share Bruce's car. The outcome was pretty dismal. I'll let Mr. Kessler himself tell that story in another chapter.

Bruce didn't come with us to Laguna Seca near Monterey in November. We only took two cars, the original left-drive Mk1 that was now repaired, and the Riverside-winning Mk2. This time Lance beat Chuck, or at least that's what it says in the record books. I think we all knew that it was a managed finish, except for Lance. He wanted to win on performance, not politics, and when he heard something about "team orders" he erupted in fury. Our boss did have a volcanic temper.

To wrap up one of the winningest seasons any team could dream of enjoying, in December we went to Nassau in the Bahamas, where I'd taken the new Hall Lotus the previous year.

Again we only brought two Scarabs, while Bruce was there in one of John Edgar's cars, a Ferrari. Bruce was the winner of a short preliminary race, but his car broke down in the main event.

RAI did better in that one. It was called the Nassau Trophy Race, a 250-miler around a rather rough 4½-mile course laid out on the airport. For the third time in a row Lance's car came out the winner, co-driven by Lance himself and Chuck Daigh. For some reason the number on the car wasn't the regular 16, but 37. I'd forgotten this detail, if I ever even noticed, but old photos show it. Mystery to me.

Chuck's usual no. 5 wore number 97, but it broke a driveshaft U-joint, which is why he jumped into Lance's seat at the refueling stop. They beat George Constantine's Aston Martin, Ed Crawford's Maserati, and the sensationally fast Rodriguez brothers from Mexico, Pedro and Ricardo, in Ferrari and Porsche respectively.

The Bahamas race was not taken very seriously, it was more of a party place, but Reventlow Automobiles Inc. could look back across a full season in which the Scarab sports car had enjoyed a sweep of nearly every race it entered.

Lance had made his point. It was clear that his quest to build an all-American sports racing competitor, and to assemble the highest-quality team to make it successful, had resulted in a unique machine for its time. With its beautiful, strong lines, superior engineering and strong Chevy V8 performance, the Scarab was way ahead of anything else of the time.

Earlier I promised to come back to a story about Chuck Daigh's

ABOVE *Lance Reventlow's great friend Bruce Kessler is at the wheel of Lance's special aluminum-bodied Mercedes-Benz 300 SL "Gull Wing" at Torrey Pines, CA, just after a small front-end crash. Crewing on Lance's team is how I learned to be a sports car racing pro.*

ABOVE *Carbuilder Dick Troutman, in sunglasses, and driver Chuck Daigh cruise the paddock during a 1958 Cal Club race weekend on an airport at Phoenix, AZ. Look how simple and casual it all was back then.*

ABOVE *Smiling Simone Olson, my boss Warren's wife, was the organizational mainstay of their family business. I learned a lot about how to run a business from her.*

ABOVE *Four young racers "bench-racing" in the pits at Santa Barbara's Cal-Club races in 1957. That's me closest to the camera, with Lance Reventlow at left, Jim Hall on the right, and Bruce Kessler just beyond Jim.*

ABOVE *Driving this under-1500 cc Porsche 550 that I race-prepared for her, Ruth Levy wins her class at the Pomona Fairplex track sometime in the 1950s. Notice the enthusiasm of the starter/finisher flagman.*

ABOVE *Ruth Levy hired me to crew for her at the Sebring 12 Hour endurance race in 1958. This is our team's little Fiat-Abarth, which Ruth co-drove with Denise McCluggage.*

LANCE - REVENTLOW

COOPER   COOPER

HOLLYWOOD

ABOVE *Lance Reventlow could afford to buy any automobile that caught his eye, and he pretty much did. But he was fairly sensible about learning to drive racecars, choosing well-proven, easy-to-handle equipment like this little English-made Cooper Formula 2 that he raced in England. The picture is on one of the promotional postcards that drivers would send out to racetracks back then, part of the usual race-by-race negotiations over "starting money."*

RIGHT *Lance Reventlow and his bride, actress Jill St. John, cut their wedding cake in 1960. Unfortunately, they divorced in 1963.*

ABOVE *In 1964 Lance wed Cheryl Holdridge, then a 20-year-old TV actress and former Walt Disney Mouseketeer. This marriage lasted until Lance died in a plane crash in 1972.*

RIGHT Road & Track *featured Scarabs on several covers. This one, the left-hand-drive Mk I, nicely shows its key design points: Traco's powerful Chevrolet V8 (converted to carburetors for street use, rather than Hilborn's racing fuel injection), steel tube "space frame" chassis, aluminum interior body panels, specially fabricated independent front suspension components, and the massive drum brakes with their radial cooling fins. The battery is carried on the right side, somewhat countering the driver's weight.*

ABOVE *The first Scarab Mk I takes shape at Warren Olson's shop in Beverly Hills (note his "Ecurie Flat Kat" team transporter in the background). From left are Chuck Daigh, Dick Troutman, Tom Barnes, Lance Reventlow (in the seat), and Warren Olson. As yet unpainted, the hand-formed aluminum body still has the original large radiator intake in the nose. Later it will be reduced in size.*

ABOVE RIGHT *From left, Phil Remington, Tom Barnes and I work on a right-hand-drive Scarab Mk II behind the Reventlow Automobiles, Inc. workshop. The white building next door is Traco Engineering. Can't get closer to your engine supplier than that!*

RIGHT *"I want to prove I can do more than inherit money," Lance said, and he accomplished that with the magnificent all-American racecars he created. He also showed some talent as a driver, but didn't become as fast as his cars. This is the first Scarab, which he drove in races and then had me modify for street driving.*

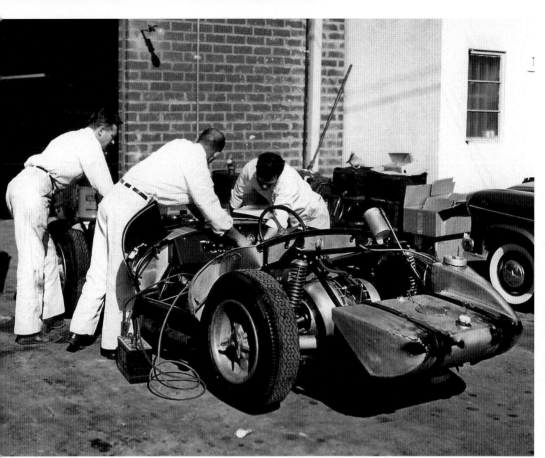

LEFT Chuck Daigh wasn't just RAI's star driver. The tough former paratrooper was as friendly as he looks here, but more significantly for the team he also had magic hands as a racecar builder and engine tuner. With Chuck's brother Harold, a former fighter pilot, the Daigh boys were a big part of Scarab's success.

RIGHT At Nassau in the Bahamas with the Scarab. I'm bent down working on the exhaust system, while Chuck Daigh has his hand on my back. His brother Harold Daigh (left) and our boss Warren Olson look on as we all share a laugh.

LEFT *Chuck Daigh's right-hand-drive Scarab Mk II, behind the adjoining Jefferson Avenue buildings with most key Reventlow crew members. From left: Tom Barnes, Emil Diedt, Marshall Whitfield, Frank Coon, Jim Travers, Leo Goossen, me (smiling at camera), Harold Mauk, Dick Troutman, Phil Remington and Harold Daigh. The car, which still bears the number 97 assigned to it for Nassau, is being readied for the 1958 Times Grand Prix at Riverside. Note the shiny extra fuel tank installed for the long race.*

Chuck's hard-fought victory for America's beautiful Scarab, beating a powerful Italian Ferrari in the hands of star driver Phil Hill, made the exciting 1958 Times Grand Prix one of the most talked-about sports car events in the country. That in turn made it a big factor behind the new Riverside International Raceway becoming one of the most important tracks in the world.

ABOVE *This is a Cessna 310 light-twin, similar to the one in which the Daigh brothers gave us such an interesting ride back to California from the Bahamas!*

—Star-Telegram Photo by AL PANZERA.
ROARS HOME—Jim Hall gets signal from Jimmy Stout as he drives past finish line in Maserati to win Sunday's feature in Frostbite sports car races.

Maserati Wins
Frostbite Feature

LEFT *One of my most satisfying races with Jim Hall was seeing him drive this Maserati, which I prepared for him, to a hard-fought victory over a Porsche at the "Frostbite" race in the rain!*

ABOVE Jim Hall and Allen Guiberson look over Carroll Shelby's shoulder as he "warms-up" Jim's 3-liter Monza Ferrari at Pebble Beach. This is just one of the many similar models handled by Carroll Shelby Sport Cars in Dallas. Both drivers often took them out to race, bringing publicity to their dealership and giving me plenty of work as Jim's crew chief.

ABOVE *Carroll and Jim thought the very sleek, ultra-lightweight little Lotus from England could beat Germany's Porsche. Despite a lot of work on it, and many repairs, it kept letting us down. Colin Chapman was a brilliant designer, but his cars weren't strong enough. Looked nice, though.*

LEFT *I really put a lot of effort into the Lotus, reengineering some details to make it more reliable, and spiffing up its appearance the way I'd learned to do in hot rodding. Painted blue and gold, and wearing Jim Hall's signature race number, 66, it sure looked great.*

ABOVE *Here I am in my own shop in Los Angeles, proudly showing a visitor the Chevy-powered Lister I built for Jim Hall. I always put a hot rodder's passion for mechanical precision and beauty into every sports car I worked on.*

RIGHT The Los Angeles Times *thought our Lister-Chevy was so interesting that they sent over a photographer and a model for some formal pictures. If you can tear your eyes away from the well-built young lady, check out the sweet engine I built. I topped it off with the same Hilborn fuel injection system that Scarab was using.*

119

LEFT *Can you can tell by my expression that PR wasn't really my thing back then? This photo shoot was cutting into my work time!*

BELOW *The last time I saw Jim Hall run the Lister-Chevy was here at Pomona in 1958, after I had gone back to Reventlow. We were there to try out a Scarab with an Offenhauser engine, but I also followed how Jim was doing with the car I built for him. He had to drop out of the race when dirt in the fuel caused a misfire. I found out that someone had removed the fuel filters that I installed originally.*

brother Harold, and here's the place. The former fighter pilot often flew Lance's airplane, a twin-engine Cessna 310, on company business. That's how Chuck and I were heading home from Nassau, with Harold as Pilot in Command and Warren in the right seat.

I'd have loved to be up there instead, but Warren had a license, so I had to ride in the back with the other passenger, Chuck. It was pretty boring back there.

Our first stop was in Miami to go through Customs. When we took off again Harold decided we needed to visit New Orleans on the way, and live it up a little overnight. So he looked around at us and asked if we saw that little bit of engine oil leaking out on the left wing. Of course we see it, we all agreed happily!

We weren't fibbing, it really was there. But I can't say it really was anything to be concerned about.

We had a great night at the clubs in the French Quarter, devouring dozens of oysters and drinking a lot of beer. Chuck imbibed more than most and when we climbed into the plane the next day he promptly fell asleep in the back, snoring noisily at my shoulder. Our pilot got a little annoyed with his brother. I figure he spent the rest of the trip thinking about ways to get back at him.

When the Los Angeles basin finally came into sight ahead, Harold suddenly shut off both engines over the Cajon Pass between the San Bernardino and San Gabriel mountain ranges.

The abrupt silence followed by a rapid descent worked magic on the snorer next to me. Chuck woke up in a panic. We plummeted 1,000 feet before Harold restarted the engines. It was a dangerous stunt, but humorous and we trusted Harold. He was a fighter pilot and that's how they behaved.

I liked Harold, although I wasn't as close to him as I was to his brother. But Harold was a really interesting guy. He was a hot rodder, and set a speed record at the Bonneville Salt Flats. As a Marine in Korea he earned a Distinguished Flying Cross "for heroism and extraordinary achievement." He was actually a professional chemical engineer, complete with a degree, and he worked for Atlantic Richfield, the oil company. He started a fuel business of his own to manufacture racing gasoline. "Cheater gas" we used to call it!

Years later Harold got into off-road racing with Steve McQueen, the racer-actor, and went on to be technical director for the group that ran those races, SCORE.

Chuck Daigh and I became firm friends. We often joked with each other about our different racing preferences, because I was a drag racer while he raced sports cars. He was good at it, he won a lot of races, especially the great Scarab triumph at Riverside in 1958. He followed that up in 1959 by winning the Sebring 12-hour in a Ferrari, co-driving with Dan Gurney along with Phil Hill and Olivier Gendebien. But he was always a mechanic at heart. In later years he started his own boat-building business in Newport Beach, and in his spare time there he kept on developing the Leo Goossen desmodromic engine on his own. He got an extra 35 or 40 horses out of it.

Kind of a rough-and-tumble guy, a former paratrooper in fact, Chuck was a hard worker with a keen sense of values who was kind and caring, although he could be something of a cynic.

Chuck and Harold came from an Irish family, and both were tough as nails and quick with their fists. They were nice guys, but you didn't want to piss them off because they'd start a fight. I really liked them.

CHAPTER 11
BRUCE KESSLER

M en of genius — that's what I call several of the race drivers, engineers, designers, constructors and mechanics that I knew in the '50s and '60s. They became idols to me, and right at the top of my list is Bruce Kessler.

He was a winning driver in the U.S. and abroad in that era. We met while I was working at Warren Olson's shop, and Bruce became a driver for the Coopers that Olson distributed. Later at Reventlow we spent a lot of time together with the Scarab he was driving. We were the same age, and we became best friends — and we still are, all these years later.

It was thanks to Bruce Kessler that we got involved with the Scarabs in the first place. He's the one who brought his friend Lance Reventlow into Warren's shop one day in the mid-'50s, when the young celebrity was looking for somebody to take care of the several cars he owned and in some cases raced.

Without Bruce's introduction, I don't know that Warren would ever have met Lance at all.

Bruce came from a creative, hard-working family that was hugely successful in business. His father started a trucking business, while his mother was the creator of the famously glamorous and classic Rose Marie Reid swimsuits. She named the apparel for a close friend from Canada who was her partner, and the brand was sold all over the world. Top movie stars wore Reid designs on-screen, including Rita

Hayworth, who was resplendent in a glittering metallic lamé swimsuit for the movie *Gilda*. All the great swimming stars in movies in the era, Esther Williams and others, they wore Rose Marie Reid.

Growing up in affluence in Beverly Hills, Bruce first raced his mother's Jaguar XK120 when he was 17 years old. After graduating from Beverly Hills High School he began to build a career as a road racing driver, and took his first victory at age 19 in 1955 at Torrey Pines in his friend Lance Reventlow's 300 SL Mercedes-Benz.

Bruce said he wanted to be a mechanic, because he thought it might help him as a driver, but admitted he had no mechanical ability. He joked that if he was ever asked to remove a spark plug, he knew he'd break it. He used to watch me working on Ferraris, Rolls-Royces, and other complicated exotics and he'd shake his head in bewilderment.

Bruce often came to watch me drag racing. One time at a Saugus event my car broke down. He was watching me fixing it so intently I felt his eyes boring through my hands.

I appreciated him telling a friend recently, "There were lots of kids hot-rodding their cars, but at 18 years old Sonny Balcaen was way past everyone else. He had this amazing ability, he was so far mechanically advanced than us. I could tell the moment I met him. He had the talent to see things that normal people couldn't see to build better parts. I'd never known anybody my age back then that had his understanding of automotive mechanics. He really was an engineering genius, doing what no one else could do. Sonny seemed to have an intuition, a mind that could see into the future. He could sense the long-term run of it. Anything mechanical was never a mystery to him. A very unusual person."

By contrast, I lacked Bruce's passion for race driving and the innate knack for doing it well. Building his experience, he raced a wide variety of cars from a tiny motorcycle-engined Cooper Formula 3 all the way up to powerful Aston Martins, Ferraris and Maseratis.

His career continued to develop through the next two years. In 1956 he continued with the little open-wheel Cooper, scoring a couple of wins, also ran a Ferrari in the Sebring endurance race, and campaigned an Aston Martin as well.

The following year he was even busier, winning again with the Cooper and two more times at the wheel of a Ferrari. Then he took a giant step, signing on as one of the drivers of a Porsche entered in the classic 24-hour endurance race in France at Le Mans. He didn't actually drive in the race itself but gained a lot of knowledge for use in the future.

This team was a good one to learn with, by the way. Their car not only finished the grueling 24 hours, they came home in eighth place.

On that trip he also got involved in the future Scarab project. After Le Mans, Bruce met up with Lance Reventlow and they headed off to England to visit the Lister factory. Lance was thinking of buying one of their cars and replacing the regular Jaguar engine with a Chevy. He didn't, as it turned out, but that was the day when the idea of the Scarab came to him.

Bruce remembers that seminal day this way:

> Brian Lister's little workshop was a converted wartime Nissen Hut, like our Quonset Huts, a long, tunnel-like place with an arch-shaped steel roof. Lister had only built one of his big, Jaguar-powered racecars at that point, but Archie Scott Brown had been very successful with it and orders were starting to come in.
>
> That one car belonged to Bernie Ecclestone — who owned a motorcycle shop in those days but had higher ambitions — and it wasn't in the shop when Lance and I were there. There was nothing but piles of steel tubing and parts and pieces of racecars scattered around. They would turn into Lance's Lister if he decided to buy one.
>
> There was nobody in the shop except Lance and Brian Lister down at one end, while I hung back at the other end of this little hut to let them talk. So I didn't hear what they were saying, but arms started waving around.
>
> Finally, Lance walked away. Outside, he and I talked over what we'd seen and agreed we could build a much better car in California. What's more, we'd put one of the new Chevy V8s in it. That's how the Scarab was born.

Back home, the conspirators filled their heads with exciting plans to build an all-American sports racer. Bruce would sit on the floor at Warren's shop and, with all his experience driving different kinds of cars, would show the guys how the best sports car should be laid out. As the Scarab evolved Bruce was the test driver.

The picture of Bruce that I'm trying to paint here is of a young American driver with ambition and talent who already had won several races. He showed signs of a good future in the sport.

Bruce Kessler must have gone into 1958 thinking, "This is My Year." He was going to be a Reventlow Scarab team driver, alongside Chuck Daigh and Lance himself. But before the cars were ready he continued racing other makes. That's why he went to Cuba that February to run a Ferrari.

I was there too, but independently. My boss at the time, Jim Hall, wasn't entered, but his dealership partner Carroll Shelby was driving one of John Edgar's Ferraris. I went along just to watch.

Havana 1958 turned out to be a disaster.

First, the legendary Juan Manuel Fangio — winner the previous year — was seized the night before the race by Communist revolutionary Fidel Castro. Not for any ransom, just to make a political declaration of strength by keeping the internationally famous Fangio out of the Cuban Grand Prix. The great man from Argentina was treated with courtesy, and once the race was over and the rebels had made their point, they released him unharmed.

Maybe Fangio was lucky to miss the race, because far worse was to happen during it.

This was one of the very old-school racing venues still in use. The course was laid out through city streets, including the broad grand boulevard called the Malecon running along the sea front. The whole 3¼-mile lap was hemmed in by curbs and trees and lamp posts, with only stacks of hay bales protecting crowds of people standing along sidewalks everywhere.

Just six laps in, a local driver in a Ferrari ran over a patch of oil and slid straight into a massive crowd standing outside a corner. The tragedy cost seven dead and over 30 injured. A red flag ended the Cuban Grand Prix then and there.

Historian William Edgar, John Edgar's son who was with the team there, repeats a story he heard that the oil that caused the crash was green, like it was just poured out of a can. Oil spilling from an engine would normally be black. More rebel sabotage, presumably, if the story is true. Castro's eventual seizure of power was not a good thing for the Cuban people.

L et us lighten the tone a little: my trip to Cuba got my name in the local paper. No, not because I had anything to do with the catastrophe. Not the kidnapping, either.

My moment of local notoriety came before the race, when a reporter from the *Times of Havana* came around looking for a story. He chose an "inquisitive young redhead" by the name of "23-year-old Raoul 'Sonny' Balcaen III, a self-educated automotive engineer... By the time he was 11, he could take an automobile apart and put it back together. He quit school in Los Angeles after the 8th grade, to his parents' dismay."

After saying I normally worked with Jim Hall, the writer added: "Sonny is working on two projects besides his duties with Hall. One project, nearly complete, is putting Lance Reventlow's classic Bugatti into condition for automotive shows.

"The other project is designing and building a sports car of his own, powered by a Chrysler V8 engine, no transmission, working off direct drive, very light with enormous brakes. The frame and engine already are built and Sonny says when the revolutionary sports car is finished, either he or Jim Hall will race it."

See? I told you I was busy in those days!

Maybe a little too busy for Mr. Shelby. He informed me that he was sitting around in his hotel room, sort of quarantined because of what was going on, bored as heck, "and I open the darn paper and there's a story about my darn mechanic!" Only he used a stronger adjective, being Shelby.

B ack to my man Kessler. In March he joined two veterans, Briggs Cunningham and Paul O'Shea, to co-drive a Ferrari to a GT class victory in the 1958 12-hour enduro at Sebring in Florida.

I don't want to even try to work out how many passes I'd have to make on a quarter-mile drag strip to log a total of 12 hours of driving time!

Somewhere along in there Kessler shared a car with the great Stirling Moss. Not a racecar, however. The two were in some little town for a race, and jumped into a rental car to go look for a café.

As Bruce told me the anecdote, Stirling was at the wheel when they came to an unpaved rural country road. This simply presented an enjoyable driving challenge for two hardy, experienced race drivers.

Pretty soon they were being chased by a police car. Well, that was no problem for Moss, he just drove faster. So the cops radioed ahead for a road block to be put up.

Of course, that too was no obstacle to the English Grand Prix driver. He simply swerved around the barrier and the pair went on their merry way.

Another of Bruce's adventures in 1958 was to try his hand at Formula 1 racing. It happened in May during the Grand Prix of Monaco, down on the French Riviera, where he shared an old, obsolete Connaught F1 car with another driver. It belonged to an English impresario named Bernie Ecclestone, who was obscure at that time but who would one day come to rule the Grand Prix roost and make himself a billionaire.

Unfortunately, the aged vehicle was too slow to enable either driver to qualify to race. That's as close as my buddy Bruce came to a career in Formula 1.

Back at Le Mans in June, Bruce finally got to run in the world-famous 24-hour race. This time he was driving a Ferrari with twice the engine displacement of the previous year's Porsche. Also, his co-driver was some hot young guy named Dan Gurney. It was all going nicely through the first seven hours, right up until just after 10 pm when Bruce sped by the pits to complete the 64th lap. He and Dan were holding fifth place.

That's when somebody crashed right ahead, unfortunately with fatal results. Bruce couldn't avoid slamming into the wrecked Jaguar, and his Ferrari burst into flames. By good luck he was thrown out of the open cockpit — this was still the era before seat belts were commonly worn — so he wasn't burned, but he did break his ribs.

Before you knew it, he was back on his feet and driving again. He finished his first event second in a Ferrari, then he notched up a third place with his little Cooper F3.

I was still working for Jim Hall on his Lister when Scarab's third sports car was finally ready. Bruce Kessler was to race this one, chassis 003, which was put together to evaluate a different kind of engine. But, as mentioned earlier, track testing confirmed that the Offenhauser four-cylinder wasn't going to be competitive, so 003 received a nice, strong, well-proven Chevy V8.

Happily for me, my deal with Hall didn't keep me from taking on other work, and I was glad when the Reventlow guys asked me to be crew chief on the third car, which Kessler would continue driving.

Scarab's big victory at Riverside that October was outlined earlier. It's when Chuck Daigh won a major event called the Riverside Grand Prix against fierce opposition from Phil Hill in a Ferrari. "American Upstart Defeats Europe's Finest!" is how I'd headline that story if I were a newspaperman. It was news that flashed across the country and put one-year-old Riverside International Raceway on the map. It was the first of what would be renowned for many years as the Times Grand Prix.

As things turned out, that was Reventlow's finest hour. As a car brand, that is. Less so for Lance as a public figure.

Here's how all that unfolded as I saw it. We went to Riverside at full strength for the first time, with all three of our "guns" locked and loaded. Lance was in no. 16 and Chuck in no. 5 as usual, with Bruce's no. 3 finally ready with its Chevy.

The only difference between Bruce's car and the others was that they both had extra fuel tanks fitted so as to run the unusually long, 203-mile race non-stop. Time ran out before the modification could be made to no. 3, so Bruce would have pull in for refueling partway through.

The *Los Angeles Times* newspaper publisher was making a big deal of the big race it was sponsoring, giving it daily publicity to pull in a big crowd of spectators. The entry was pretty strong, including rising local stars like Richie Ginther, Masten Gregory, Dan Gurney, Phil Hill, Ken Miles and, of course, SCCA national champion Carroll Shelby.

Widening the focus to Indycar racing, because this event counted as a round of the short-lived United States Auto Club (USAC) Road Racing Championship, we had several 500 drivers like 1952 winner Troy Ruttman, future winner Jim Rathmann, and Unser brothers Bobby and Jerry.

Spicing it up with international flavor — and thereby catching the notice of the European press — were British star Roy Salvadori and France's Jean Behra.

My role, as I've said, was to look after and manage Bruce Kessler's no. 3 car. During practice my guy was getting used to his new-found horsepower and, like all racers, I thought we had a chance to win.

But managing our boss was outside my job description. During a practice lap Lance lost control and spun off the road — not exactly an unknown occurrence for Mr. Golden Boy — and hit something hard enough to disable the car.

Here is Bruce Kessler's own recollection of that weekend:

> Lance had set up his car, number 16, with its weight distribution biased to favor turns to the right, because the 3.3-mile Riverside lap had more of those than left-handers. He figured any speed he lost when turning left would be more than made up by going faster around the more numerous right-handers.
>
> I guess he didn't figure on losing control of the unbalanced car in the left-hand Turn 7. He spun off hard enough to damage the chassis. The crew took it back to the shop in L.A. but weren't able to fix it quickly enough to make Sunday's race.
>
> Lance came to me and said, "Do you mind if I share yours?" Sure. "Can I start the race, and hand over to you at the pit stop?" OK.
>
> I didn't think anything about it at the time, but in hindsight I wish I had.
>
> Riverside would be the longest race any of us were used to doing, except for long-distance ones like Sebring. Most of the Ferraris and other cars had big enough fuel tanks to go the 203 miles, but the Scarabs didn't. Lance's and Chuck's got extra tanks installed, but not mine. So I would have to stop to refuel.
>
> But because I would start the race with much less fuel load than the others, we hatched a plan that I would go out in front as fast as I could go. We knew Phil Hill in the Ferrari was our strongest opposition, so the idea was to draw him into going so hard that his car would run into trouble.
>
> Phil didn't know I was intending to make a pit stop. Nobody did. We all tried hard to hold onto that little secret.
>
> That was still the game plan when Lance took over the no. 3 and started it in the third fastest grid spot, on one side of the three-wide front row. Chuck Daigh was on pole on the other side, with Phil's Ferrari in between.
>
> John von Neumann was in a Ferrari on the second row,

right behind Lance.

It was a standing start, not one of the rolling starts they use now, and when the flag fell and Lance dumped the clutch, his car hesitated a little. I don't know if it was too much wheelspin or if the engine bogged, but he wasn't accelerating as fast as usual.

That meant von Neumann behind suddenly had to get on his brakes. Only trouble is, the Ferrari he was driving had the old-fashioned pedal arrangement that put the gas pedal in the middle, where the brake normally is. So you can see what happened when von Neumann instinctively stomped on the pedal he thought would stop him.

The Ferrari rammed the Scarab right in the tail. Where the fuel tank was.

Lance kept going, and we didn't see any fuel leaking out, so we were surprised when the officials waved a black flag at him. They hadn't seen any fluid coming out either, I heard later, but they wanted to make sure.

So Lance came into our pit — which was at the inbound end, where cars came off the last corner and veered left into the pit lane, which was to the driver's left in those days. The officials told the guys to take off the rear of the body so they could inspect the fuel tank. Sure enough, there wasn't any leak, so they said OK, go back out.

I was just standing there with my hands in my pockets and didn't expect it when Lance turned to me and said, "Pull your hands out of your pockets and get your helmet. You're driving."

He caught me by surprise. I was unprepared mentally to just jump in and go out racing then and there. So I was pretty excited when I blasted away. I had the whole length of the pit lane to accelerate and I was going at a terrific speed when I got to the end and about to race out onto the track. I sure wasn't expecting to see a red flag. It was all I could do to pull up. Why in heck were they stopping me?

Nobody told me anything. I looked back and I could see Lance running up toward me. Obviously he didn't understand either, and he was really hot. When he got to the start line he suddenly turned and ran across the track — the race is still going — to the officials at the start line. They started arguing and I heard, though I didn't see, that Lance took a swing at somebody.

When you stop and think about it, communications weren't very good in those days. Apparently the guy who stopped me at the far end of the pit lane hadn't got the word the guy at the other end had cleared me to go. And of course Lance had no idea why I got stopped.

But if he hadn't lost his temper and run across a live racetrack and got into a physical confrontation with the officials, my car wouldn't have been disqualified.

In which case, I would have made the race. This was the last of four races in that year's USAC Road Racing Championship. I'd already earned points earlier that year, finishing second and third at Lime Rock and Watkins Glen with a Ferrari in the same team Richie Ginther was driving in. If I could have gotten one more point at Riverside, that would have made me series champion over Dan Gurney.

Hindsight doesn't do you much good, but I wish I'd argued with Lance when he wanted to be the one to start the race.

It wasn't the year Bruce had wanted with Scarab. In the end he only got to do two race weekends with "his" car no. 3. Most racers are optimists, so they'll talk about "well, there's always next year." And even though his 1959 wouldn't be with the Scarab sports cars, which were being sold, he could look forward to the Formula 1 project.

Meantime he opened the new year in March at the Pomona Fairplex track by racing for the Nisonger spark-plug team in a Chevy-powered car named Sadler. Bruce won a minor preliminary called a Consolation Race, but then in the main event, the opening of the new season's USAC championship, the car went off the track and crashed heavily. Bruce suffered severe concussion, in fact he was in a coma for days.

Effectively his racing career was over.

He did run a little in the following year, and managed an eighth place finish at Road America in a Porsche, but after retiring a Lotus from a race at Riverside in February 1961 he hung it up.

I'm sure I'm not the only one who regrets that Bruce Kessler never had a chance to fully develop his talent as a driver. But like me, once my friend left racing he found another career that ultimately brought him great success.

Movie making.

Bruce was hired as a technical adviser in movies that involved motorsports. Before he knew it he began writing a script of his own, which he also directed and produced as the short 1962 film, *The Sound of Speed*.

The story was of Lance in the driver's seat testing the Scarab F1 at Riverside. It was a silent movie except for the sound of the engine changing gears and shifting.

Bruce told me his screenplay was based on a story he'd written in high school titled, "He Almost Died." Lance read it and suggested it be adapted to a movie.

It focused on the third Formula 1 Scarab, which I worked on to get it ready. The movie was filmed at the Riverside track. Lance was to be the driver, with the small crew on camera consisting of Chuck Daigh, Warren Olson, and Paul Camano handling timing. They all appear in the film.

The script has the driver being signaled to come into the pits, refusing to do so, and staying out on the track for several more laps, going faster and faster until he finally loses control and spins out. The scene typified Lance's own streak of independence that showed itself now and then.

Sound of Speed only had engine exhaust sounds. Bruce didn't shoot dialog, because that was going to be the most expensive, hard thing to do. There's a scene in *Lawrence of Arabia* where you see the key actor as a tiny speck on the horizon, and there's no dialogue for minutes. Well, Bruce came up with that idea long before director David Lean.

As it turned out, Lance couldn't play the role of driver. He'd put his hand through a window and was unable to drive. So Chuck Daigh did double duty, stepping into the car for on-track action sequences as well as standing in the pits with stopwatch and clipboard as chief mechanic. Warren Olson starred in his real-life role as crew chief, and so did crewman Paul Camano. Four guys, one car, 20 minutes; that's all it took to launch a cinematic revolution.

Bruce Kessler did a lot of creative work on his movie, and here's what made it unique: he mounted a movie camera on the car. I had quite a bit of involvement in that camera set-up and other equipment, and enjoyed the challenge. Bruce wasn't the first to do this, but I think the wide distribution of *The Sound of Speed* brought the technique to the attention of other filmmakers. Today onboard cameras are standard equipment in Formula 1, Indycar, NASCAR and other racecars, greatly improving television coverage.

Bruce Kessler's groundbreaking movie won accolades at the Cannes Film Festival. It was also nominated for the Academy Awards, only to get disqualified because someone said its release date was falsified. The film needed to be in release in a major theater prior one week to judging. That decision put the movie on the front pages of the Hollywood trade media, the reporters writing that it was the best to represent the U.S. at Cannes.

Garner's role led to his being selected for other movies and documentaries about racing. John Frankenheimer's *Grand Prix* was the most notable. There was one in 1968 in which Chuck Daigh did most of the driving. Garner also started his own racing team.

For Bruce Kessler, *The Sound of Speed* changed his path in life. His next Hollywood venture was designing all of the race action as director of the second unit on *Grand Prix*, as well as for Howard Hawkes on *Red Line 7000*. He went on to make many other movies and television series including *The Rockford Files* (again starring Garner, who did his own stunt driving), *The Flying Nun*, *Mission Impossible*, *Knight Rider*, *Mike Hammer*, *Renegade*, and *The A-Team*.

There was another interesting fallout from Bruce's link to Hollywood. In the Scarab race shop we had what you'd call several characters coming in and out of the place over the years. One mechanic Bruce recently remembered was Jack Russell, whose mustache was so large and wide he was nicknamed "Handlebars."

One day Handlebars asked Bruce if he knew anyone in the movie business. It turned out that our mechanic had been a paratrooper in World War II, and between jumps he and his buddies had a hobby of writing what were called caper stories. One of them was about how to rob a Las Vegas casino.

Just a little later, in 1960, there was the release of the first movie called *Ocean's 11*, in which Danny Ocean, played by Frank Sinatra, gathers a group of his World War II compatriots to pull off the ultimate

Las Vegas heist. Together the 11 friends plan to rob five casinos in one night.

In the movie's list of credits, it says it was "based on a story by Jack Golden Russell."

When Bruce met up with Handlebars years later, Jack told him that he was helping author James Michener write his 1992 book *South Pacific*. Michener included a note of thanks to Jack Russell on the acknowledgements page.

One other side of Bruce: like so many of us in racing, he wanted to learn to fly. There's an extensive training curriculum for that — it's not the same as driving a car — and I remember Bruce telling me that during his first lesson his instructor said, "You're the first student I ever had that can fly straight and level!"

N ow that Bruce is retired, he spends more time on the water. Born to a family of fishermen in Seattle, he has a love of boats. He owned an ocean-going yacht, *Zopilote*, and with his wife, Joan, he circumnavigated the globe over a three-year period, the first captain to do so in a small power boat. His next one, similar to the first, was *The Spirit of Zopilote*, now moored in Maine. A large, scaled-down copy of it is displayed in a glass case in the lobby of the Del Rey Yacht Club in Marina Del Rey, California, where the Kesslers live.

I myself am not quite ready to retire from all the activities in which I still have an interest. One of my final working connections with Bruce, although we continue to socialize, was when I was helping to establish the Petersen Automotive Museum.

He became the final driver to be honored for the Fabulous Fifties, after which the practice was terminated. Bruce and I and the very few of us left from our Golden Age racing world are fortunate to be able to keep closely in touch, reminiscing. Our memories span many decades. We have often taken parallel paths while diverging drastically at times, Bruce with his movie career, and me with IECO, my wines, consulting, and a toe into Economics. He calls himself a fisherman these days, and is enjoying the fruits of his many experiences, while my curiosity continues to keep me involved in various interests.

CHAPTER 12
THE STREET SCARAB

Rather than try to replay 1958's successful season all over again in 1959, Lance turned his ambitious mind to Formula 1 and sold off the two right-hand-drive Mk IIs. He kept the American-style prototype, the left-drive one he'd raced as no. 16.

But not as a keepsake. He came to me and said to make it street-legal for him. He wanted to take his world-famous, championship-winning red hot racecar out of his home garage and blast around Beverly Hills.

Well sure. Who wouldn't.

For that to happen it needed to be pretty heavily modified and then registered with the Department of Motor Vehicles. I checked with our local DMV to make sure I understood how to conform to their rules.

I did the work next door in Traco's side of our combined facility, with all the facilities and equipment I needed. Looking back, I remember that hardly anyone on the racing crew paid much attention to what I was asked to do. The car would no longer be a racer and therefore of little interest to them.

But the project appealed to me tremendously because I was a born hot rodder. I grew up turning ordinary cars into special ones, and this was just reversing a process that I enjoyed. It called for creative ingenuity, making do with what you had or could find.

I have to say that when Lance's request fell into my lap I was utterly delighted. Although I generally do not show a lot of emotion when inside I am actually thrilled to the core, that time I remember shouting out an uncharacteristic whoop of joy!

Thinking about what needed to be done, I figured it would be a quick and easy job. Traco built a new Chevy engine for it, with a lot of input from me.

I knew we had to swap out the Hilborn racing fuel-injection system for progressive carburetors, so that the car could run smoothly and economically at ordinary street speeds. I got a manifold to install three Rochester carburetors on the Chevy V8 engine. To link the three together I created a progressive throttling system, enabling the car to run on the center carburetor and burn less fuel when it was cruising. When the driver needed more power, all three carbs would come into play and really move!

Although I softened the suspension a little for a better ride on the street, I left the braking systems alone and kept the tires the same, so it would still feel like a racecar. But open-pipe racecar noise would not go down well in Beverly Hills, so we had to quiet down the exhaust system. I recruited Phil Remington and Emil Diedt to refine the exhaust system with a special arrangement that made the car look like it still had huge racing pipes, but actually there were dual mufflers in the back of the fenders so it ran quietly for the street.

Next we tackled the dashboard. I wanted to replace the pedestrian black-and-white Stewart Warner gauges that were in the racers with the nicer-looking kind that Mercedes used in the 300 SL, so I bought a bunch of the popular German VDO instruments, including a speedometer, tachometer, and all the oil and water temperature gauges.

To mount the spiffy new gauges Phil shaped a beautifully curved dashboard with a nice visor hood like a passenger car, instead of the flat, utilitarian piece it had before. I had Phil's masterpiece finished in black crackle paint. Then to go with the rest of it I had a special Italian steering wheel made, a wood-rimmed Nardi, the most famous and top-quality product in the world.

Hang on, I was far from done. Deciding to add insulation barriers inside the door panels, I took the car to my drag racing buddy, Tony Nancy, who owned a trim shop and had been a friend of Lance long before the Scarabs were built. Tony upholstered the seats and added padding to them for greater comfort. He even embroidered the Scarab emblem into the Scottish vat-dyed leather seatbacks.

The racecars didn't have radiator grilles, so we made one and I hand-filed a steel version of the Scarab emblem to be welded on it. Phil Remington made an indent for the license plates with inside lights illuminating them. Then we had the whole thing chrome-plated.

Bumpers. Hmmm. The bodywork was thin aluminum paneling hand-formed by Emil Diedt, so the slightest traffic incident would ruin it. But there were no Department of Transportation rules for bumpers in those days, so we made racing car style "nerfing bars" to protect the rear end.

We left the beautiful Scarab nose alone. I figured that keeping the front end looking good was up to the driver.

The windshield for Lance's car came from a 1955 Porsche speedster. We installed French-made Marchal headlights. There were stop lights, a horn, an emergency brake and even seat belts, although at that time they were not required.

The entire project took about three months. I spent countless hours on it every day and night, with Phil and Emil's help. Traco tested the engine on their dyno before they gave it to us, so I knew we were getting that part right.

Then I drove it down to the DMV to get it registered in the state of California. The car legally passed all tests that were required back then. The DMV rep walked all around the sparkling blue Scarab and listened to it run. I don't think the guy knew what the hell the car was, probably thought it was some weird foreign make, but he didn't find anything wrong. All I knew was, I had designed the Scarab street car to pass the DMV test and pass it we did.

I think that was one of my proudest moments.

I was totally responsible for the whole car. To me it became a neat piece of hot rodding. That's how I looked at it, taking this sports racer and turning it into a road-going vehicle.

The Reventlow Scarab street car, which I finished just before going into the U.S. Army, was registered first in 1960, then 1961 and again in 1962. The license plate number was RUR 467, and the validation number was 5021690. The registration also noted the engine number, N361069CAL, the make and model as "Scara" (the "b" was left off for some reason — well, I guess some might think this racer-for-the road was a little "scary"), and its body type as RDS (roadster). Also noted on the registration was the name Lance H. Reventlow and his address, 1309 Davies Drive, Beverly Hills, Calif. No zip code in those days. The registration fee was $200. A year later the fee was reduced to $148.

Lance still had the Scarab street car in 1972, when he lost his life in an airplane crash in Colorado. His widow, Cheryl, put the car on display at the Briggs Cunningham automotive museum in Costa Mesa, California.

Cunningham, of course, was Reventlow's predecessor in striving to take on International racing with an American automobile. It was neat that Briggs was happy to display our car — even though we had defeated him on the racetrack! Briggs was a good friend to me, and helped me with my Corvair turbo project.

Subsequently, car collector and racer Don Orosco bought the Scarab street car and reversed my alterations so he could campaign it in vintage events. Troutman and Barnes were still together at the time, so Orosco had the original builders put it back to its original racing configuration. Today it's owned by Rob Walton of the Walmart family.

CHAPTER 13
MY BANTAM BOMB

Balcaen's Bantamweight Bomb. That's what a magazine writer called my dragster. It's the only complete vehicle that I ever built and raced, but it was a successful one, a winner.

Winners go down in history. Whatever the drag racing record books say about my name, it will be thanks to that car, which I started building in my home garage as a precocious teenager. Despite all the success I've enjoyed since, I'm still very, very proud of that youthful achievement.

That's why I've written this dedicated chapter: to tell the whole story, the true story. My old car is still famous in drag racing annals, but over time certain mistakes and misrepresentations have crept into various accounts. This is my opportunity to set the record straight.

Three things in particular need to be clarified. One, contrary to what some people claim, it never was a Bonneville Salt Flats car; two, it had nothing to do with any Miller oval track racer; and most importantly, I was the first to complete a job started by others. I'm the one who made a finished dragster out of it. I won a lot of drag races driving that car.

There's more, but I'll get into details as we go along.

As I outlined in Chapter 4, all during my teenage years my early fascination with fast cars — the hot rods I was seeing everywhere — had done nothing but intensify. In the beginning it was exciting enough to be competing in my mother's hopped-up Chevrolet coupe, but the more speed I tasted, the more I wanted.

Drag racing was making me a racer; maybe it's more accurate to say that the racer already within me was finding its outlet.

When I started driving I was too young for a driver's license, and that was still true the first time I drove a real dragster on a dragstrip. I was only 14. That thrilling opportunity came thanks to my friendship with Frank Startup and Ed Donovan. Their Startup & Donovan partnership was one of the best and most innovative in early hot rodding. Frank was the driver, as well as a great mechanic. Ed was the engineering genius. At the time, in fact, he was studying engineering at Santa Monica College. That was before he went on to work for Meyer-Drake, the Offy people. Frank owned a bicycle shop and was a locksmith too.

My new buddies were both seven or eight years older than me, which is still quite a gap at that stage of life, but they took a liking to me and seemed happy to have this kid come along and be part of their little team at the races.

Donovan and Startup were very astute about motor racing, very scientifically oriented, and good, honest, straight people. They didn't try to put people down like so many in drag racing do, or try to be competitive with you. There were no games being played like we saw so many times in racing.

Both were big fans of four-cylinder engines, and they normally ran a Ford from the early '30s in a really funny-looking, stripped-down car called a "rail job." That nickname was a natural, because those cars were little more than a pair of totally exposed old Ford Model T chassis rails that carried the engine, the fuel, the driver and not much else.

None of us had much money to spend on racing, so we had to use 20-year-old engines, but we tried to get the very best of them. In the Ford four-cylinder world the ideal was the final version of the Model B engine. Ford kept on improving it right up until the end of production in 1934, and those last Bs had enough last-minute improvements that we called it the "Model C" — although that wasn't an official Ford designation.

We wanted that one because it had the best internal oiling system of them all. The B improved on the older A by having a pump to feed lubricating oil into the crankshaft main bearings. The older system simply relied on the oil being splashed around as the crank revolved. Not good enough for us racers.

The so-called "C" went a step better by adding pressure lubrication to the connecting rod bearings as well. It also had a counterweighted crankshaft, which improved balance, smoothness, and durability as it revolved at high speed.

I'm aware that what I've just said contradicts certain stories people have put up on the internet, but I was there and I have personal knowledge of the difference. We could have never, never used Nitro in that engine without oil pressure to the rod bearing surfaces. We had to have the strongest possible starting point when we muscled it up to much more power than Henry Ford ever imagined.

Getting that power required almost everything about the engine to be modified for racing, with special pistons, rods, cams, etc. The Startup & Donovan rail also had one of the popular Fargo four-port cylinder heads on it. In addition to providing better airflow into the engine, Fargo's aftermarket heads had two spark plugs per combustion chamber. That let us fine-tune ignition timing to get more out of the nitromethane fuel we used.

Our sport was still in its infancy, and a lot of drivers at the time used regular gas from the pump, and they produced plenty of horsepower. But when we used Nitro we were getting maybe three times as much! We couldn't measure it, it was just a guess. It could have been even more.

For most people Nitro was hard to get, but I knew a good source thanks to my mother giving me that Thimble Drome toy as a young boy. So when we needed some I'd go down to Ohlssen and Rice in Long Beach and pay $25 for five gallons of Nitro.

Nitromethane is produced as a cleaning solvent, but the oxygen its molecule contains makes it a powerful racing fuel too. The horsepower boost is enormous, like double or even triple. Setting up a dragster to burn Nitro makes it a Top Fueler.

Nitro is dangerous stuff to handle, though. It's kind of like liquid dynamite. A mixture of air with the fuel has a tricky characteristic of setting itself on fire if it's compressed beyond a certain critical point.

What does that mean? That the fuel-air mixture crammed into the combustion chamber can ignite spontaneously and prematurely, without waiting for the spark plugs to set it off at the correct instant. The prematurely high pressure would stop the piston from rising in the bore with a heck of a shock. It's like when the gunpowder explodes inside a rifle barrel. "Hydraulic-ing" is what we called it when it happened in a dragster engine. Best case, you lose power. More likely, you lose your engine. Break the connecting rod and blow the top off the piston, anyway.

Another thing about Nitro, the engine needs to burn a lot more of it than ordinary fuels, so you need larger-diameter dump tubes in the carburetors. To make those we drilled out the carb bodies and fitted much larger lines made for hydraulic brakes.

Also, because you couldn't use floats in the carburetors due to the all the engine vibrations, you took the floats out along with the needle valves they controlled. That made what was called a bypass fuel system.

Of course, I'm talking about the period before fuel injection came in and made carbs obsolete.

Starting the engine was a very laborious process. You didn't dare to start up from cold with Nitro in it, just the methanol that was our starting fuel. It's the type of alcohol that Indy cars use. First we primed the carburetor with just plain methanol and got the thing going on that. Once the alky level dropped the Nitro would come in. You could tell because nice yellow flames would be coming out of the headers.

Some people would dilute the nitromethane with methanol, because of the risk, but you have to push it to win. Everybody wanted to know how much the competition was prepared to risk. Guys would come by our pit and ask, "How much Nitro didja put in?"

The standard reply was, "The can, the lid and the label." Meaning, 100 percent. Actually, we put in a tiny bit of ethyl ether, about one percent, but the other 99 percent was pure nitromethane.

Nobody knew this stuff at first. Everybody had to learn it for themselves. We were pioneers, and we were top-notch mechanics and fabricators and home-schooled engineers. We had to be. You couldn't buy anything, you had to invent it and make it yourself.

Eddie Donovan was especially good at it. Nobody told him how to do it, but he had a mind that could figure it out. That's what made him the genius he was.

Eddie and I liked to experiment. One time Donovan said, "Let's trick the fuel up with some hydrazine!" That's a chemical compound that NASA used in space rockets, so among us it was known as "Rocket Fuel." Boy, did we get more horsepower!

But now that I'm older and wiser, I realize we were playing with some nasty stuff. For one thing, hydrazine can self-ignite like Nitro.

But worse, it can badly damage your health. The chemical is seriously toxic. It's known to burn skin tissue, to poison your neural system, and to cause cancer.

So, kids, don't mess around with "Rocket Fuel" like we used to do!

We had fun with our fuel experiments, though. There was a racer nicknamed "Mike the Armenian" who was sponsored by his fellow countryman, Ed Iskenderian. "Isky" owned a cam-grinding business among his other interests. He gave away camshafts for free to some drivers.

This didn't sit well with Donovan. He played a trick on them by adding food coloring to our fuel mix, turning it bright green. When Mike the Armenian saw it he said, "Jesus! That's green death! Donovan has got secret fuel!" A perfect psyche job.

The first time Eddie and Frank let me drive their "digger," as such extreme dragsters were called, was a single-car trial run at Saugus Speedway. At 14 I was way under-age, but Donovan handed me a pair of old plastic and rubber aviator goggles to wear along with my "brain basket" (what we called our helmets). "Here kid, put these on, they won't be able to tell how old you are." They fit tight to my face and were so big they almost covered it.

Sure enough. When I rolled up to the starter he didn't question me. He just waved his flag and off I went. I think I ran 120 mph. Man, that felt fast.

Once you drive a real racecar that's all you want to drive. Hopped-up street rods just don't do it for you anymore.

To be a racer you need a racecar, and in those days there was no such thing as buying new ones. You either found an old, well-used dragster that somebody no longer wanted, or you built your own. Most commonly, probably, people combined the two approaches, and that's what I did.

Sitting in Frank Startup's shop — which was his mother's home garage — was an unfinished Lakester project car that belonged to a good friend of his named Laird Pierce. Nicknamed "Lefty," Pierce owned a company in Ontario, California, named PARCO, which meant Pierce's Plastic and Rubber Products Company. I think he handled O-ring seals, which are important in engines and is probably how he and Startup met. In later years Pierce would become better known for racing Unlimited hydroplane boats, but back in the early '50s he was a dry lakes hot rodder.

Contrary to a published magazine story, which repeated several of those errors that I hope to correct, Pierce did not build the car for the Bonneville Salt Flats in Utah, just for the California dry lakes.

He didn't start with an old Indycar chassis, either. The frame was made for him from scratch, using a pair of straight, stiff box-section rails with hand-fabricated kickups where it had to go over the rear axle.

Another misstatement: Pierce didn't complete the car, and it had never run before Frank Startup showed me the chassis in a corner of his Los Angeles garage. Really, there wasn't much more to see than the stripped chassis, a '29 Ford rear axle with a Halibrand quick-change differential, and a center-mount Franklin steering box. There wasn't any engine or transmission. It didn't even have a body.

Frank said to me, "Sonny, why don't you do something with this? Don't you want to fool around with a six-cylinder engine?"

I did. I liked the four-cylinders that Donovan and Startup were using, we were getting great performance out of them, but I wanted something different. At the time nobody was using the GMC six in drag racing. I saw there was enormous potential for development.

By that time I was 17, I had left school to work as a mechanic, I had learned a lot about drag racing, and I had saved up enough money to buy these bare bones of a racecar.

Why a dry lakes car when I wanted to be a drag racer? Back in those days there wasn't much difference. Strange as it may seem now, the cars meant for top-speed runs through the measured mile across the wide, flat, geologically ancient dry lakes up in the desert were basically similar to ones built for short-distance acceleration along the new quarter-mile drag strips scattered around town.

Another difference was their appearance to modern eyes: both Lakesters and Dragsters actually looked like Indy 500 cars of the time, with the driver sitting up behind the engine between wheels that stuck out in the wind, not enclosed in streamlined bodywork. Remember, back then we took our marching orders from Indianapolis guys. They were the best, so we did what they did.

Full-bodied streamliners were seen on the lakes, of course, mostly at the super-fast Bonneville Salt Flats, but the sport's rulebook had a classification structure that offered plenty of more affordable options to ordinary people. You could pretty much take any old car you had and hop it up for speed runs anywhere. Doing it yourself, to suit yourself; that's what hot rodding is all about.

My new dragster-to-be came home with me to my own mother's garage in Playa Del Rey. It was 1953 and I was bursting with a 17-year-old's energy and enthusiasm. I set to work getting or making parts that my future racecar needed. It needed a lot of parts.

Take a breath, this might get a little more technical than some of you will care about. But for me this stuff was meat and drink and dreams.

Let's see. I needed a box-section cross member to bolt onto the front end of the chassis, to hold the front axle and steering and so on. I had a guy weld that up for me, to my design. But I fabricated pretty much everything else myself.

I made up my own steering wheel. Steering linkage. Mounts for the engine and transmission that I would get and install. I welded up the spur gears inside the differential, so both rear tires would lay power down equally onto the track. I cut holes in those chassis rails.

"Cut holes in the chassis?" Well, as I've mentioned before, I was a devotee of German race engineering, and in particular a great Mercedes-Benz engineer named Rudolf Uhlenhaut. I call him my Great Guru. Mercedes racing cars of the '30s, which dominated the Grand Prix scene in those days, had lightening holes in their chassis rails. It was to save weight, and thereby improve the power-to-weight ratio.

I had a German mentality about engineering, and if the Germans drilled holes in everything to make the car lighter, so would I.

You have to do it scientifically. You don't drill holes where it could cause a structural problem, just where it's excess weight. Metal that's along for the ride without contributing any strength.

I can't say how much weight I saved, I never bothered to weigh the pile of circular pieces of scrap metal I cut out. But my finished car really was "bantam weight." Beyond the chassis work, I hand-built an all-new body from scratch, including a belly pan for better streamlining. Mostly I used very light magnesium panels, which saved more weight over the ordinary aluminum most people were using.

The one exception was the long, bullet-shaped nosepiece. That had to be aluminum, because it doesn't mind being bent and hammered and shaped into three-dimensional forms. Mag is too stiff and brittle for that, but it's happy enough to just be curved one way or another, like the side of a body.

Once all the panels were done, I fixed them to the chassis frame with spiffy aircraft-style Dzus fasteners. Then, because I admired German racing cars for their superb engineering, I painted mine to match those fabulous "Silver Arrows."

When my digger was finally ready to go and we put it on a feed scale, it was 1275 pounds. That's really, really light for a car with as much power as mine had.

Horsepower! That's not the only thing you need in a dragster, but it's the first thing. I decided my best way to get it was the six-cylinder GMC truck engine made by General Motors Corp.

This was a relative of Chevrolet's classic "Stovebolt," which was the engine in my mom's 1946 Chevy, "my first racecar." I was very familiar with that, so the bigger, stronger truck version wasn't hard for me to get on top of. It displaced 302 cubic inches compared to the passenger car's 235, so that was more torque and power right there, and the engine was built tough to handle heavy duty. That's exactly what I intended to give it.

Having been to the Sprint car races at the Ascot dirt-track speedway, I had seen that the GMC was popular because of its torque. But nobody was using it on drag strips. To me, it looked like an entrepreneurial opportunity to do something new in my chosen sport.

I found a good GMC six, took it home and started making a drag race engine out of it. That was an ongoing, evolutionary process that went on for the next several years. Week by week, piece by piece, it turned into something far removed from the original truck engine.

The biggest change was to a new cylinder head, but that didn't happen right away. For a while I kept the stock head in place, contenting myself with hour upon hour of hard work with a grinder to enlarge and smooth out the intake ports so they'd flow more air. More air, more power.

The GMC, like the smaller Chevy, was known as a "three-port" engine, referring to the way the intakes for the six cylinders were siamesed in pairs. Usually, you'd put three carburetors on it, but sometimes you'd use five carbs. They'd be on the left-hand side, as the driver would be looking at it.

Also on that side were four exhaust ports, even though this was a modern overhead-valve design. The older side-valve layout (aka L-head or Flathead), such as on Ford's Model B or its famous V8, pretty much required same-side valves because manufacturers didn't want to put in more than one camshaft. That made economic sense, but stuffing all the ports together on one side restricted flow and therefore handicapped the horsepower potential.

That was still the case on the stock Chevrolet/GMC, despite it having its valves up in the head, clear of the cylinders in the engine block. That would have freed up the exhaust ports to run across to the opposite side, for a "cross-flow" layout that removed the constraints on airflow. In fact all of the V8s that GM was beginning to produce were that way.

But on the stock Chevy/GMC six-cylinder inline engine from that era, if you look at pictures you can see all the ports lined up on the left side of the head. There's one exhaust either end, then alternating pairs of siamesed intakes and exhausts in between. Let's call them "X" and "I" and the 12 ports line up like this: X, I+I, X+X, I+I, X+X, I+I, X.

As a racer I would have preferred that the GM engine designers had taken the opportunity to design a cross-flow head, but of course GM hadn't assigned them to make a drag racing engine. That little job was left up to us hot rodders to do.

So we did. A former Lockheed aircraft engineer named Wayne Horning came out with a beauty of a new cylinder head for the overhead-valve GM six. It was a proper cross-flow head, with separate ports for every one of the 12 valves. I had to have one. Actually the one I got was made by Horning's former business partner, Harry Warner, who bought the business and kept the brand name "Wayne."

On the "Wayne 12-port head," as it's known, there were six individual intakes on the left, where that many carburetors or fuel injectors would stick out sideways. On the right-hand side, the six exhaust primary pipes, or headers, could be blended into various configurations as they took the exhaust gas to the rear. Doing tricks with the pipes can increase power, if you do it right. It has to do with harnessing pulse waves oscillating inside, but let's not make this too techy, OK?

I guess I should apologize if I'm boring anybody with all this talk about engine airflow. For me it's fascinating, practically a passion, the key to everything else about engine performance. It's what I built my career on, first as a racer and then as a businessman.

First time I raced my new car was on the Santa Ana dragstrip (aka John Wayne airport) when I was about 18. At that track you started on a little downgrade, so you got a nice little send-off, but then you had to be careful with the steering and not get the thing sideways.

At that early stage the car didn't have its body yet, and I was still using the original seating position that it came with, which had me sitting up high over the rear axle with nothing around me but wind. I guess it was about as precarious as it looked, and I won't claim the car was pretty, but it sure was fast. It got to 129 mph right out of the box. I was very happy with what I'd built.

Over the next few years I raced all over SoCal, places like Colton, Saugus, San Fernando, Mickey Thompson's "Lion's" strip next to Long Beach, down to San Diego, up to Bakersfield to run with The Smokers, and even all the way to Half Moon Bay near San Francisco. Over the next few years I won a lot of races at San Fernando and Santa Ana in particular, took home a bunch of trophies.

One time in 1956 at San Fernando I did a really fast run that made news — but the reporter spelled my name wrong. Somebody named "Valcaen" got the credit for that one.

I think my best race in that car was in 1957 at Colton. I knew it was good the instant I saw Ed Donovan's face right after the run. Usually when I arrived back in the pit he was scowling. The sound from the engine always told him how it was running, and if it sounded ragged he'd say, "You were shootin' ducks out there."

This time he had a big grin. When that GMC was firing strong and hard on all six it made a beautiful tone. "You sounded like a pine board going through a buzz saw!" he said. My elapsed time was 9.6 seconds and the trap speed was 151 mph.

Donovan was a genius with engines. Because I was running Nitro, he made me some new valves out of titanium, to take the heat. When he started developing his famous dual-plate slipper clutch, my car was so powerful that I tested his invention for him.

That clutch was very effective with a high-power engine, but it was tricky to handle. The clutch springs were very, very strong so there would be no slipping, but even though I was a young, strong guy it was tiring to hold the clutch in until you were ready to release it.

There were no starter motors, so they had to push-start the car with a truck or something. Once it lit off, you had to hold the clutch down while they rolled you back to the start and, sometimes, you had to wait while the other guy got ready to go. That was quite a workout on your left leg. If you ever let it go accidentally it could have caused a disaster. I was always a little worried I might kill some spectators.

We didn't know how many horsepower a drag race engine put out, we were just guessing. But we were sure it was more than our dynamometers could handle. "Don't run it on the dyno," we'd joke, "it'll tear it right out of the floor!" Donovan estimated that my GMC with the Wayne 12-port head and fuel injection must have had around 1000 hp. That doesn't seem too impressive nowadays, but it was a big number back then. He worked it out from the weight of the car, the speeds I was doing, and the amount of fuel that was burned in the race.

Fuel quantity was critical. You didn't want to carry more than you needed, because of the extra weight, but if you ran out even a split second early you were done for the day. That happened to me one time at Bakersfield. It was the end of a bad day.

It started because in those days it was still an infant sport. We didn't have drag chutes to slow you down at the end. No highway-type guardrails either, just white lines and rows of parked cars and crowds of people. The only safety measures were beds of sand to snag your wheels if you ran too far. Sand could be really treacherous. I was nearly killed in a sand trap that day at Bakersfield.

My car was so fast that the instant you went through the lights you had to toggle a switch on the steering wheel to kill the magneto, twist a valve to shut off the fuel, and haul on the brake lever. We only had rear brakes, none on the front, so they weren't that effective. It could get a little hectic, trying to get the thing stopped from high speed.

At least they always gave you a nice straight shut-down areas.

Not this time at Bakersfield!

On my first pass of the day I got to the lights, shut off the power, started trying to brake... and I saw the shut-down area jogged to the left!

They didn't have drivers' meetings in those days, so I never heard that they had to kink the end of the strip to keep you out of a farmer's field.

Dragsters don't turn real well. I couldn't make the corner and went off into the sand, which at 150 mph wasn't as soft and smooth as it looked, so I was rattling around inside the roll cage and it screwed up my shoulder. Separated it, so at least it wasn't a major injury, but it was no fun. It broke a rear wheel, too.

I figured I was done for the day, but I got back to the pit and Donovan said, "You can drive, let's keep going." When you're racing you're so full of adrenaline you don't feel pain, so we got the car back in shape and I ran some more races and won again and again. At the end of the day when I was really ready to quit, Donovan sais, "You're top eliminator. Get ready to run the Final."

Night had fallen. The only lights were spectator headlights lining the strip. I rolled up to the start alongside the other car, which was the Nesbitt's Orange (their sponsor's name) with a big Chrysler V8. It was gonna be nice if my GMC 6 could blow him off.

To this day I still wonder if the guy deliberately screwed me up by continually killing his engine. They made it look like they were having trouble, but all this time I'm sitting there burning fuel. My tank was a surplus aircraft oil tank, a "kidney tank" they call it because of its shape, which I put on the car because it was small and I only would need enough fuel to make a normal pass.

Trouble is, this one wasn't normal, I got delayed at the start. So by the time we finally left the line and I got down the strip to the timing trap, which was 132 feet long, it was like somebody pulled the plug on my engine right in the middle!

I was ahead of the guy at that instant, I could see him out of the corner of my right eye, but when I lost power-abruptly he made it by to win.

Donovan accused me of shutting down too soon, but no, I just ran out of juice. It wasn't until I got home late that night that I started feeling pain. It would have been wonderful to beat a big Chrysler.

I had a couple other nasty incidents in my drag race career. One time I was running against a twin-engine Triumph motorcycle called "Double Trouble" when, halfway down the strip, out of the corner of my eye I saw him losing control and veering toward me from the left-hand lane. I don't know how we didn't hit each other, it was real close. I still get chills when I think about that one.

The other time was the one time I ever agreed to drive a Funny Car. Funnies aren't like diggers, you sit down inside a closed cabin. I launched, and instantly exhaust fumes filled the cockpit and I started feeling sick and I couldn't see. No more Funny Cars for me.

Dragsters were in my blood. I loved racing them, and the long hours of working on my car were the best times of my day. But I was getting so busy with other things that I couldn't take that time. My digger was sitting all mothballed in my shop over next to Bill Murphy's Buick agency in Culver City.

A couple of guys came along who were running Bonneville and wanted my GMC 12-port engine to put in their streamliner. Up until then I had always said "no way" to Sprint car racers who tried to buy it, but the streamliner people made a great offer and I finally agreed. I sold it to them for quite a lot of money in those days, I think about $2000.

I kind of had a pain when it left, but they ended up putting it in a streamliner and taking it to Bonneville and going very fast, well over 200 I believe. I felt good about that.

That left the empty chassis sitting in the garage, until my friend Nick Arias said a drag racer named Frank Iacono was interested in buying it. Again, I was offered a lot of money and accepted it.

My car's new owner put in another 12-port GMC, like I did, but changed or rebuilt practically everything else on the dragster. At the rear end, where I had sat out in the open air to save the weight of extra bodywork, he made a shroud around the cockpit and added a new tailpiece that was rounded off along the lines of Indy cars of the time.

Then he covered over my "Silver Arrow" paint with an orange-and-black scheme of his own.

And remember all those holes I'd cut in the chassis to trim off useless pounds of steel? Iacono laboriously filled them all in again to make it look better.

Well it was his car now, and he had the right to do what he wanted to do. But where I had been interested in performance, he was going for pretty.

Later on that car got a Chrysler Hemi V8 and kept on racing for many more years. Iacono kept the car on track longer than I would have, I'll give him that. Later Pat Ganahl bought the car, and over time it became something of a legend. In fact, I'm proud to note that today the car I created is on display in the NHRA Museum. It's the longest-running dragster in history.

However, when *Hot Rod* magazine featured it on the cover a long time after I sold it, I was surprised to see that the writer of the story

RIGHT This General Motors Corporation (GMC) inline-six and I had a long-running love affair. Because it was based on a truck engine, which was bigger and stronger than GM's similar six sold in passenger cars, I was able to get a lot of horsepower out of it. How much? Again, it pegged the dyno, so I had to estimate it was around 1000 hp.

ABOVE My "Bantamweight Bomb" at the Saugus drag strip in 1957, with me second from right, between the starter at the end of the line and Indy driver Cal Niday on my other side. My self-built and personally driven car had set top speed of the day, and won the Top Eliminator final race. This angle shows the nice, clean line of the body I made out of magnesium (body sides and belly pan) and aluminum (bullet-shaped nose). My choice of an inline-six engine let the car be slender, good for aerodynamics.

ABOVE *When I first built my top-fuel dragster, I mounted my driver's seat above the rear axle. Later I relocated it lower down and farther back, "slingshot style." Notice the large Indy-style exhaust system I put on the left side of my six-cylinder GMC. I clocked 136.53 mph at the Santa Ana drag strip in this car.*

ABOVE RIGHT *Now with its "back seat" but still without a body, my new rail tries a Donovan and Startup Ford engine. That's actually my friend Frank Startup at the wheel. Frank said it was fast and stable, but I had my heart set on GMC power.*

RIGHT *Here my digger has its six-cylinder GMC as it accelerates off the start line at Santa Ana, the first home of properly organized drag racing. Our strip was actually a taxiway alongside the runway of what is now the major airport in the area.*

How it looked in action at the dragstrip, my big inline-six pulling strong and big rear tires digging hard. What fun! Frank Startup is driving here, wearing my helmet. I would let others take over my car to give me their impressions and advice. I wanted to keep improving it.

ABOVE *Here is my bodyless "bomb" posed in the driveway of my grandfather's Playa Del Rey house, which was now my mother's home — and my "race shop!" I guess the oil stains give that away.*

ABOVE *This angle gives a clearer view of how I relocated the driver's seat to behind the rear axle. My hand-made magnesium/aluminum bodywork is now in place. I deliberately didn't add rear-end bodywork in order to save weight.*

Owner-driver Sunny Vulcaen at work on his outstanding Dragster during San Fernando program Aug. 19. Spotless machine is powered by 302 cubic inch GMC engine running Wayne 12 port head. Potent combo poses constant threat to popular OHV V-8's with Top Speed to date of 142 and Elapsed Time low of 10.13 seconds.

Sunny Vulcaen, nearest camera, in his beautiful 302 C.I. GMC powered Dragster challenges Top Time winner Jim Miles (hood? body?) for Top Eliminator of San Fernando meet Aug. 19. Vulcaen won in close race at 131 in 10.13 seconds.

ABOVE Newspaper clippings from the San Fernando drag races. My name was misspelled, but the story is correct. Winning with my nitro-burning, GMC-powered Top Fueler was a regular event.

ABOVE Digging hard for record speeds in my own Top Fuel dragster, which I built with my own hands. Maybe the best times of my life!

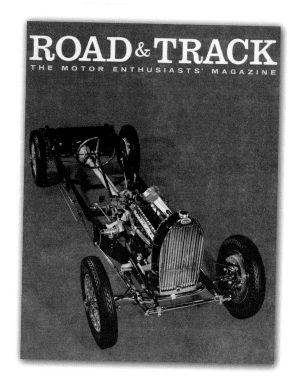

ROAD&TRACK
THE MOTOR ENTHUSIASTS' MAGAZINE

RIGHT While I was working at Warren Olson's shop in 1956, at the age of 20, Lance Reventlow had me do my first-ever "ground-up" restoration on one of the rarest, most idiosyncratic vehicles in automobile history — this Bugatti Type 57SC. John and Elaine Bond, publishers of Road & Track *magazine, came by one day and were so excited by the quality of my work that they had the bare chassis professionally photographed for the cover, along with a full-length feature story.*

BELOW My restoration of this magnificent French classic included having it painted a beautiful coat of proper French Racing Blue. But Lance later had it repainted orange! He meant it as a joke on "pur-sang" Bugatti admirers. That's the way he was. Here it's pictured at his Beverly Hills house in 1957.

RIGHT I always thought that Bruce Kessler could have been one of America's best drivers, maybe even as good as Dan Gurney (at the left here). A nasty crash at Le Mans ended that dream, but Bruce went on to a great career in the movie and TV business.

RIGHT Bruce, a close friend of Lance, gave the new Scarab its first trial run against opposition on March 2nd, 1958, at Phoenix. During pre-race practice he shattered the existing track speed record, but did not go on and race it. Satisfied the car was fast, the team returned to Culver City to continue development. This was the only time this original, left-hand-drive car ran as #23.

ABOVE *Lance was the driver for Scarab's first official race entry, which was on April 13th, 1958, at the Palm Springs airport. The shapely new American contender was the center of attention! This gang of admirers includes Carroll Shelby, the tall figure at the right with the big grin. Unfortunately, engine problems kept the Scarab from racing that day.*

LEFT *Bruce Kessler and Steve McQueen, two guys who shared two interests. Which one do you suppose they're discussing here, race driving or filmmaking?*

ABOVE Bruce was supposed to be "my" car's only driver for 1958's Times Grand Prix at Riverside. But then our boss, Lance, crashed his own Scarab #16 during practice, and insisted on stepping into #3 to start the race. Maybe my face shows how I felt about that. Bruce had the same reaction — that's him just behind me, back turned and walking away. The plan was for Lance to stop halfway through the grueling 200 miles for Bruce to take over. But we never got past halfway.

At Santa Barbara in 1958, Kessler drove the third Scarab with an experimental Offy engine. Note the hood scoop, which wasn't on either of our other two cars. This race proved the Indy-type four-banger, designed for alcohol fuel, didn't make enough power on gasoline. Plus, engine vibration was severe. So I swapped it out for one of our regular Chevy V8s, which was much more suitable for road racing.

ABOVE *A top-down photo of the street Scarab, the original left-hand-drive one, showing the overall graceful design of cars during its epoch. The beautiful styling was the work of Chuck Pelly, with further development by the metalworking geniuses at RAI.*

ABOVE RIGHT *Street Scarab's interior showing the special instrument panel, which Phil Remington fabricated to house VDO instruments under a shrouded hood.*

RIGHT *Padded leather-upholstered seats were installed for highway comfort. Notice the Scarab logo sewn into the seat back. The late Tony Nancy's elegant taste resulted in a superb interior.*

LEFT *A close-up of my filed-by-hand Scarab emblem framed into a hand-crafted grill insert. It was a lot of work, but gave Lance's unique roadgoing sports car its own special identity.*

ROAD TESTS: VOLVO 544 B-18 SEDAN, APOLLO-BUICK GT

Salon: *Scarab Chevy Sports Car* *Brabham F-1 in full color*

NOVEMBER 1963
FIFTY CENTS
50c in Canada

ROAD & TRACK

THE ENTHUSIASTS' MAGAZINE

ONE OF A KIND — A SCARAB FOR THE STREET

⚫ SCARAB

LEFT *My street-converted Scarab on the cover of* Road & Track *magazine. The car sits atop Lance's property in Beverly Hills, CA. The excitement that this thrilling sports car raised among enthusiasts made one think that the Reventlow car could have preceded the Shelby Cobra into production, had RAI been commercially inclined.*

LEFT *Lance Reventlow drives his street Scarab down Beverly Hills' Benedict Canyon Road. The "civilized racing car" was street legal and fully licensed in the state of California. After Lance's death, the original left-hand-drive car was "de-civilized" back into a racer for vintage events.*

credited the new owner for all its success — without mentioning all the races I won! He did mention me, but neglected to acknowledge that I was the original builder and driver. He never even bothered to call me to ask.

I wish people would try to get it right, and give credit where it's due.

As I look back over those wonderful days, I see it really was the Golden Age of Racing. It was an historic time. I can still feel the excitement of being part of it all.

CHAPTER 14
AMERICA'S
FIRST F1 CAR

F ormula 1 is basically a European thing, but most of the world considers it the top level of car racing. That's despite there being many other forms of competition vehicle. The long list includes sports cars, Indy cars, stock cars, rally cars, dragsters, land-speed streamliners, motorcycles, off-road buggies and trucks, airplanes, powerboats and so on. Each of them has its own multitude of faithful fans, many of whom know next to nothing about F1 and care less.

But from a global perspective, more people are most likely to follow the high-performance, high-tech, highly expensive open-wheel single-seaters known as Formula 1 Grand Prix cars. They're what the official World Champions drive.

That's the giant step that Lance Reventlow took next. He was the first American ever to build his own F1 car.

Flush with spectacular success in his debut season of sports car racing, when RAI won nearly everything we tackled hands down, 23-year-old Lance had no trouble imagining that a Formula 1 Scarab made in America could challenge the world.

Late in 1958, when decisions were being made, that season's results meant he would be gunning for Ferrari of Italy and its World Champion driver Mike Hawthorn, along with Stirling Moss, the driver who had only just missed the championship by a single point. Moss had been driving for Vanwall, a British organization that took the 1958 constructors' title — the first year this new award was bestowed.

The F1 starting grids also featured established teams BRM, Cooper, Lotus and Maserati, and great drivers such as Jean Behra, Tony Brooks, Peter Collins, Graham Hill and Wolfgang von Trips. Not to mention American newcomers Phil Hill and Carroll Shelby.

Should be a piece of cake to beat 'em all, right?

Well, there were a few headwinds. For one, Lance became determined that his all-American F1 contender was to be built practically from scratch by Americans in America. Nothing wrong with that, except that very, very few of us had any experience at all with F1.

No other American F1 car existed at that time. There was no local industry making F1 components like engines, transmissions, brakes, wheels, tires... nothing that we might buy off a shelf to ease our task.

Our driver Bruce Kessler had tried out one F1 car, not a competitive one, for only a few laps of a very tricky track he didn't know.

Maybe a few of the rest of us had watched a Grand Prix here and there, but only by traveling overseas. There was no GP of the United States back in 1958 — the first wouldn't be until the end of 1959.

Newspaper coverage was mostly about "stick and ball" sports. TV coverage of any kind of racing was rudimentary. Internet? What?

Our only way to find out what was going on in F1 was through enthusiast magazines. America's *Road & Track* did a good job, but it was a monthly, while copies of the English weekly *Autosport* came by sea mail. In either case, news of events arrived long after they happened.

Racing evolves much quicker than that. Whatever "new" engineering information the magazines brought us was already out of date when we finally read it. We were seriously out of touch with the latest trends.

And a vitally significant trend was developing over there: the so-called "mid-engine revolution." Thanks to Cooper, the entire concept of the F1 car was changing rapidly. The long-traditional layout, where the driver sat behind the engine, was falling victim to a new breed of designs with the driver up front. These cars were smaller, lighter, more responsive and much, much faster around a twisting road-racing circuit.

I think it's fair to say that, when the decision makers at Reventlow planned the F1 Scarab they intended to race in 1959, they had no real grasp of what they would be up against that year (in fact the cars weren't ready until 1960).

However, Lance did have one vital thing going for him: top quality people.

Warren Olson, RAI's manager and guiding hand, was lining up the best race engineering and design talent in the industry. The staff grew to as many as 24 people, which looked like a crowd in those days. Most important were those tasked with creating the first Formula 1 engine ever manufactured in the USA.

Leo Goossen was the most renowned engine man in America, based on his tremendously successful work over several decades with the Offenhauser, or Offy. But that was just one of many important engines and other racing products to flow from his fertile mind.

Goossen began as an assistant to the brilliant Harry Miller in the '20s, then further developed Miller's basic engine concept in the '30s with company successor Fred Offenhauser. Leo stayed with it during the postwar years when the manufacturer became Meyer and Drake Engineering. But the double-overhead-camshaft, four-cylinder engine still was called an Offenhauser, it was still winning the Indy 500, and Goossen's hands were still on it.

Really, no one in America was a better choice for what Reventlow needed. Our F1 road race engine couldn't just be an Offy oval-track model, we had tried that, but understandably Goossen drew on his lifelong experience with that to design the Scarab.

His new one was no copy of the old standby, though.

Don't worry if you're not a nut about nuts-and-bolts, I'll steer clear of most of the technical stuff, but two special features stand out about the Scarab.

One, instead of standing it upright like most other engines that have their cylinders all in one row, Leo designed this inline-four to tilt over almost sideways. Think of picking up your suitcase from the ground and laying it down to fit in the trunk. For our new racecar, the benefits were both a lower center of gravity, for better handling, and a lower hood line for less air resistance and therefore higher speed. That was a good feature.

One less good was called "desmodromic valves." To put it simply, instead of relying on commonplace coil springs to shut the valves that let air in and out of the engine as it revolves, Goossen added a complex extra mechanism to keep them closed when they should be sealing the internal pressure. Frankly it was a mistake for our engine, a lot of trouble for no benefit.

Leo's wasn't the one to blame. Lance made him do it.

Young Count Reventlow, a keen car guy whose towering ambition was unrestrained by cash-flow concerns, knew that Mercedes-Benz chose desmodromic valves for its championship-winning cars a few years earlier, and he demanded that Goossen do the same for his Scarabs.

Trouble is, Lance wasn't an engineer, and didn't realize there was another side of the story — as there always is. Desmodromic camshaft and valve mechanisms are very intricate to design, involving extra cam lobes and strangely shaped cam followers with forks that embrace the valve stems. Everything must be manufactured to painstaking precision, and keeping it all adjusted properly is a never-ending pain.

Also, this extra apparatus is only needed on engines that operate very fast, so fast that the valve springs begin to oscillate. That means the valves will bounce on their seats, letting air leak through and losing horsepower.

The Mercedes-Benz F1 engine of 1954–55 divided its 2.5-liter/152 cubic inch displacement among eight cylinders, which made for smaller, lighter pistons operating through a shorter stroke distance. That engine might be able to spin fast enough for desmodromic valves to be of some value (if maybe more to the advertising department than the race team, those fabulous cars were going to win anyway).

Our four-banger of the same size couldn't reach high enough revolutions per minute to realize the theoretical advantages of positively closing the valves. Without that "improvement" Goossen's Scarab engine could have been lighter, simpler and less troublesome. The car might have been completed sooner.

But that's hindsight. At the time I probably was as enthusiastic as Lance.

And fair disclosure: in my more mature years I have been a keen owner of Ducati motorcycles, which feature — guess what — desmodromic valves. After many years of experience with them, Ducati knows how to manufacture the intricate system to give great results. At Scarab we didn't have any desmo experience at all.

Anyway, Goossen went ahead with the desmo design, and in doing so he had the benefit of actual engineering drawings of the Mercedes engine. But how in the world did he come by those? By Travers and Coon handing them to him.

Preston Lerner's book *Scarab* revealed that a few years earlier

Jim and Frank were hired by Ford Motor Company to go to its museum in Greenfield Village, near Detroit, and disassemble and study the straight-eight engine of a Mercedes racecar. The German company had allowed it to be on display there, but I'm not sure permission extended to examining every internal component with micrometers!

Ford had no immediate need for the data, but when Jim and Frank heard Lance say the D-word they said, Hey, you know what?

So Leo sighed and got to work on his own interpretation of the Mercedes valve mechanism. Overall head of the project crew was Art Oehrli, another engine man with long experience at McCulloch Superchargers. Jim Nairne and Ed Iskenderian did most of the machine work and dyno testing, using the Traco dynamometer.

Marshall Whitfield was Warren's choice to design the car itself. At 23 and fresh out of engineering college, he understood racecar dynamics from some experience in driving them. But he'd never designed any car of any kind.

Marshall was a brake man, in fact he came to Scarab from Douglas aircraft, where he had been working on airliner braking systems. A good engineer can design anything, all he has to know is what the job is. But the RAI team wasn't sure what to tell him, not at first.

For those who might not know the complexities of designing an automobile, it's more than just sketching out how it's going to look. When you look at a design you only see the overall car, but to me, that's just the skin. The complexities are underneath that skin, just like the skin on the human body covers our organs and anatomy. The whole mechanism, whether it's the driver or the car, is very, very intricate and every part has to work in perfect harmony. If you're designing a brand-new racecar, a machine you hope will be better than anything already running around the track, there are a million places where you have to get it just right.

Although we were a little out of touch with the latest developments in F1, as I explained earlier, we were not ignorant of rear-engine racecar designs. Coopers and Porsches constructed that way were familiar to us, and news did filter through that Stirling Moss won the 1958 GP of Argentina with a mid-engine, open-wheel Cooper car powered by a four-cylinder engine.

Later that spring Bruce Kessler would have seen another such car take the Monaco GP.

But both Moss and Hawthorn scored most of their championship points that year aboard traditional front-engined models. Furthermore, most cars all across America carried their engines up front, and remember how oriented we were toward the Indy 500. There might have been a feeling that building cars "backwards" was a silly fad that would fade.

Taking emotion out of it, the reality was that going Formula 1 at all was an enormous undertaking. Better to take our baby steps on terrain we knew. So Marshall Whitfield started designing a front-engined F1 car — maybe the last one ever.

Caution wasn't the only factor behind Scarab's conservative approach, though. Another was Lance Reventlow's adamant insistence that his cars be all-American, without any foreign components. That caused a real problem with the brakes.

Scarab sports racers had been equipped with drum-type brakes, a technology that was almost as old as the automobile itself. Ours were modernized as much as possible in the '50s, with heat-dissipating aluminum fins surrounding traditional iron drums that were extra wide for more surface area. As it happened, Marshall Whitfield's father had been an inventor of that concept, called the Alfin process. They worked well enough for our sports cars to win all those races, although like everybody else our drivers had to take care not to use them too hard, which could overheat them. By the end of a hard race there might be no brakes left.

However, a revolution was going on in this area too, and disc-type brakes were proving to be superior. Jaguar sports cars had proven how effective discs were by winning the grueling Le Mans 24-hour race multiple times. Formula 1 was rapidly adopting discs too, because they allowed drivers to go harder without running out of brakes due to overheating. Naturally Scarab would follow the latest trend, right?

Not if Lance couldn't use ones made in the USA, and there weren't any that were suitable. Easy enough to resolve, just buy some F1 racing hardware from Europe. No way. He was making American cars and they had to be all-American.

Lance was an inveterate reader of books, newspapers and magazines from Europe, and from them he gleaned the famous water-brake idea. Cunningham had experimented with such a concept, and even though they abandoned it, Lance was determined to try it on his Scarab Formula 1 car.

His notion involved a single brake mounted on the rear-wheel driving mechanism, thus acting on both rear wheels. The idea was to keep the brake at a consistent temperature, so it wouldn't fade, by means of bypassing engine cooling water through a housing around the brake drum.

Lance described all this to our designer, who drew up blueprints for how to make such a system. Warren and the crew spent a lot of time and money on building and testing the novel device, only to run into a major problem: the extra heat load kept making the engine run too hot. Also, the extra volume of coolant increased the operational weight of the car, and that handicap would only increase if an extra radiator was installed to help the first.

We just couldn't make it work right, no matter what we tried. In the end, Lance had to accept that his water-cooled brake idea wasn't practical. Common sense took over and the Scarab was adapted to take modern disc brakes. Imported from England.

Does all that seem like a waste of time and resources? Racers see it differently. Such setbacks are a normal part of developing any new technology, especially anything in motor racing. To win you must push the envelope. If you come up with a new idea, you must try it — before somebody else does. They might wind up beating you with your own idea.

If it doesn't pan out — most brainstorms don't — you didn't make a mistake by taking the risk. That's how you learn and move on.

It was Lance's fierce drive to be competitive that resulted in almost every part on the new F1 racer being custom-made. That meant plenty of time-consuming work to design and make the pieces, along with analyses of stress, and then development and testing. As a result, the RAI crew expanded to more than 24 people. They were sweating countless hours, with Lance more and more impatient and anxious for the completion of the first three F1 cars.

A draftsman who was also an engineer was hired to sketch out the initial body design, then Phil Remington and Emil Diedt constructed it out of sheet aluminum panels.

Lance's pocketbook supposedly was bottomless, so we did have enough funding for the project, but Simone Olson kept his money on a tight leash. I remember how careful we had to be with our costs, which seemed to be rising by the day. We had to watch every penny, analyzing budgets and how much we could spend on materials. We were conscious of pricing in everything we did, and a time clock helped keep us productive.

Observing these methods helped me later when I ran my own businesses.

Every day in the shop I was able to work with and observe at first-hand the best in the business, Lance's dream team. I've already mentioned some of the great talents in that little building on West Jefferson in Culver City, but I want to say more about Phil Remington, the team's genius fabricator. I was most admiring of how he made his decisions.

"Rem" was a local, born and bred in Santa Monica. It's reported that in World War II he signed up by claiming to be older than he was and managing to fudge the Army's eye test despite being color-blind. In the Air Corps he worked on aircraft engines, and served as a flight engineer on a B-24 bomber. Outside the military he raced hot rods on the dry lakes, built some of the great old racecars for Indianapolis, and also developed engine-swap kits and parts for hydroplane racing boats. He was a terrific ideas man and a masterful craftsman.

Chuck Daigh called Phil Remington "the electric motor," because he was always working!

After the Scarab years he went with Carroll Shelby on the Cobra and Ford GT40 programs, both far more successful than Reventlow's. Phil wound up with Dan Gurney's All American Racers, working on Dan's Formula 1 and Indianapolis Eagle cars, as well as helping build cars for the Can-Am, Trans-Am, Formula 5000 and IMSA sports car circuits, a massive undertaking.

Defying his advancing age, Rem kept on working right to the last. Dan memorialized his longtime right-hand man and close friend by leaving Phil's apron on his workbench right where he laid it on his last day in the shop. Nobody touched that bench except to keep it clean.

Emil Diedt was another master craftsman I admired. He was magic at shaping metal into beautiful car bodies, and had been famous for a long time when I met him. Before the war he was part of the team that built the 1935 Ford Indianapolis Miller-Ford team cars for Henry Ford.

Emil and I were "brown baggers," that is, we brought our lunch to work. It was usually sandwiches, which Emil called "somonabitch" in his deep, accented Austrian voice. The two of us would sit and eat together, and I'd sketch racecars, what I thought they'd look like in the future. It seems kind of cheeky now, looking back, that I'd proffer my drawings to this great designer. But he'd good-naturedly give me his input, his opinions.

Interestingly, although we were building F1 cars, I was drawing Indycars. Hot rodders like me took our marching orders from the Indy people. Those guys were the best. We tried to build parts that were more precise than theirs, with better welding and better fabrication techniques.

"Crabby" Travers was another mentor to me. Jim was half of the Traco engine partnership with Frank Coon. The crew nicknamed him "Crabby" because he was always complaining and was extremely arrogant. That didn't bother me, I really loved the guy.

Eager to learn from Travers, because I considered him a master craftsman, I followed him around and assisted when asked. At times, I think he took advantage of me. He was building a big powerboat right next door at the Traco shop, and I'd help him work on the boat every evening without compensation.

Not many people know it, but there was tremendous animosity between Warren Olson and Jim Travers. Warren, of Norwegian descent, was a stoic and managed to put up with Travers' "holier-than-thou" attitude for the sake of the project.

It was common knowledge that many Indycar builders regarded themselves as the elite in the world of motorsports, and the Indy 500 truly was the biggest deal in the U.S. back then. Jim obviously felt superior to most of the Scarab crew and felt all along that he should be running the project, not Warren.

I admired them all, but Travers would probably have been able to spearhead the building of the car better than Olson. I think Warren was intimidated by Jim, causing confusion. I also believe that the whole issue later hindered work on the Formula 1 car.

Art Oehrli would always be around, too. Art told me that even in the cradle he could smell metal and machine oil in his father's shop. Art's father and uncle emigrated from Switzerland and were among the first builders of piston and radial piston engines for Pratt & Whitney, the aircraft engine manufacturer.

Art produced horsepower that you'd never seen before, but he smoked like a chimney, and coughed, even when working on engines. One day "Crabby" said to me, "Don't let Art die in the shop. Drag him outside if he collapses!" I decided he was joking.

If one just looks at the finished Scarab Formula 1 car without preconceptions, it was an impressive piece of work. It was very beautiful, not only in how it looked but also in the craftsmanship that shone out of every part of it. If any of your fingerprints were on it, you couldn't help but be proud of it.

Although I held German engineers in the highest regard as being way above everyone else, I saw that Lance's crew were beginning to produce an exceptional car. Ultimately it would be famous, although we didn't realize it at the time.

One of my responsibilities was to make the gearboxes. I started with a standard Corvette manual transmission, took out its four-speed gearset, added a fifth gear, and installed it all in a custom-made housing.

Another assignment had me conducting analyses of the desmodromic valve gear in the lay-down four-cylinder engine. We had a working prototype of the desmo system for the exhaust and intake. We analyzed the system in motion, watching with a strobe light to see how it functioned at various RPM. The strobe light appeared to stop the mechanism while it was actually going, letting me see how it was behaving, how the oil was being distributed over the rotating surfaces, and how it wore. We'd figure out what kind of materials we could use to make it stand up to very heavy duty.

Leo Goossen, of course, was the prime engine designer. Jim Travers also had a lot to do with it, and others in our shop made small but vital contributions as well.

Working with Chuck Daigh on this gave me immense respect for him. He was as good at working on cars as he was at driving them.

Earlier I described the scene as our first engine burst into raucous life on Traco's dyno. The sound excited everyone. There was a sense of promise in the fume-filled air. We wanted to believe we had created another winner.

U nhappily, I wasn't going to be around to watch it win. Warren Olson intended to send me to Europe early as an advance man, because he knew I had lived in Italy as a boy and spoke a couple of languages well enough to set things up before the whole team arrived.

But then a letter came from Uncle Sam ordering me to join the U.S. Army. A "Draft Notice" was something young men received routinely in those days.

Lance tried to intervene with the military, claiming I was critical to the company and that I needed to complete my work as a key person on an urgent project. I'm not sure the Army realized he was talking about a frivolous thing like a racecar, but he succeeded in procuring a six-month deferment for me.

It was enough time for me to finish Lance's Scarab street car and also to be involved in early testing of the F1 Scarab, especially of the desmo engine.

It turned out I was right about those intake ports. As I remarked in the opening of this book, I had a hunch that they needed to be bigger to flow more air and make more power. Also, I thought we needed a better supply of the oil that lubricates the rotating parts of the engine. Starve the engine of oil, and you potentially destroy it.

As the young kid on the crew, I knew my opinions didn't count for much, but I was firm in my belief and sure enough, the engine wasn't producing all the horsepower it should have been for its displacement.

S carab's first Formula 1 race was the Monaco Grand Prix in May 1960 on the French Riviera. Unfortunately, by that time I was otherwise engaged, defending America by learning how to march in step and fold bedsheets to perfection at Ford Ord in California. Some news from Europe did reach me, though, and I was really excited to hear how "my" team was doing over there.

Not so well. The practice sessions in Monte Carlo weren't encouraging. The cars proved to be well off the pace of their competitors, almost completely out-horse-powered and definitely out-handled.

After Daigh fiddled with the cams and valve clearances, the engine managed to breathe a little better, to provide 30 percent more power. But getting the power hooked up to the road was another matter. After Stirling Moss took a few laps, he said, "It drives like an Esso truck!" Lance enjoyed repeating the comment.

And it was a fair comment. The front-engine Scarab carried all its fuel way back in the tail, causing problems with weight balance as the fuel load lightened during a race. The new breed of mid-engine cars had their fuel in the middle too, alongside the driver. That meant the handling balance stayed the same.

Mid-engine cars had won nearly every race in 1959 and topped the World Championship, and were on their way to doing it again throughout 1960. Our sparkling new Scarab was two years out of date the day it made its debut.

The two-car Scarab team was unable to qualify for Monaco. RAI immediately went off to Zandvoort for the Dutch Grand Prix, hoping for happier results. This time they qualified and made the grid, but a dispute ensued with officials and Lance angrily withdrew his entries before the start. Chuck and the rest of the crew were pretty pissed off about that.

Undaunted, hoping that third time would prove lucky, the team immediately headed to the Spa-Francorchamps race circuit that speeds through the Ardennes forest in Belgium. At last the Scarabs made the start of a Grand Prix, but failed to finish it. Lance was forced to retire early on with a blown engine, thanks to the inherent oiling problems, while Chuck, drifting the second Scarab perfectly around the fast corners to the delight of the crowds, kept going until an oil leak pitted him.

It was a bad race for other reasons, too. During practice Stirling Moss and Mike Taylor crashed their Lotus racecars and sustained serious injuries. Even worse, two British drivers were killed during the race itself.

Despite all that went wrong, I'd have loved to have been there because of my Belgian heritage, but I was busy obeying marching orders in Northern California.

The depressed RAI team set off for the next GP at Rheims, France. This time Lance stepped down to let the more experienced American driver Richie Ginther have a shot. That shot missed too. More engine problems kept both Ginther and Daigh out of the race.

RAI packed up and came home.

The final Grand Prix race of 1960 was on American soil, at Riverside in November. Here at last was familiar ground. Surely Scarab could make a good showing at what could be described as its home track. But confidence — and resources — were only high enough to enter one car. The team had had worked hard on it, finally increasing oil flow to the main engine bearings, and also taken weight off the car itself.

During practice Chuck Daigh qualified 18th, toward the back of the grid. To the Scarab F1 guys that might have had the feel of an improvement, but it was a massive eight seconds slower than the pole-position time — and four depressing seconds off the pace Chuck had achieved with the victorious sports-racing Scarab two years before. The F1 car was a huge contrast to its predecessor.

However, on Sunday afternoon Chuck gave the German driver Wolfgang von Trips (Lance's houseguest in an earlier chapter) a challenging race before he fell back to finish 10th, two laps behind Trips. The Scarab was five laps behind the first-place car, but at least Reventlow Automobiles Inc. had scored its first ever finish in F1.

Incidentally, I was pleased for my old boss Jim Hall, who drove a good race in a Lotus he owned to run fourth for a while, only to drop to seventh at the end when the transmission failed.

How I wish I had been there to see it all. But the Army wouldn't let me have that weekend off. So the only times I ever saw the F1 Scarab on a track it was a test track. All I know about the races are stories from other people. It feels like I missed out on some important history.

Stirling Moss, recovered from his injuries in Belgium, started his Lotus from pole position at Riverside and gave a textbook demonstration of how to win a Grand Prix. Winning the World Championship was Australian Jack Brabham, taking the title for the second year in a row with a Cooper — another mid-engined car. The front-to-rear revolution was complete.

An interesting side story about Brabham: he came by the Scarab pit one day during Riverside practice and took the car out for a brief test. He was as good an engineer and mechanic as he was a driver, and when he came in everybody clustered around to hear words of wisdom from the two-time champ.

But little was gleaned from his ride. "Black Jack," as they called him, was almost totally non-committal, except for a few vague sentences which the Scarab guys weren't quite sure how to take. Chuck Daigh wondered if Jack was deliberately giving him false feedback.

I don't know what the point of that would have been. It was the end of the F1 season. Scarab had not been any kind of a threat to Brabham.

We could barely make it into races, let alone finish them.

All of our hopes and dreams had come to an ignominious ending.

RAI's dismal Formula 1 season devastated us all. Over time I have tried to piece together why the F1 version of the Scarab failed as far as the engineering side was concerned.

One fundamental handicap was not jumping straight into the rear-engine revolution, which was just beginning when the project got underway. But I've already explained why RAI chose the more conservative road.

Also, we were under-powered, which we should not have been. I don't wish to second-guess the famous Leo Goossen's original ideas, his genius is well established in history, but my personal judgement was that, as I noted earlier, we needed bigger intake ports and better oil circulation to the bearings. I could see and "feel" that these important factors weren't adequate.

That feeling was my hot-rodding instinct. This instinct of mine I could liken to painting a picture. You could almost feel the next color going on before it actually does. This came from intuition built up over years of hot-rod engineering. I just knew.

These faults were eventually discovered and corrected, but too late.

When Reventlow closed up shop, Chuck Daigh took some stuff with him, including at least one engine. He moved to Newport Beach, where he started a powerboat business, but on the side he kept working with the Scarab F1 engine. He finally succeeded in increasing the horsepower by a lot, and also figured out how to make the bearings live. "How did you do that?" I asked.

"I fixed the oil galley and enlarged the intake ports," he explained. My mouth almost dropped open. So I'd been right all along! Chuck's analysis was a great vindication of my own earlier theory. I felt really good that Daigh and I thought the same way about the design of the engine.

Beyond those two fundamental factors, though, Chuck had the luxury of development time that RAI had lacked. Critically, as he gained experience with the desmodromic valve gear, he discovered that we had been handicapping performance by leaving clearances too loose.

That was intentional, because we didn't completely understand the novel (to us) push-to-open and pull-to-close design. We thought that looser clearances were necessary to keep the two sides of the system from fighting each other, which might bind the whole thing up.

But when Chuck decided to trust Goossen's design and snugged up all the clearances, the engine came to life. I think he said he got 35 to 40 more ponies out of it.

That would have made America's only Formula 1 engine competitive with Europe's finest.

CHAPTER 15
SOLDIERING FOR UNCLE SAM

My military service was at Fort Ord near Monterey, California, a big basic training center where fresh recruits were sent in those days. Most of them then went on to other posts, but they assigned me to become one of the training instructors, so I remained at Fort Ord for the next year or more.

Not my idea of paradise. By that time Laguna Seca raceway was already in operation on a corner of the property, but I never was able to get a weekend pass to go and watch. I could hear the engines in the distance, that's all. I was totally cut off from what to me was civilization.

Well, not quite totally. One day a fellow soldier saw my name on a roster and came to find me. He said, "Hi, I'm John Drake. My dad's Dale Drake, he and Louis Meyer make racing engines."

Well, sure I knew that! The Offy engines that Meyer and Drake manufactured were as good as it got! John and I stayed friends for a long time.

My father was still hoping I would like being a soldier, and stay in the military life and follow him up the ranks. His idea was that I would go to Officer Candidate school and become a Warrant Officer in helicopters. "It's a natural for you," he'd say. "You have mechanical ability, you love to fly, you have high IQ, you'd enjoy it."

I bowed out. He was a military man through and through, a born soldier, a warrior. He had it in his mind that I would finally see the light and become a warrior like him.

But I'm not a soldier. I didn't care for Army life.

We carried M1 rifles left over from World War II strapped across our chests. It was pouring with rain one day when we had to do our usual 50 pushups in the mud, then we'd be called out for having a muddy rifle and told to "clean that son of a bitch!"

That might have been the same time my father flew in for a visit. We were on bivouac down at Fort Hunter Liggett, camping out and doing field maneuvers, and it was raining like hell. We were slogging along with parkas stretched over all the bulky, heavy gear we had to carry. I looked up and I saw this helicopter land and Major Balcaen stepped out. With him were four other officers. They were there to inspect us or something.

Well, that caused me a lot of trouble with the other guys in my squad. "Goddam, Sonny, you're a blankety-blank Major's son! You're privileged! You're being treated better than us!"

That wasn't the case at all, in fact I think I got away with less than the other guys could. And I know it made me a special target of a certain drill sergeant.

Sergeant Cherry was a true dictator. He enjoyed demeaning me because of my father, I guess, and often made me work in the kitchen on KP duty, and waiting on the NCOs in the mess hall. He also liked to deny me weekend passes.

But Dad could pull rank on him when necessary. He and my stepmother used to drive down from Sacramento in his yellow Thunderbird, obtain a pass for me, and take me out to a great restaurant for dinner in Monterey. A treat, for sure.

He also gave me a beat-up old Dodge to drive around. But then one time when I wanted to drive up to visit my parents in Sacramento, Sergeant Cherry refused to give me a weekend pass. My dad called and asked me why I wasn't up there yet. When I told him the reason, Dad said, "Get me the Executive Officer!"

That soldier was a young lieutenant who was told to "Take Sergeant Cherry, stand him up tall against a wall, and tell him the facts of life!" I soon got my pass and left for Sacramento in my Dodge. Curiously enough, I never saw the sergeant around after that.

As for flying helicopters like my father had suggested, I did do that. But not in the pilot's seat. I was just one of the observers stationed in the open side doors of the twin-rotor Sikorsky helicopters that we called the Flying Bananas. Appropriate nickname, because it was enough to drive me bananas, the boredom of patrolling the base hour upon hour, looking down at the racetrack I wasn't allowed to see from the ground.

My father finally accepted my rebelliousness, and he arranged for me to finish up my enlistment in the Active Reserves in Los Angeles.

So in late 1961 I returned to civilian life, finally finished with my Army active duties except for being posted to the Reserves. It was a joy and a great relief to be done with orders, commands, uniforms, and regimentation. My service had been a thorn in my side as a freewheeling entrepreneur who valued independence.

Still, perhaps I needed to experience the discipline that my father did as a career officer of the U.S. Army.

But what would I do next? What kind of work would I find? I had been away for many months and a lot happens in the racing world over that long a period of time.

PART III

CHAPTER 16
ENTREPRENEUR

My service in the Army marked a major transformation in my life. While enduring what I saw as wasting too much time in monotony and purposelessness, I seemed to feel a big, powerful spring in my brain that was winding up tight. When I finally hit the street as a civilian, all that pent-up tension and energy released explosively.

It's the point when I truly became an entrepreneur.

Simply going back to Reventlow wasn't an option. First of all, the team was running out of gas and weren't hiring. But I don't think I would have taken a job there anyway.

Although I still loved car racing and still wanted to be involved, I no longer wanted to be a hands-on racer. There was more to life than twisting wrenches and standing on gas pedals. Ever since I was a boy I had known I was born to be a businessman, an entrepreneur. It was time to get serious about that.

The next few years were a whirlwind. My days and nights became a blur of working, working, working. It's hard to look back and say just when certain things happened, they all seemed to happen at once. But to make sense of it here I'll split it all into categories.

Lance Reventlow had undergone changes of his own while I'd been away. His futile effort to establish an American Formula 1 team had cost a lot of money, money that wasn't really his to spend. Behind the scenes his mother, Barbara Hutton, still had control of his trust fund and she only indulged his ambitions while it looked like Scarab was going somewhere. The success her son achieved with his sports cars in 1958 must have satisfied her.

But he'd talked her into spending a lot more money on his F1 ambition, and 1960's dismal outcome broke her patience.

At the same time, Reventlow Automobiles Inc. was coming to the end of the five-year limit that the IRS places on unprofitable business enterprises. If you can't make money by that time, it looks like you're not taking it seriously, so you're not entitled to tax breaks.

Lance did try to shift gears, by setting up to manufacture Scarabs for sale. That called for a larger facility, so he acquired vacant property at 1942 Princeton Drive in Venice. It was very near the Marina Del Rey yacht harbor, and only a few miles from the old Culver City place. Here he erected a new, designed-for-the-purpose brick structure with plenty of shop space on the ground level, including an in-house dyno facility, plus a smaller second floor for offices. RAI moved there early in 1961.

That part of the story is short and sad. Everything was against success. For one thing, the international F1 rules had changed, drastically reducing engine size to a maximum of 1.5 liters. Scarab's desmodromic 2.5 was now illegal as well as inadequate.

Over in England an alternative series was being offered, something called the InterContinental Formula, which allowed engines up to 3.0 liters. This pleased diehard horsepower fans, and for a time it seemed there would be a worldwide market for such cars. RAI took a stab at the Intercontinental, sending one of the front-engined cars over for Chuck Daigh to drive. But everything was still against him — engine, chassis, weather, his knowledge of the tracks, the strength of the opposition. Worst of it was a serious crash in torrential rain that broke his pelvis and some ribs. Tough guy Chuck walked all the way back to the pits before he would admit he was hurt.

The Scarab team then designed and built an all-new open-wheeler, a modern mid-engined car with a small, lightweight General Motors-made Oldsmobile V8, but that proved fruitless as well.

One more thing to try: a two-seater sports car version of the mid-engine V8 design. That was actually a pretty good car and had some racing success. But it didn't bring back the glory days of 1958. Buyers didn't beat down Lance's door. He closed the Scarab business early in 1962.

He hung up his crash helmet, too. Our feeling was that he realized that he just didn't have what it takes to be a top driver, and lost interest. That happens to people. Besides that, when his mother cut off the money it wasn't only to prevent him squandering it, but also that she thought racing was far too dangerous a sport for her only son to be doing. Perhaps Daigh's crash strengthened that feeling for both mother and son.

Also, there was a rumor going around the racing community that Lance shut the shop because he owed taxes and the IRS was breathing down his neck. There was some truth to the rumor.

Princeton Drive didn't stand idle for long. My old boss and friend Carroll Shelby was starting up his own automobile make. A master wheeler-dealer, he persuaded both a small English car manufacturer called AC Cars and gigantic Ford Motor Company to cooperate with his dream for a hot sports car he called the Cobra.

He saw that the former Scarab place in Venice was an ideal spot to manufacture it. Shelby quickly leased the property, taking over a magnificent, fully functioning race shop overnight. What's more, Phil Remington came as part of the deal, as did several others including Warren and Simone Olson.

The personnel were important. Reventlow had the best builders, mechanics, designers and engineers all working there, and in my opinion these people aren't lauded often enough. Famous race drivers get all the cheers, but without the people on the shop floor many drivers who take the checkered flag wouldn't be able to do so.

Let me expand on that. I think Dan Gurney was one of the exceptional few who recognized this. A couple of years afterward, when he started his own business — in partnership with Carroll Shelby — he took care to hire the best talent available, including Remington and others who had been at both Reventlow and Shelby in Venice. But Dan added another vital ingredient: himself as a driver.

Not only was Dan Gurney one of the finest drivers America has ever produced, he also had an innate ability at engineering and technical innovation. In economics there's something called the law of comparative advantages, meaning that when drivers become good at what they do, then the workers become good at what they do, especially the team managers. This in turn transfers back and boosts the driver's success.

Shelby American moved into the former Scarab shop in March 1962, and by October the powerful, fast little Shelby Cobra sports car "Powered by Ford" won its first race, which was out at Riverside.

I was getting involved with Shelby about this time, for the second time, but not as an employee. Now I preferred to work on a consulting basis, not only because I like being my own boss but also because I had a lot of other things going on.

When the Army discharged me from active duty, I went to work for William Doheny, the CEO of the oil company Unocal. Bill was the grandson of E.L. Doheny, who was the pioneer of the rich Southern California petroleum industry, being the first driller to strike "black gold" and making a huge fortune from it. A successful entrepreneur, in other words. Doheny became a philanthropist, and is remembered on several place names around Los Angeles.

The company his grandson William headed up, Unocal, had been one of the early beneficiaries of his grandfather's wildcatting success. Unocal's gasoline brand was Union 76, and that company was a big sponsor of auto racing, no doubt because of my new boss's personal enthusiasm for motorsports. He had sponsored the famous California driver Ernie McAfee, who is remembered for driving bright blue Ferrari with the number 76. He also owned a dealership with McAfee's name on it that sold Ferraris, OSCAs and Siatas.

Incidentally, Warren Olson had been McAfee's ace mechanic before I met him at his own shop and then at Reventlow's.

Ernie's tragic death in 1956 at the wheel of one of Doheny's Ferraris was a heavy blow to Bill, who dropped out of the sport but kept McAfee's name on the dealership. It was on Sunset Blvd., and that's where I reported for duty.

Bill had gotten the franchise for NGK, the Japanese spark-plug brand, and wanted somebody to go out and sell them to all the mechanics at the racetracks. By then I had a reputation as an engine man, and the racers would trust my judgment. So I became the representative for NGK, just like Dick Jones was for Champion.

I'd go around to the crews telling them how great the NGK products were and how they could improve their cars' performance. As a race engineer I was able to explain exactly how to use the spark plugs as they related to their particular racecars and the conditions of the day.

If you think about it, unscrewing a spark plug is the quickest way to open a window into the inside of the engine. Because it ignites the fuel-air mixture inside the combustion chamber, it lives in the very heart of the action. The temperature and quality of the fire leaves its mark on the plug, and by examining it with a loupe you can tell a lot about what has been going on inside.

By being well educated about doing that I could help the guys tune their engines, advising whether the carburetor mixture needed to be leaned or enriched, and if the plugs they were using were "too hot" or "too cold," which is shorthand for the heat range those particular spark plugs were made for.

I enjoyed and embraced all of it, being back in the pits with its smells and noises, and it was how I was making my living.

What's more, I was doing so without getting my hands dirty!

As a retired racer, what interested me the most now was seeing how the drivers, mechanics and teams were handling a race. They had me thinking how I'd do it differently and realizing how pedestrian, basic, and even naïve I thought some of their ideas were. There were so many small changes that could have made a big difference between winning and losing.

But selling spark plugs wasn't all I was doing. I became an inventor at the same time.

My invention, which I patented, was an improved intake manifold for the Chevrolet Corvair engine. We used to call the Corvair the Poor Man's Porsche, because both those cars had air-cooled engines in the back end and all-wheel independent suspension. I had a lot of experience with the Porsche, and I could see the Corvair could benefit with a better induction system, so I designed and made a new manifold. "Crabby" Travers was very helpful to me with this part of it.

I bought a new 1960 Corvair, red in color, then designed and fabricated my new manifold in my garage and sent it out to be machined. I ordered other parts to go with the package. It was all the trick stuff that I always did to improve a car's performance, like modifying the ignition system and exhaust and so forth, anything I could do to make the ordinary car a little better. I just took my racing experience and built special mechanical parts that you couldn't buy in those days. I always took it upon myself to modify cars, it was just my nature to try to make them better, and in those days there was a big market for it.

Doing the work was one part of building my fledgling business, but I figured that some magazine publicity would help. A way was made clear when a friend from racing introduced me to Jack Dulin. He worked as a mechanic for a fine old gentleman who ran Indy cars and whose Lincoln-Mercury dealership in Inglewood was very successful.

Jack knew Bob Petersen, the publisher of Petersen Magazines, Inc., and took me to meet him. "Pete," as he was known, suggested I call one of his editors, Ray Brock. The result was a great story in the magazines about my invention. After that, I bought small ads in the Petersen publications and realized how well advertising worked — business took off!

Orders would come into a PO box, and I'd be building parts in my garage or subcontracting stuff out, the manifolds, special steering arms, shifting mechanisms and so forth. Then I'd assemble it all and ship it out.

That was the beginning of what would become my company, IECO, which stood for Induction Engineering Company. I first used that name in October 1962, when I was still working for Bill Doheny to sell NGK spark plugs while producing performance parts for the Corvair on the side.

But that's not all I was doing in those days. In 1963 I was attending college part-time to get a degree, which meant adding homework to my already-overloaded life. Reading *Barron's* magazine and the *Wall Street Journal* was another way to further my education.

Beyond that, when Shelby started making his Ford Mustang Shelby GT350, I worked for him setting up the inventory for his Ford accessory parts system. Plus that, I worked with Pete Brock in another building on the marketing and advertising of the Shelby products, doing catalogs and so forth.

So it was a really busy time of my life, but I rarely let it affect my internal insistence on perfection as far as feasible.

Pete Brock was another one of the highly talented, capable people that Shelby's big personality had attracted like planets. In fact I'd go so far as to say Pete is one of those rare, true Renaissance Men. His accomplishments have been in fields as varying as car styling, product design, team and business ownership, photography, writing... it seems like he's good at anything and everything.

I believe Pete was one of Carroll's first employees, if not the first, dating to the time when Shelby had started a race driving school at Riverside and hired Brock to be chief instructor.

Renaissance Man was a very good race driver too. He was so keen on racing that he quit his job at General Motors, where he had been the stylist for the Chevrolet Stingray racecar that established the lines for the immortal 1963 Corvette "split-window" street coupe.

How come he had gone to work for GM Styling? He was a graduate of the famous Art Center College of Design.

Shelby knew all that, of course, and had moved Brock from the driving school into the Cobra project. They wanted to take on Ferrari head-to-head in international GT competition, and knew that the standard open-cockpit Cobra wasn't fast enough. It had the engine and chassis, but it needed a more streamlined body with a closed cockpit to stay with the Ferrari GTO on long European straightaways, especially at Le Mans. So Shelby promoted Brock to an executive position as the designer for what became known to history as the Cobra Daytona Coupe.

I became involved the day Peter Brock phoned and said, "Shelby would love you to come down here and straighten out the parts and accessory business for us."

Shelby's "Li'l Cobra" venture with FoMoCo had turned into a Big Business when Ford introduced the Mustang and decided to make a sports car out of it. For the transformation, Ford shipped brand-new Mustang Fastback bodies-in-white — meaning they weren't finished cars — from the assembly line in San Jose, California, to Shelby American in Venice.

There they basically became factory-made hot rods: more powerful engine, revised suspension meant for hard racetrack duty, stronger brakes, better radiators, etc. By leaving out the small rear seats — which were pretty useless anyway — the vehicle became a sports car in the eyes of the Sports Car Club of America. All that, and topping the job off with special styling cues and boldly flamboyant "racing stripes," also changed how the public saw the Mustang.

When it first came out as a "1964-and-a-half" model, Ford pitched it as a "Personal Car." It was good looking, but not very interesting to performance enthusiasts. Car guys began to call the Mustang a "secretary's car."

But suddenly there were Shelby Mustang Cobra GT350s, and magazine road testers raved about their performance and handling. A limited run of hardcore, racetrack-focused GT350 R-models started winning races all over the country. Mustangs started selling like double-whopper bacon cheeseburgers to fast-food fans.

Why the "GT350" designation? The story goes that Shelby got so exasperated with everybody's indecision over what to call the car that he sent one of the guys to measure the distance between the two shop buildings and that was the number: 350 feet.

No focus groups. No high-priced marketing consultants. No endlessly long sign-off process. Just one Top Guy making a snap decision based on instinct, information and intelligence. That's how it has to be in racing, and it works in business too.

And Shelby Mustangs became a big business very quickly. Even though Carroll and Ford set up a second, separate building around the corner from the Venice race shop, it was too small to handle all the orders. In March 1965, only a few months after production started, the entire Shelby American operation, GT350s along with Cobra production and race team, picked up and moved to a pair of large aircraft hangars on Los Angeles International Airport (LAX).

When Pete Brock called me, I declined at first, explaining that I was busy with an idea for my own parts company, and I was planning to expand to various manufacturers. I considered myself well on my way to earning my fortune. I told Pete, too, that my racing days were behind me.

However, they persuaded me to come in as a consultant, not an employee, to set up Shelby American's parts and accessories program and inventory. Also, I created catalogs for Cobra accessories such as T-shirts from Japan, key chains, jackets, and so on. That business became a huge success and gained much publicity.

In terms of the GT350 itself, Ford shipped new but incomplete cars to us, and we'd add ancillary parts to make them Shelby's own. We gave the engine more power, and beefed up the suspension for better handling. We installed a different exhaust system that was good and noisy, as hot rodders love, and added hood pins like the NASCAR guys used. There was a tachometer to show engine speed, of course.

I personally dealt with Koni, the shock absorber titan, to build shock systems for the Shelby Mustang. I also had something to do with designing the distinctive aluminum valve covers and exhaust systems for the engine, and special wheels for the car.

All of these additions were really to make it look like a sports car to compete with General Motors' Corvette, but of course it wasn't a "real" two-seater. People loved our Mustang anyway.

Now, of course, anyone can buy a brand-new Shelby Mustang with all the hot-rod accoutrements already in it.

Talking about those special GT350 wheels makes me remember a story. Outside of Shelby I had a special deal set up with the Harvey Aluminum company in Harbor Gateway near Old Town Torrance to do the pouring for an exclusive wheel I was designing for other passenger cars.

When the company owner, Mr. Harvey, an industrialist and philanthropist, heard that I worked with Shelby, he and his staff naturally asked to meet him. I called Carroll at his house in Playa Del Rey and told him he had to get over to Harvey Aluminum with me right away.

"Goddam it!" he said. "I really gotta get down there?"

"Yes," I told him, "and you have to wear a tie."

Shelby disliked wearing neckties and most of the time his shirts were open-necked. It was pretty obvious he preferred to stay home, but I'd set up this deal and didn't want to lose it. I went over and picked him up, and the folks at Harvey were thrilled when we showed up. We talked with Mr. Harvey about their process and of us making some of the investment in the castings. The Carroll Shelby wheels were subsequently poured there.

Our wheels were unique, a different sort of look compared to other makes. I felt that if we had a special design it would appeal to more people and thus Shelby American would sell more cars. The look of a wheel is an important part to buyers. My wheels were sand-blasted in places to give them texture and other parts were polished. The wheels were very original at the time.

Another time Shelby was really annoyed with me because one of the editors at Petersen Publishing had been loaned a press car from our dealership, and he brought it back an utter mess. I'd handed it over to the editor in pristine, sparkling condition and he returned it spattered with dirt and mud. It was as filthy as if it had been through a junk yard.

After I gave the guy hell, he called Carroll and I was immediately called on the carpet and told never, ever to scold anyone in the media again.

It took me a while to calm down. I was upset because the car hadn't been treated with respect. I heard a few other stories of journalists trashing cars to test their limit, but mostly the writers brought our cars back in good shape — although almost always out of gas.

It was a crazy, busy period. At the same time I was working for Shelby I was also taking classes and studying for my degree, plus creating my own catalogs of Corvair components and accessories, making and placing ads in magazines, redistributing parts, having customers' orders manufactured, picking them up and taking them to my home where I packaged them at night in my garage, and shipping them out during my lunch break at Shelby's. The Corvair orders became the nucleus of my business, strictly mail order. That's known as direct marketing, or today as online or Internet shopping.

Best for last: besides all that I also was sort of the Shelby American company pilot!

C arroll was a longtime pilot, ever since he'd been taught to fly in the Army and became a flight instructor in bombers. He never was sent into combat, but he never lost his love of airplanes, and he owned a lot of them over the years.

At the time I'm writing about he had a Cessna 206, which is a high-wing, single-engine utility airplane that can carry six people or some cargo, depending on the mission. Shelby's company used it a lot for business purposes, but Carroll rarely piloted it himself, because he was always so busy. So he often requested me to take the plane up. He liked to impress his guests by having me taxi "the company plane" right up to his office door at LAX to meet them. I would ferry his friends, racing guys, investors, himself, and others around to various places, usually to racetracks where he'd take dignitaries and corporate sponsors.

My friend Ken Miles was a little jealous of me for being the company pilot. He had always wanted to fly and he was older than me, so why would Carroll pick me instead of him? Well, I had been a licensed pilot since I was 16. Ken had never even taken a flying lesson, as far as I know. But racecar drivers are like that, their egos reach the sky!

There were times when Shelby would take the 206 on personal trips himself. There's one anecdote I still enjoy a chuckle about.

ABOVE *Lance Reventlow tries out his new Scarab Formula 1 car in the spring of 1959. It's not hard to imagine him thinking, "We're gonna win the World Championship too!" I can tell you that I had the same hopes!*

RIGHT *Our Scarab Formula 1 engine was the first ever to be made in America. The international rules of the time limited displacement to 2.5 litres, or 152.6 cubic inches. Designer Leo Goossen, along with other engine specialists at Reventlow Automobiles Inc.,*

chose a four-cylinder inline configuration, and canted it nearly on its side to allow for a low body design. Its most significant mechanical features were "desmodromic valves." This system, pioneered by Mercedes-Benz a few years earlier, used a dual camshaft mechanism to both open and close the engine's valves, rather than relying on conventional valve springs to close them.

RIGHT Count Reventlow about to conquer The Principality. Posing happily in the pit lane at Monaco, debuting his very own, all-American F1 car, doesn't Lance look like he expects to be king of the Grand Prix world. Just a dream, alas.

ABOVE Lance Reventlow and Stirling Moss confer about the Formula 1 Scarab's handling and performance characteristics at Monaco. The great British driver had been asked to turn a few laps and give his assessment. It was negative.

ABOVE RIGHT Lance Reventlow takes the Formula 1 Scarab around a tight left-hand corner at Zandvoort, Holland. Our flamboyant boss loved his "beat-up looking" crash helmet, painted in the US Air Force "day glow" paint.

RIGHT Today, one of the two surviving Scarab Formula 1 cars is in the excellent hands of historic car racer Julian Bronson. Now with Offenhauser power, it has scored wins in various vintage events, including here at Monaco — where the American Formula 1 hopeful first appeared in Europe back in 1960.

Sadly, the Formula 1 project failed to take the world by storm. However, when this car received a Chevrolet V8 heart transplant, it started a revolution in movie-making. Bruce Kessler's innovative short film, Sound of Speed, was a breakthrough in how to make the excitement of motorsports come across on the silver screen.

ABOVE *Carroll Shelby left a huge mark on the auto business, not only in the USA but worldwide. The tall, lanky, warmly genial Texan was not only a very strong racing driver, winner of Le Mans as well as national championships in America, he was a born entrepreneur. Out of his boundless imagination and ambition, fueled by inexhaustible energy, came the iconic Cobra sports cars, which gave birth to a dynasty — Shelby Automotive. His name lives on.*

ABOVE *Carroll himself was taught to fly by the US Army, and continued piloting a series of his own aircraft in civilian life. But as his growing businesses took up more and more of his time, he often had me ferry people around for him. The company plane I flew a lot was a Cessna U206 similar to this one.*

RIGHT *Carroll's idea of a corporate hat. Becoming an industry mogul meant appearing more formal, but really, inside he was still the same Ol' Shel who built his first image as "that Texas chicken farmer who drives in his overalls and wins all the races." Learning from him as I worked in his Shelby Mustang accessories program taught me a lot about starting my own car business. Carroll personally gave me this portrait of him.*

ABOVE My friend Pete Brock with the landmark Cobra Daytona Coupe he designed for Shelby. Thanks to Brock's new, ultra-streamlined body with its distinctive "cut-off" tail, what had been an open-top sports car became fast enough to defeat Ferrari's GTO on the high-speed straightaway of Le Mans, ultimately making Shelby the Manufacturers' Champion for 1965.

The shop building behind is where Pete and I later worked together in Carroll's aftermarket business.

RIGHT The cover art of one of my IECO catalogs, featuring a wonderful painting by famed automotive illustrator George Bartel. The brand name meant Induction Engineering Co, because it was founded on the first home-built induction manifold that I made up to get more power out of the small flat-six, air-cooled Chevy Corvair engine.

ABOVE *This is the IECO corporate headquarters I put up on Broadway Avenue in Santa Monica. A far cry from my mom's little garage in Playa Del Rey! The building was designed to show the precision and detailing that went into all products that IECO engineered and developed. Note the use on the building of "Swiss-style" graphics, which was in vogue in the 1970s. Unfortunately, the structure is gone now.*

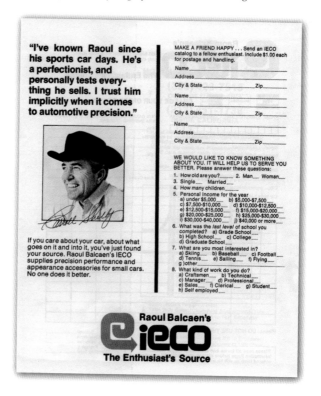

RIGHT *Carroll Shelby was helpful to me in starting IECO, and generously did this advertisement as a favor to us. We used it as a research piece to develop algorithmic links to customers' potential needs.*

LEFT *This formal executive photo of me was taken by a business publication in 1963, after the founding of IECO. I was just 27.*

BELOW *The IECO Vega that I developed in 1973, pictured here at speed in the Malibu hills. With our mods to its standard engine and chassis, this car could beat the specially produced twin-cam Cosworth-engined Vega that General Motors came out with later. GM got the idea to make its own "performance car" after the overwhelming success of our IECO "Hot Rod" — which still has a cult following today.*

ABOVE *A basic little Chevrolet Vega four-cylinder, single-overhead-cam engine, which IECO transformed into a 190-hp street machine for driving enthusiasts. Chevrolet's own Cosworth-developed twin-cam engine couldn't outrun it.*

ABOVE *With Bob and Margie Petersen at their superb Scandia restaurant on the world famous Sunset Strip.*

ABOVE *At Machu Pichu in Peru, standing at the start of the Inca Trail. This ancient ruin is now a spectacular UNESCO World Heritage site deep in the sacred valley of the Inca Indians. On this unusually clear day the Huayna Picchu and Moon Temple ruins can be seen in the distance.*

ABOVE This is me at the entry plaza to the Taj Mahal in Agra in the state of Uttar Pradesh, India. A very beautiful and unique structure to visit for the world traveler.

ABOVE *Taking a quick break from a long ride, motorcycle buddies in Yosemite National Park in front of Half Dome mountain are, from left, Dan Genter, David Kaiser, Randy Sugarman, and me.*

ABOVE *My wife Franziska standing next to her Ducati GT1000 with me and my Ducati ST-3S, ready to take a weekend ride in the "twisties."*

One winter he flew up to Lake Tahoe with a lady friend. Overnight the weather closed in, with a low overcast obscuring visibility of the mountains. Carroll wasn't rated to fly on instruments, so after an attempt to spiral around looking for an opening in the clouds he aborted the flight and landed back at Tahoe. He drove his girlfriend back to L.A. and phoned me to go up and get his airplane.

I told him I'd do it if he'd pay for my girlfriend to fly up with me commercially, so she could act as my navigator for the flight home. She was a great pilot herself. However, Carroll groused about the extra expense, so I had to carry out my important mission alone.

A more usual flight was back and forth from Shelby American's base at LAX to a testing or practice session, mostly out at Riverside. It's a long drive but a short flight. To make it even shorter, we'd just land on the track's big, long back straight. It was wide and a mile long, so it might as well have been an airport runway.

Except that smack cross the middle of this "runway" was a stout bridge sponsored by Champion spark plugs. Race cars could zip underneath no problem. For an airplane it could be a little trickier.

One time Shelby had some VIPs coming into Los Angeles airport, and he told me to fly them out to Riverside. I was happy to, I love to fly.

So I got into my own little Cessna that I kept at Santa Monica airport, flew it down to Long Beach airport where Shelby's bigger Cessna was, and flew that back up to LAX. The Shelby American hangars were on the south side of the airport, next to some charter hangars.

I picked up his passengers and we set off for Riverside.

Whenever I landed at Riverside, the nearby March Air Force Base, which controlled the area, would always have me stay north of them so as to not interfere with their own operations. Fair enough, Boeing B-52s are bigger than Cessna 206s. But it meant I would be landing toward the south, which usually involved landing with a tailwind. That increases the plane's speed across the ground and it takes more distance to slow down. But the RIR back straight was plenty long enough, under normal wind conditions anyway.

This particular day the wind was from the northwest and pretty strong, maybe 30 or 40 knots. That stiff a tailwind made our flight in from the west shorter than usual, but it made my downwind landing much tougher than usual.

Ramping up the tension, on board I had the son of the vice-premier of Japan plus five other dignitaries. So that was a full load of "souls on board," as they say in aviation accident reports, and what's more, thanks to that helpful tailwind we hadn't burned up as much fuel as usual. Now as I lined up with the runway, the combination of a heavy aircraft and strong tailwinds meant we were scooting along over the ground at a dramatically higher speed than normal.

The situation was a little twitchy, but I told myself I could handle it. Other places I'd flown were even tighter. When I attended music festivals in Ojai, California, I'd land in a farmer's small field that was studded with telephone poles. A good pilot can land on a postage stamp, pilots tell themselves, and I knew I was a good pilot. But this time at Riverside it was a little different.

First and foremost, I had passengers on board. Secondly, on the ground were some impatient drivers and crew chiefs, who had been forced to interrupt their testing program with Shelby's Ford GT40s for the Le Mans race and wait for me to get my airplane off their darn racetrack.

Another wary eye on me was the air traffic controller at March, standing ready to divert his big, lumbering nuclear bombers in case this fool private pilot aborted the landing and violated his airspace.

I almost had the plane wheels-down when suddenly the Champion bridge was looming right in my face. I had to get under it, there were no options left. By dropping the flaps full down and working the controls to counteract the tricky wind I just made it, although I felt something strike the plane as we zoomed under the bridge.

My passengers disembarked safely, and began bowing, smiling, and thanking me. I am sure they were much less relieved than me, because they hadn't realized the difficulty of the situation.

As it happened, I had scraped the tips of the propeller blades, only slightly but the plane needed to be checked over by a certified aircraft powerplant mechanic. My passengers went back to Los Angeles in a pair of Mustangs. I don't remember how I got back, but it wasn't by plane.

Wait, the story gets better. When the engine was inspected and pronounced airworthy a few days later, I went back to Riverside to bring Shelby's 206 back home. Along for the ride came a friend I'd met when I was lifting weights. He was Steve Merjanian, who became a famous weightlifter and ran Arnold Schwarzenegger's gym in Venice,

California. Steve weighed 290 lbs.

What a mistake I made by inviting Steve! The extra "ballast" required me, once again, to give the take-off my full attention. At least I was heading north this time, facing into the wind, which would help with my buddy Steve's weight.

We gained airspeed quickly, so the plane was soon ready to rotate and lift off, but I had to keep the nose down until we got through the Champion bridge. By that time we were going so fast that the instant I lifted the nose wheel the plane jumped off the ground.

And the crosswinds started drifting us toward the line of telephone poles right alongside the track! Man, I pulled the stick right back, maxed the engine, and the left wing just squeaked by those poles.

I realize, looking back, that I took unnecessary risks that time and probably other times as well. I was a young guy, 26 years old, and there were chances I took then that I would never take later.

Although occasionally I went to the races, I was never a big part of Shelby's actual racing program. I never touched an engine, because I had become a Shelby executive.

In point of fact I felt like an old racer — at 27 years old! I had been racing since I was 14, I'd had great experiences, worked with the best people in the racing community and I was grateful for it all, but now it was time for me to ensure that my own business grew.

My ambition was as fierce as ever. I was intrinsically motivated and had dozens of ideas I wanted to see come to fruition.

Occasional I did go to races, though, such as the time I bumped into an old friend in the pits. Bobby Rahal, winner of the Indy 500 and lots of other races, was now a race team owner. We had lost touch, but said he often read about me in magazines and wondered why I had gotten out of racing.

I told him, "I no longer race because I wasn't making any money. I had to get out."

Rahal laughed and said, "Yes, that's true for all of us."

CHAPTER 17
SHELBY AS I KNEW HIM

C arroll Shelby became my friend almost the moment I met him, and even after we both left racing this bigger-than-life Texan remained a big part of my own life. Even in his final days, when confinement in an intensive-care unit closed him off from most everyone else in the world, he and I had the kind of relationship where he could call in the middle of the night and ask, "Sonny, we want to know which jets you put in the 45 DCOE Weber carburetors?"

During my time working with Shelby I found out what a great promoter he was. In fact he was a genius of a promoter. Finally, I realized his secret: he promoted himself. Not the Cobras, not his parts inventory or the catalogs, nor his drivers. He had a great meet-and-greet personality, was affable, always smiling, and ready with a handshake. If buyers liked you, I observed, they'd buy your products.

And it worked like magic. It would have worked whether he was selling apples or birdseed. Simple as that. It was a good lesson for me.

This brings to mind a story about the 1964 Indy 500. I had been invited to dinner at Shelby's one evening back in 1963. After the meal we adjourned to the living room to have another glass of wine to digest the black-eyed peas and vegetables his Danish housekeeper prepared. She was an excellent cook and this was one of Shelby's signature dishes.

During dinner the phone rang and Carroll excused himself to take the call. I asked if he wanted me to leave so he could have privacy, but he insisted I stay. A heated conversation ensued with what I gathered was the director of the Goodyear racing program. Shelby had acquired that program as part of the Reventlow Automotive buyout. On the phone he was very firm and almost demanding: "Don't you worry. I will tell you again, A.J. Foyt will be racing on Goodyear tires at the Speedway. I assure you of that!"

Since Brooks Firestone and I were friends, I shared this story with him many years later during a dinner together. When he heard it, he said, "I have a connection there," and went on to tell me the story. I'm including it because it's a significant part of the battle between Firestone, having been the Indy-only monopoly, versus Goodyear's attempt to unseat them. Brooks especially wrote the following for my book. It's genuine racing history, not a web-related distortion!

Several of us Firestone executives were on hand, including my uncle, Ray Firestone, who was the Chief Executive and designated to present congratulations as we waited for our driver, Parnelli, in the winner's circle. We had been the winning tires for every Indy 500 race previously and we expected to win again. We were making a film about it for television and it was a big deal for our advertising and promotion campaigns.

The race began with all the usual excitement, but heavy rain began falling. This was one of the few times the race had been stopped for fierce rain and held over from Sunday to Monday, Memorial Day. Tuesday was a Firestone Board meeting and it was determined that all the executives needed to fly on the company planes back to Akron. They had a meeting with the film company that made the 25-minute special for our company each year to be shown around the country. The final scene of congratulating the winner was an important element. As my uncle needed to return to Akron it was decided that a guy named Firestone, me, would be the designated winner's participant in my uncle's stead. The film company and all our public relations and racing staff were so notified. I was briefed on how to get there, and was given all the necessary credentials. The Indy people were informed so that I could be in on the action.

The race resumed on the Monday and all went well with

Parnelli Jones ahead of A.J. Foyt by, I believe, at least a lap by five laps to the finish. He was driving the turbine car and in good shape. His lead sponsor was Andy Granatelli and the car was the STP Special. I knew the Granatellis and we gathered together at the entrance to the winner's circle in anticipation and the excitement of the finish.

The atmosphere was incredible with the race two laps to go. We were all going out of our minds, and the PR and race people were making sure I was briefed and ready for my appearance that would be filmed and televised on cue. The Granatellis, of course, would be the lead personalities, but my brief moment of congratulations was important to our film and publicity, etc.

Then, the incredible happened! At one lap to go Parnelli's car broke some minor part and the car was forced to drive off the track and stop on the backstretch grass verge. A.J. won the race on Goodyear tires, the first time in history for our arch rival!

We were in desperate confusion. The PR and racing people didn't know what to do. The film crew were all set up and ready to film. My credentials and moment were ready and the Indy staff were ready for me. I don't think the Goodyear people were even there. In the moment of incredible winner's circle excitement I barged in anyway, and was filmed and photographed congratulating our arch rival A.J. who looked a little surprised to see me as we knew each other. We shook hands, said all the right things, and the moment came off OK.

We flew back to Akron and I went straight to my Uncle Ray, who was a fairly soft-spoken guy. I told him what I had done, hoping that it had been the right thing. He replied that he would not have done that himself but it was probably OK for me to have done. So much for my big moment at Indy!

Not all was roses in the Shelby world, however. Some who had dealings with Carroll were less than enchanted with certain aspects of his character. He was often called a lovable and clever scoundrel. He picked up the nickname "Billie Sol" after a big scandal involved a Texas oilman of that name, Billie Sol Estes, who defrauded farmers of mortgages on their ammonia tanks, and other matters. Some people, at the time, named anyone they thought acted in a criminal way as a "Billy Sol."

But that's racing. I knew many in the racing world who didn't always stay on the straight-and-narrow path when it came to their business dealings. To most of us, whether Carroll Shelby was of the same ilk didn't matter. We loved him. He had this charisma, and he gave us our head to be creative and independent. If he agreed with a proposal, he'd let us go out and do our thing. He didn't really want to know the details, he was interested in the big picture, the end result.

Unfortunately for Shelby, Warren and Simone Olson had entirely different ethics. Simone, a graduate of UCLA, was very smart. She effectively ran Shelby's business, doing the books, writing letters, and handling the various relationships. I loved her. She and Warren were an incredible team, a terrific couple who often invited me over for dinner.

But they were becoming more and more stressed about our mutual boss's business ethics that a day came when they rather abruptly resigned.

In my opinion, racers by their very nature prefer to be totally independent. I mean, hardcore independent, including me, and especially the older racers in their day. Roger Penske is a great example. He always went his own way and became highly successful doing so.

So although it's in my own nature to strive always to deal scrupulously ethically with everyone, as a racer myself I understood those who ran a little fast and loose. I used to talk about Shelby with a girlfriend of the time, Stephanie, and as she had a different viewpoint our discussions gave me a lot of insight.

Her father was a famous psychiatrist who treated many of Hollywood's celebrities, and was a friend of movie star Burt Lancaster. Her mother was a renowned cellist who played with the Los Angeles Symphony. So with Stephanie's background it was inevitable that she'd have an analytical mind, and we often discussed pretty deep subjects, including the theories of psychoanalysts Sigmund Freud and Carl Jung. I enjoyed our debates.

Naturally we talked a lot about my work with Shelby, and at one point she said he was just using me. I replied that if that was true it was fine with me because I was having a great time!

But I am sure Stephanie influenced the way I was evolving mentally.

I was still taking engineering classes then, paying the tuition from my own earnings. However, the classes were kind of boring, as I already knew so much as a top racing mechanic. So I dropped engineering and took up biology, chemistry, and comparative anatomy instead. I thought I might like to become a doctor and later a psychiatrist, like my girlfriend's dad.

I was completely fascinated with the specialty of mental illness and emotional disturbance, and with the way people behave. It all helped me deal with people like Shelby.

Steffie owned an MG sedan and I offered to hop it up for her. She liked speed, although she also enjoyed riding around for fun with me on my little Vespa motor scooter. An iconic Italian product, it sold in the millions in its heyday around the globe.

America was in the midst of the hippie movement, she more than I, and its tentacles were everywhere. One evening I told her how my dad had become a bureaucrat in the Army. Hippies were not in favor of bureaucrats. Steffi leaned close to me from where she was riding on the back seat of the Vespa as we dodged traffic along Wilshire Boulevard, and whispered in my ear, "You know, Sonny, your parents will mess you up (except she used the f-word instead). If you stay that way then it's your own fault!"

Her wise words rang a bell for me like no one would believe. We became closer than ever.

I also developed a close friendship with her father, who had trained at the Menninger Clinic. I had a great admiration for him and he became a trusted adviser to me.

Throughout my life I have had the good fortune to meet people who became my mentors, not only in all forms of racing, but also in business and in life at large.

Another was Dr. Mandel Sherman. He had been a professor at the University of Chicago. He was in his 70s then, while I was still in my 20s, but he became another great influence in my entrepreneurship and was kind enough to tell me that he had great respect for my intellect. We constantly exchanged ideas, but my full attention was always directed toward him. He was pure wisdom!

Speaking of mentors, I will always be grateful to Carroll Shelby for teaching me how to promote my business, how to get publicity, and how to approach the media. He was a genius at that. He even taught me how to speak to editors when I went to the magazines to ask for articles on IECO. I'd have appointments not only with the car magazines but also business journals and business editors at newspapers.

For extra publicity I had my own IECO-modified GT350 Mustang that was part of a pool of cars that I'd delegate to journalists and editors to test drive for a day or two. I wasn't the only businessman doing that but I was instrumental in providing the press with special cars not available from anywhere else.

A group that worked at Shelby's loaned Ford cars to Hollywood studios for placement in movies and today it has become common, pricey practice. I had other friends who did the same for their products, such as champagne. One friend put Dom Perignon on the map by getting it into the James Bond movies. They now call it "product placement."

Carroll was a great guru to me in many ways. Many years later he said, "Sonny, I gotta tell you, you were a great mechanic and a great businessman. I was so proud of you for starting up your own company when you opened your automotive business and made such a success of it." That was music to my ears from such a legend.

CHAPTER 18
PETE BROCK

P ete Brock is an important and visionary figure in motorsports and the Golden Age of Racing. A man of many talents, he is most famous for his styling work on Chevrolet's breakthrough 1963 "split-window" Corvette, and then for his scientifically aerodynamic body for Shelby's championship-winning Cobra Daytona Coupe. He also started and operated a highly successful racing team for Datsun (now called Nissan). Pete's shop, Brock Racing Enterprises or BRE as everybody knows it, won a total of four US National Championships. But that barely scratches the surface of a true Renaissance Man.

I have known Pete as a close colleague, a business partner, and a friend for many, many years. He and I worked together off and on. At one point we formed a company called Performance Design Associates, PDA, which was run under Carroll Shelby Enterprises. We rented offices in the Princeton Street building in Venice after Shelby relocated to LAX airport. Carroll needed more space to ramp up production of the Ford GT350s and finish up the last of the big Cobras, the 429s.

Pete and I first met in Nassau, the Bahamas, when I was with the Scarab guys at the Governor's Cup race in 1958. A fellow my age approached carrying his design portfolio, and appeared eager to show it to me. I guess he selected me as I was the youngest Scarab team member, a contemporary of his, and perhaps he thought the older guys wouldn't pay any attention to him.

I was still drag racing whenever I could fit it in, and most in our business knew my reputation from the winning car that I built and drove, as well as my work with Reventlow's Scarab team. In addition, I was well-recognized as a race engineer-mechanic with Jim Hall, which probably gave me a certain prestige as far as Pete was concerned.

The reason he wanted to speak to someone on the team was that he wanted to show some sketches for a proposed new body for the Scarab. I replied that we were happy with the original that Chuck Pelly had designed, and although we had modified it slightly, it was fundamentally Pelly's design and it was winning races for us.

Pete would have produced a great alternative, no doubt about that. His career is crammed with great racecar designs, projects, and start-ups. And he's not only a car stylist, far from it.

At age 16 he bought a 1949 MG sports car, then turned to his hot-rod side by installing a Cadillac engine in a 1946 Ford convertible, with which he won the Oakland Roadster Show. Well-travelled throughout his childhood, he spent time in Europe and Mexico, and studied at the Art Center College of Design in Los Angeles.

I was told that Pete's mother was a very wealthy artist and poet who lived in France, but he didn't rely on her for funds. His grandfather, E.J. Hall, was an engine designer who co-founded the Hall-Scott Motor Car Company, then co-designed World War I's famous Liberty L-12 airplane engine. So Pete had plenty of mechanical oil in his artistic blood.

He also had a passion for photography, and was a familiar face later on as a photojournalist. I understand his camera career goes back to the early Pebble Beach road races near Monterey that wound around the twisty roads near The Lodge, some of them unpaved back in the day.

At the age of 19 he was an intern designer with General Motors working with their Vice-President of Design, Bill Mitchell. Pete said that his time with GM was the best education he ever received, because he not only worked with some of the top designers in the country, he also learned about Corporate America and how it functioned.

In his spare time Pete was also working on his obsolete, junkyard mid-'50s Cooper that had run at Le Mans. He aspired to be a racecar driver too.

His early styling concepts for the 1963 production Corvette were also the basis for an earlier prototype racecar called the Corvette Sting Ray racer. Breathtaking to me in its pure elegance, sleek simplicity and style, it was a masterpiece, a sculpture that personified speed.

My friend Brock could have made a great career for himself in Detroit, but like most of us he longed to be a race driver. As soon as he reached the age of 21, SCCA's minimum for a racing license, he quit his job at GM in Detroit and returned to California. He set up a race shop at his home and continued to rebuild the Cooper, teaching himself in the process how to turn his design on paper into reality in his shop.

When it was ready, he took it to the track for two years, along with a Lotus he ran. Inevitably, he met Carroll Shelby, who offered Pete the job of running Shelby's new driving school at Riverside, the Carroll Shelby School of High Performance.

One day Shelby told Pete he had more important things for him to do than teach rookies how to race. So the driving school was taken over by Bob Bondurant, who turned it into the largest driving school in the world.

One of Shelby's first assignments for his new designer was to create a symbol for Shelby American, a brand logo to be used for advertising, merchandise, crew uniforms, business cards, letterheads, accessory items, and insignias for the cars.

I've already described how Brock brought me in to handle Shelby's accessories business. They both knew I worked for Lance Reventlow and that RAI had set up the best racing team on the planet.

Pete had often been on the Riverside track back when we were finishing up with the Scarabs and I'd take them out there to test. We'd exchange notes and opinions quite a bit about our test results, and I was encouraged to hear that Pete thought I looked at my job on a very sophisticated basis. He said I wasn't just a guy out at Riverside with wrenches, but was figuring out how to engineer things better and improve everything, taking my skills learned through many years of racing experience and coming up with solutions.

Brock opined that I always had modern ideas, a great sense of design and style, and coming up with some great, great work. Coming from the legendary designer Brock, I very much appreciated his words.

Later at Shelby's, Pete and I had a mutual friend, graphic designer and talented artist Rick Runyon, who was renowned for working with Saul Bass, the Oscar-winning movie title and poster designer. After Pete sketched and worked on the blueprints for Shelby, Rick did all the finished work on them, as he did for me with my IECO catalogs.

At the same time I was handling Shelby's accessories department, and studying business at school, while also busy getting my own business off the ground.

Eventually Pete and I were going in such different directions with our careers that we agreed amicably to part ways.

Pete had designed another coupe body for the second-generation Cobra, the big-engined 427. But he couldn't move past getting a single prototype built in Italy because Ford, which controlled Shelby's projects, did not want any competition for the GT40. So Brock also decided time had come to move on.

Pete had a dream of creating Brock Racing Enterprises, BRE, for drivers who needed a design and development service. He started that from home in 1965, and by 1969 had opened a business in El Segundo, California. The BRE place was always pristine clean despite housing an engine assembly plant, fabrication and grinding, and a machine shop.

At first Pete had a contract with Hino, a Japanese manufacturer of diesel engines and commercial trucks, to create Japan's first-ever racecar. Then, after Toyota acquired Hino, Toyota had Brock build a beautiful little prototype for them. That led to the consideration of having BRE run a racing team for Toyota's new 2000GT, a competitor for Datsun's 240 "Z-car."

But then Shelby got wind of it, swooped in and sweet-talked Toyota into handing him the program instead.

Whereupon, being a born racer with that essential never-say-die attitude, Brock went directly to see Datsun's U.S. President, Mr. Katayama, and landed their racing program.

Brock initially hired engine specialist Art Oehrli, with whom I had worked earlier on the Scarab F1 project. But after Shelby went with Toyota, so did Art. Brock replaced him with John Caldwell.

To begin with, BRE made winners out of Datsun's little 2000 roadster, seeing it rack up eight SCCA victories with driver John McComb. It quickly became clear that the car was unmatchable for speed and power. Its success boosted sales. Among the drivers who became BRE customers were SCCA national champion Bob McQueen, who bought the car that twice won the National Championship.

Gene Felton was a "privateer" who bought the McComb car in 1970 after asking Pete to add a roll cage. One time Felton related that his BRE engine for a Road Atlanta race arrived very late. He had to install it himself and promptly put it on the pole! Second pole was another successful privateer, Dave Frellsen, who became the five-time National Champion with his own 510, 610, and A510 cars.

We all considered Pete Brock's entries the best-engineered Datsuns in California due to BRE's pursuit of perfection, a path I always sought to tread myself.

Meanwhile, the Shelby Toyotas had quietly disappeared. They were nice, but not competitive. With my old friend and mentor Phil Remington running the program as crew chief, the cars were solidly prepared and testing went well, but indications were that the racer couldn't qualify because of carburetor rule changes, and it was raced only one season, in 1968.

For 1970, Brock tackled Datsun's 510 sedans and 240Z sports coupes. That's when BRE's image went big time, with driver John Morton winning SCCA titles two years straight with Brock-prepared 510s and 240Zs. Brock was totally vindicated.

Meanwhile, my IECO was becoming a major aftermarket parts supplier. Colleagues sympathized when the Corvair was terminated and my parts catalog for it became obsolete, but I was mollified somewhat with Pete telling me that in his opinion I had taken a rather mundane automobile and developed a lot of interesting equipment for it, resulting in a really fabulous car. He also admired how advanced my marketing ideas were. Praise from a master!

Brock ended his involvement in motorsports after the 1972 season and turned his considerable talents to creating a company that manufactured hang-gliding products. With his phenomenal marketing skills, he built Ultralite Products into the largest company of its kind in the world. Not content to merely produce the hang-gliding equipment and unable to leave racing behind in any form, he saw an opportunity to develop the sport of long-distance hang-gliding competition.

But racecars continued to draw him and he returned to motorsports as a photojournalist and an author of books including those on the Daytona Cobra Coupes and the Sting Ray.

Meantime he created a new edition of his immortal Cobra Daytona Coupe, which is roomier and more civilized than the original racer but offers all the performance that Cobra fans expect.

As of this writing, he has his own company called Aerovault, which is manufacturing a highly successful aerodynamic enclosed trailer he designed to haul cars with security and efficiency. Pete built his own machinery and uses special fabricating techniques not available elsewhere to produce these excellent haulers.

They have no competitors. I sure would have liked having one of those when I was trailering Jim Hall's racers all over the country!

CHAPTER 19
MY OWN COMPANY, IECO

That spark of entrepreneurial ambition that ignited when I was a boy in Naples, Italy, became a full-blown fire within me as I reached adulthood. My years in racing had afforded me good, close looks at how bold risk takers like Carroll Shelby, Jim Hall, Warren Olson and so many others that I admired had achieved success.

I came to realize that they were working mostly for themselves at what they loved, and were living their dream. It was time to live mine.

Taking my own experience and expertise with racecars and engines, and putting it to work at inventing, designing and marketing high-performance automotive parts; that was what I was good at.

I had not only the creativity and know-how, but also a good business sense. I knew how to set up and run a company, and due to my ongoing studies for degrees I became more skilled at management. I had no doubt that I could be my own boss running my own company.

It was interesting to me that so many of us in the auto industry were, essentially, entrepreneurs who had started as racers. If you think about it, the kind of personality and drive that it takes to succeed on the racetrack is very similar to what's needed in the hard, hazardous, intensely competitive world of the business office.

But it's also true in the wider world beyond motorsports. I remembered being inspired by my mother's friend Sonja Henie, the ten-time Olympic champion skater who became a movie star. She had garnered a lot of publicity during her career and was able to capitalize on it by starting a business marketing ice skates, clothing, and other skating-related products.

Her success in this field encouraged me to use my own knowledge about engines and cars to create a sales catalog that would include my own product inventions, as well as those from other aftermarket manufacturers.

My problem was finding the time, but happily, at one point in 1963 Shelby took a break and I took advantage of it. I was still working for NGK, but now I had the time required to create my first serious entrepreneurial enterprise.

I named it Induction Engineering Company, or IECO (pronounced "EYE-co" without regard to the "E"). The word "induction" of course referred to my original product, the induction manifold that I created to boost the performance of Corvair engines, but I had plenty of ideas beyond that. My corporate vision for IECO included a small catalog of other engine performance parts, some of which I planned to invent and have manufactured for me.

By this time I had become serious about education and was going to college. I started taking engineering classes, then switched to life sciences because I wanted to be a doctor, but finally settled on studying business. I graduated with a BS and an MBA in finance and economics.

With a good grounding on the mechanics of business, I started figuring out how best to use quantitative thinking and counting everything in percentages. I developed algorithms that were far ahead of their time. It was marketing analysis for merchandising, and I was a pioneer in the concept for small businesses, doing it all mechanically with no computers. I was confident that IECO would technically be a great program that I put together after much thought and planning.

My first focus was on the small, sporty Chevrolet Corvair, a fresh, affordable small car with a modern look, a rear-engine design and independent suspension on all four wheels. All this was in stark contrast to the cars made in America at the time. It was America's answer to the German VW and, more appealing to automobile enthusiasts like me, it looked like it might be Raoul "Sonny" Balcaen's answer to a Porsche.

It was a car that looked like being a winner with the public, and I was right. As soon as it went on sale it became highly popular. But for some people it lacked performance and handling. That's where I would come in.

From my years as a race engine builder I saw that the Corvair's six-cylinder, air-cooled engine could quite easily be modified to be more powerful, and my long experience with sports cars pointed to many additional ways the vehicle could benefit from upgraded parts.

Although I was still in my 20s, my motor racing background was solid and lengthy, and I found plenty of energy, to say nothing of new ideas, to start the new business while still fulfilling my various other duties and responsibilities. It required that I be working all day and half the night week after week, but I was up for it. I was full of confidence. Thus, I began IECO.

To test my products I bought a bright-red stock Corvair coupe and used it for development work, taking everything apart and trying out and evaluating various innovative mechanical parts and options.

My modified engine was tested on the dynamometer, and there was a really substantial power increase, an exciting result. When we drove the modified car on its first trial run, I was delighted by its impressive throttle response. The car could still idle along in any gear, but when you stomped on the gas the IECO Corvair responded quickly and smoothly.

We also outfitted my coupe with wider wheels and tires for better cornering and stability. And more special upgrades were to come.

All these would be made available through my 25-cent catalog. With the products decided upon, Pete Brock suggested I talk to his artist friend, Rick Runyon, to help me design and produce the catalog. For the cover of the publication I turned to my good friend George Bartell, a renowned automotive illustrator whose beautiful work often graced magazine covers. For me he painted the picture of the green IECO Corvair on the cover of my catalog. Reproductions of it have become the thing to have for Corvair collectors, and George's large, original painting of the car still hangs on my wall at home.

To illustrate the interior pages of the catalog I took photos of all the parts that we were offering, and I also wrote all the descriptive text to go with them. I sized the catalog to fit into a #10 envelope. It was an instant success. We received over 1,000 hits from our magazine ads right away.

The reason my parts stood out from everyone else's was because I invented or modified several of them, knowing what was needed to hop-up a car. In addition to the induction manifold I had invented, I added high-performance components and accessories to transform the nice little Corvair family car into a sports coupe, or what car enthusiasts with my own particular background still thought of as a hot rod.

I made sure that car owners could only buy the items from our own IECO catalog. Many of them were exclusive to us, so I didn't sell through other firms.

Initially, the catalog targeted only Corvair owners, although other makes would follow. I followed this first catalog up with larger versions that contained bigger pictures and more text.

The first product listed in the catalog was a Dyno-kit, a tune-up performance package of parts not used on the factory Corvair. My first invention for the car, a four-barrel, Ram split-intake manifold that accepted a higher-performance carburetor, was the first one ever to come on the market back then. In addition to my special manifold, I designed "trombone" exhaust headers and extractors, again to improve power and performance.

As business grew, I went on to also develop enhancements for the car's braking system, using special bronze brake linings that were ahead of their time. There also were special steering arms to make steering quicker and more responsive, and a quick-shift gearshift mechanism.

All of these were manufactured exclusively for IECO by top-quality specialists. I believe the parts are still available, 50 years later, and at least some have been duplicated from my originals.

In fact, the manifold proved to be so popular it was illegally copied and produced by other specialized hot-rod engine companies, including Offenhauser, ELCO, and Edelbrock. I ended up having to file suits against some of them, as I already held the patent on its design. I won, of course, and thankfully the settlement more than covered the lawyer's fees, but it was a long process as most lawsuits are. I learned a very valuable lesson: avoid lawsuits.

Business was brisk. Within weeks of magazine articles and ads promoting IECO, and through talks at Corvair owner's clubs and other venues, I had to hire extra help to get the catalogs out to customers.

Looking back, I see that once I had my IECO system running well and learned more and more about selling retail directly to the consumer, I had become an early pioneer of the concept of the online buying we have today. I was excited that my entrepreneurial vision was materializing.

Carroll Shelby, of course, had the inside track in terms of selling performance accessories for the Ford Mustang, as his name was famous worldwide. He came and asked me to write ads for him, which I was happy to do.

The Vega, a new small car from Chevrolet, was completely different in concept compared to the rear-engined Corvair, a front-engined vehicle like a miniature Camaro. It too developed a strong enthusiast following. Just my kind of customer.

The Vega four-cylinder engine was something new in American industry, because its cylinder block — the basic core of the engine — was cast in aluminum instead of the traditional iron. That shaved off some weight, but the technology was new and I believed that there also was some strength and durability lost in that early implementation.

The cylinder block was an advanced aluminum alloy with a high content of silicon, so the engineers thought they could dispense with the iron cylinder liners, also known as "sleeves," that such engines normally incorporated to prevent undue wear as the aluminum pistons raced up and down.

But during testing of my hopped-up motor I saw there was in fact some damage to the pistons, so I used an old hot-rod technique to rebore the cylinders and insert a durable cast-iron sleeve into each one. In effect I reverse-engineered Chevrolet's new, troublesome, all-aluminum experiment back into one of the tried-and true old designs that had been serving us perfectly well for decades.

As well as my sleeves, I also designed a new IECO piston that changed the shape of the combustion chamber, thus raising the compression ratio and releasing more power. Along with high-performance Weber carburetors from Italy, larger valves and other upgrades, IECO customers had 190 horsepower under their right foot, a substantial increase.

Not neglecting the rest of the Vega, which was a nice-handling little car that seemed to invite people to drive it hard, we went on and developed a complete catalog of racing gear for the Vega, all the bits and pieces it takes to turn a street cruiser into a racetrack bruiser. To allow customers their choice of just how far they wanted to take the performance increase, we offered various packages of replacement components in different stages of tune.

IECO's improved Vega was such a major development that word spread far and wide, wide enough to reach a certain official at General Motors, where it struck a nerve. I received a phone call from the engineering executive in charge of product performance at Chevrolet. His purview included the Vega, and he was not pleased that I had found fault with its innovative but imperfect sleeveless aluminum four-cylinder engine.

"Sonny, this is Vince Piggins. You're claiming that you can do something better than we can. Never say you can improve on a GM product."

His tone was not cordial, and I was speechless at his utter arrogance. I felt I was being threatened. The message seemed to be that I must never, never say I can improve a GM product, or else. You can imagine how the competitive racer in me reacted to that.

To be clear, there was no connection between our IECO parts and Chevrolet. My company was entirely independent.

A couple of days after the Vega catalog was first mailed out my assistant called me.

"You'd better get down here early today," he shouted into the phone.

"Why?"

"Six bags of mail filled with orders have just been delivered!"

That was one of the most exciting days of my life, proof that my instincts had been right and the business was a success. For an entrepreneur, that was happiness. We had orders coming out of our ears.

"No need to improve a GM product," eh? I'm glad to say we had no hassle from Mr. Piggins at General Motors.

Improvement was required, however, on my own attitude toward delegating authority. I am a control freak. It's a typical failing of entrepreneurs. We don't trust anyone to do something as well as we think we can handle it ourselves. People like me feel a need to control everything. We hate to hand over a critical job to someone else.

That's all very well for a solo operator, maybe, but as even a very small business starts to grow, more and more people will be needed. Too much needs doing for one person to do it all; increasingly, that single person finds it essential to delegate certain responsibilities to others.

I was able to stave off the inevitable for a while, for the genuine reason that I could only afford part-time employees! But when IECO's growth curve reached a certain point I simply had to start sharing the workload.

Guideposts on how to delegate responsibilities had come from my observations of how publishing pioneer Bob Petersen ran his own empire. Because of the very nature of his many enterprises, right from the beginning he had to bring in people to handle things he didn't have time for. Delegating is the secret to good growth with a large institution. I encompassed Bob's ideas into my own business venture, hard though delegating responsibilities was for me. It really was an effort.

IECO did not develop any equipment for the bigger Chevys or Mustangs with their V8 engines, except for one brief fling with my own ideas of how a Mustang could be improved. That experiment confirmed that those niches were already well filled by other companies.

But when Ford brought out a small, four-cylinder car named the Pinto, I developed a catalog of parts for it and they were popular too. Then IECO added products for Hondas, Toyotas, Datsuns, and Volkswagens.

I was pleased that my racing experience provided me with the expertise to build components for all the passenger cars I had catalogs for, and supply people with parts they wanted that were not available in stores.

But it all took time. I needed to process my ideas, give them a gestation period, poke around them until all of a sudden, Bam! My ideas gelled. I also designed the tooling and my people fitted the different parts together to assemble them.

One of our most exclusive products was the Recaro performance seat from Stuttgart, Germany. It became the top-of-the-line seat for racers, rally drivers and enthusiastic drivers who appreciated extra support and quality. I became a great fan of the Recaro seats, and installed them in the Vegas.

Occasionally retail stores approached me about selling my catalog products through them, but I always declined. My mail-order business was thriving, I was making really good money and I had earned a reputation for excellence and honesty.

As a plus, I was still known for pioneering the fastest GMC-powered fuel dragster in the U.S. along with having worked with the greatest of racers. The lessons I'd learned from the great Ed Donovan, Rex Mays' famous mechanic Pete Clark, Traco's Travers and Coon, and many others, was paying off in a big way.

One reason for my IECO success, I believe, was that I kept my prices moderate. I also made sure never to renege on a client, and to fulfill orders promptly.

A good name is vital in any business. It was very gratifying to see that owners who modified their cars through our catalogs referred to their cars as IECO Corvairs, IECO Vegas, and IECO Pintos. This fact also attracted the attention of automotive writers. We were featured in several magazines, club newsletters, and journals. *Car Life* magazine photojournalist Jim Wright devoted a long and detailed article to my company, emphasizing our contributions to sports car racing and to the Corvair itself. Two more very favorable articles were by Bud Lang in *Chevy Power* magazine, and by Marlan Davis in *Hot Rod* magazine — the "bible!"

Knowing that enthusiasts range from technical amateurs to the mechanically knowledgeable, I set up five levels of car parts and accessories with which to modify a Corvair and other models. Level 1 components were easy for owners to install, and most of them needed no tools. Level 2 required only a few tools and some patience if you were short on experience, but installation was still pretty easy. The average do-it-yourselfer could handle Level 3 with only a couple of hand tools at the ready. Level 4 required some savvy and a good set of tools as well as tuning ability. Level 5 was for the professional owner-mechanic who was right at home fixing his engine, or was close to a good repair shop.

My business was based on hardware, but it ran on software (a term that had only just been coined). Credit cards were coming into widespread use, and IECO was the first company in the automotive mail-order industry to accept American Express, Visa, and Mastercard. We also were among the first to add an 800 toll-free number for telephone orders.

I have always liked to be on the cutting edge of new technology, and with IECO booming we bought our first office computer, a Wang Winchester disc drive. We had been controlling our inventory by hand, so computerizing it was a huge step forward. I discovered that even a fledgling software user could prepare computer algorithms (another unfamiliar term back then) to greatly boost our efficiency, but with the potential clearly there I hired a professional software programmer to work for me part-time.

As early as 1971 IECO was utilizing the computer not only for inventory control, but also invoicing, shipping, and customer information and statistical analysis. The data helped us figure out just who our customers were and how we could serve them even better. And we developed a unique part-picking system for shipping items, another way to utilize algorithms.

I believe I recognized the dawn of the personal computer age long before Bill Gates of Microsoft created their programs. I remember sometime later attending the first computer show held in the basement of the Biltmore Hotel in Los Angeles. Bill Gates, Paul Allen, and Steve Jobs were there, but I bought the Wang long before PCs came on the scene.

In retrospect I do have one regret. Although mine was one of the first small businesses to computerize, I should have developed updated software for a regular marketing program. I should have immediately taken what I'd learned about mail order and gotten into the infant computer PC business with software. I missed the boat on that.

I ECO had become profitable enough by 1970 that I was able to buy some land and erect a stunning new 7,500 square foot building on Broadway at 15th in Santa Monica. I had it designed by an architect, and my girlfriend of the time, Stephanie, created Swiss-style graphics on the outside of the store in time for a wonderful Grand Opening. The move cost a lot of money, but as an investment it was a huge success. Business kept increasing and the number of my employees grew.

Annoyingly, I came up against all kinds of Santa Monica city bureaucracy. I already had disdain for bureaucrats and that struggle only ramped up those feelings.

On a very much lighter note, I acquired a marvelous new friend and team member. His name was Hieronymous. He was a mixed German Shepherd that a friend of Steffie's was going to give away, and I offered to take him as I had grown up with animals and loved them.

Hieronymous was part coyote, I think, and noble-looking. He hung out at the back of the shop, wandering about snuffing at things and sleeping under a work bench in the warehouse. My showroom and office in the front of the new building were off-limits to him, but I enjoyed having him around. Stephanie was in San Francisco going to school, and when I drove up to visit I'd take the dog with me in my Mini Cooper. He took up just about every square inch in the rear of that small car.

After he died I bought a purebred German Shepherd from a breeder. We named him Hans. Later in life I had two chows that looked like miniature lions with their puffy fur. One dog I often thought I should have was a Belgian Malinois, but I never did.

It took me ten years of attending school part-time, but finally I completed my B.S. and M.B.A. degrees at the University of California, Los Angeles. That long slog sure showed my industriousness and hard work ethic!

Thus freed from at least one of my responsibilities, I plunged into building IECO project cars for magazine publicity. These were exciting days for me and my crew, and to see the cars and the details of how we accomplished the modifications was a thrill. Our results appeared to be great stories for auto magazines as I was frequently asked for interviews.

The downfall of the Corvair began when consumer protection activist and lawyer Ralph Nader claimed that the car was dangerous. One of his arguments was that unbalanced handling characteristics, which he claimed was caused by the rear engine placement and the rear swing-axle design, made the Corvair "Unsafe At Any Speed" — the title of a book he wrote to condemn the car.

The media loves a scandal, and worldwide publicity resulted in basically killing sales of the first-generation, 1960–64 Corvair models. Chevrolet totally changed the 1965 model's rear suspension, transforming it into an even better car, but the damage to the brand was fatal.

I felt Nader's accusation was spurious, and I came to the Corvair's defense. He came up with statistics that he said proved his point. But the irony was that the Volkswagen Beetle had a very similar design for decades, and yet no similar negative statistics were seen for the German car. However, Nader's criticism saw the end of the Corvair and in 1969 it was discontinued.

It was gratifying during all this to receive a letter from GM's executive vice president Ed Cole, after I had expressed my admiration for the small car. Cole had directed the origin and development of the Corvair as its chief engineer, and when he sent me the letter he had become Executive Vice President of General Motors (in future years he was to be president of the whole company). The letter, which was dated September 7th, 1967, reads:

Dear Mr. Balcaen,
I appreciate your kind remarks about the Corvair and for sending me the framed materials which you provide to members of the Classic Corvair Club.

It is gratifying to know that there is so much interest being expressed in this fine car and that you have been able to organize such an enthusiastic group of owners.

We, too, believe that the Corvair offers something completely different from the average American car. Its sales over the past eight years certainly indicate that it won the approval of a sizeable segment of the American public. While sales this year are down because of some very unfair and groundless criticism, we are hopeful that the Corvair will enjoy a resurgence of popularity in the years ahead.

Thanks for your thoughtfulness in writing and best wishes for your continued business success.

Sincerely,
E.N. Cole

Ed Cole had designed a great car, air cooled to compete with the wildly popular Volkswagen Beetle, and with more power and size for American roads and American families. Despite offering more space and comfort, it was economical. And it really was fun to drive.

It is true the swing-axle rear suspension designs on both cars, VW as well as Corvair, seemed unusual to mainstream American buyers — although European motorists had long been thoroughly accustomed to its characteristics, as so many automakers there had used swing axles for decades.

To cater to any concerns, one U.S. aftermarket company came up with a stabilizer bar for the rear of the VW. Chevy tried to build one for the Corvair, but wound up going in whole-hog by totally re-engineering the car for 1965. The new rear suspension was unique, the first-ever independent system for an American car. Jim Hall helped to test the new model at his Rattlesnake Raceway in Texas. It worked great, and the car could fly around corners.

But the damage Ralph Nader did was a fatal hit job on the Corvair. The headlines made him out to be a big consumer advocate, which I didn't think he deserved. When Nader became famous, he created a huge non-profit firm, taking in donations from those who thought he was an environmental savior.

But coming from my standpoint as an automotive engineer, I questioned whether knowingly or not he distorted his conclusions for the common man. I knew very well there were solutions to Nader's attack on the Corvair. I heard that he did no factual testing himself. Whether he did or not, the end result was that two highly costly class action lawsuits against General Motors ruined the reputation of the little car, which was a great, great product.

Headwinds struck IECO too. As government agencies in California began to crack down on what they claimed were polluters, I was going to have to make some serious modifications to my engine parts. I scrambled to conform to new legislation. Serious changes would have to be made. Did I want to go through that process?

Then a recession hit the marketplace. Capriciously, and counter-productively, local city tax officials decided to impose increases.

In a discretionary environment, I was selling products that the general public didn't have a need for. Only those who were rabidly passionate about speed and performance in their cars continued to come to us. IECO's sales went soft and I began to run below my break-even point.

At this critical time, 1973–74, the Arab oil embargo rocked the globe. Gas supplies dropped and prices skyrocketed. Some people became desperate enough to steal gasoline from other people's tanks, using siphons.

Aha! Rather than sitting on our hands, we at IECO realized we were being presented with an ideal opportunity to create means to address both problems for our loyal customers with Corvairs, Vegas and other cars.

We worked out ways to increase fuel mileage for engines, while a friend of mine came up with an idea for an anti-siphoning device. We felt good about doing something positive to help people through a tough time; of course, it was a way to revive our business too.

Unfortunately, a single uninformed newspaper writer misunderstood what we were trying to do. This person from a small, local paper apparently heard one side of a story, but despite having no automotive knowledge at all, made no attempt to contact me for my side of it. The matter was trivial, but of course any smell of scandal swiftly excites the noses of other "reporters," who gleefully spread the distortions without understanding the topic or bothering to research it.

This "fake news," as we call it today, caused me enormous trouble. Considering how I prided myself on honesty and integrity, the allegation that I was falsely advertising things that could save gasoline wounded me deeply. I felt railroaded.

It hurt my business really badly, too. Everything was piling up against us. Needless to say, IECO went downhill. Eventually we made a comeback, but I came to be very wary of government and the press.

Finally, I burned out. I was just overwhelmed with a costly divorce, coping with adverse legislation, a financial setback in the bond business that I invested in; I was exhausted by trying to figure out what to do about it all.

After 20 years of building and running my business, I decided it was time to sell IECO.

I found a buyer more quickly than anticipated. He was Thomas Keller, the grandson of K.E. Keller, former president of Chrysler Corporation. Unfortunately, IECO went bankrupt three years after he bought it. That was sad news for me. I had poured my heart and soul, to say nothing of hard work, into building the business and making it a huge success. But as always, I moved forward with minimal regrets.

On the plus side I had earned a sterling reputation as an expert in my field and running a fine company. Sales had increased tremendously until recently, and buyers were lining up to bid to buy me out. It was gratifying to realize that my company was so highly regarded in the auto industry.

An honor I prize highly was my induction into the SAE, the prestigious Society of Automotive Engineers. Two of my friends at Peterson Publishing, who were SAE members themselves, so admired the work I had been doing at IECO that they nominated me.

I attribute IECO's success to years of education, determination, training, and learning the ways of business from experts in their field as well as from car constructors, mechanics, owners, drivers, and racing automobile owners. I also thank Carroll Shelby because he always gave those who worked for him their head if he agreed with their ideas.

In my own case, I was able to couple my abilities with luck and knew how to recognize a golden opportunity when it showed up. Meeting Pete Clark, unsung hero Phil Remington, Warren, Shelby, Lance, Kessler, Ed Donovan, and Jim Hall, among others, gave me a life in racing and business I could never have envisioned. Jim Hall once told me he noticed I never let anyone get the better of me. Well, that's a pretty good philosophy to live by, in any field of endeavor.

While I was running IECO I studied finance and always had money invested in the stock market and bond markets, although the market was depressed at the time. I invested quite a lot of money into the high-interest California tax-free municipal bonds with big coupons, so that I didn't have to pay taxes, thereby conserving capital.

Friends asked how I managed to become an expert at all of these money matters, and I responded that I learned it from actually doing it. I gave myself an education in finance by studying the markets, banking, bonds, and securities, and asking questions.

Several years later, in 1985, I began a consulting practice. Today, I see myself as an economist.

But that's only one side of who I am now.

PART IV

CHAPTER 20
ADVENTURES IN GASTRONOMY

Divesting myself of IECO did not end my involvement in racing and its peripheral industries, but it did afford more time to pursue other areas of life that interest me. So in addition to setting up a consultancy in performance parts with clients in several businesses, I got into the municipal bond market and also set up a few small businesses.

One of those grew out of my love of great foods and wines. In particular I had studied wine seriously. At last I was free to look for ways to turn my hobby into a profitable sideline.

"America's Great Taste" was what I called this new venture. I partnered with a like-minded friend of mine, Eugene Morris, who was the marketing director for Merle Norman Cosmetics. Our business plan was to offer a catalog of only the finest, most exclusive specialty gourmet products from all around the United States.

After researching companies throughout the U.S and going to several food service conventions, Eugene and I began asking a series of housewives, mostly friends of ours, to be on a judging panel. Eugene designed a logo, which we trademarked, showing a star with a fork stuck in the middle. He was a great ideas man, and suggested we travel around the 50 states to see and sample the food and wine products that each state specialized in.

It was a fascinating exercise. One memory is that we were going to obtain crab and salmon from Alaska, which was very special.

But as my enthusiasm deepened, a friend warned me that I might be getting into real trouble with such a business. He was a very smart guy. He pointed out that, if people were going to buy maybe $10 worth of food, for instance, and it was also going to cost them $10 to ship it, they would most likely decline. Food is perishable, unlike car parts.

After considerable thought I took my friend's advice and decided against the venture. But that decision didn't by any means diminish my love of fine dining.

My wife, Franziska, and I made a pledge to try out premium restaurants all around the world. We would focus on those awarded three stars by the series of Michelin Guides.

Here again, a connection to automobiles lured me on. The guidebooks are published by the French tire company, Michelin. Hoping to sell more tires to motorists back in the early 1900s, the two Michelin brothers who founded the company came up with the idea for a book listing gourmet French dining spots that necessitated a drive in one's car, thus affecting wear and tear on the tires. A clever ploy.

Many places required a lengthy drive, but the Michelin Guide assured motorists that dining there was worth it. Fine dining is very important to many people everywhere, but to the French it's part of their national heritage.

The restaurants were graded by assigning them stars from one to three. To be awarded even one star the cuisine, service and ambience had to be "Very good." Two stars indicated "Excellent, worth a detour." Three stars were awarded only to restaurants that provided such an exceptional dining experience that they were worth a special trip.

At first the findings were targeted toward the motoring community in Europe, although today the publishing focus has expanded worldwide. There are Michelin Three-Star restaurants in many countries, including the USA.

These distinctive red Michelin Guides became my "bible," so to speak. I consulted them for everything on a trip, including hotels and other places to lodge for a night.

Franziska and I trust the Michelin Guides because we admire their objectivity. The judges visit a restaurant without the knowledge of the owner or chef. The ratings are assigned by anonymous, independent diners, and are thus free of fear or favor.

We visited several of the French and Italian Michelin restaurants when we were in Europe. We always liked to visit the kitchen and speak with the chef. One time, in Lyon, France, a city known for its gastronomy, we ate lunch at the world-famous Paul Bocuse restaurant. Monsieur Bocuse was still alive at the time, and our visit was kind of a pilgrimage for us. He cooked in the classic French style, and it became quickly obvious to us how he earned his unmatched reputation after comparing it to many others.

This brings to mind a story about a dinner with Lance Reventlow. He and I were driving north in his Mercedes-Benz 300 SL Gullwing from Los Angeles to Bakersfield, California, to attend the drag races. On the way home we stopped at an Italian restaurant in the San Fernando Valley for dinner. The food was mediocre and Lance sensed my unease. Having grown up in Europe, he was knowledgeable about cuisine. As we went out the door he turned around to the maître d' and piped up, "My compliments to the chef but the food was terrible!"

I can't neglect to add another incident on that memorable drive with Lance. His 300 SL had an extra-large gas tank holding 30 or 40 gallons. I felt obliged to pay my share, of course, and made my offer as we were driving through a small town.

Just then we happened to pass their local five-and-dime Woolworth's store, at that time a fixture along the main street of just about every town and city in America. As we flashed by, Lance waved at the Woolworth's and said, "Sonny, don't worry. There's the old bastard that's buying the gas!"

When my wife and I travel in Europe we look forward to meeting up with other gourmet couples who share our passion for dinning at Michelin restaurants. We usually set up a rendezvous and stay at Michelin-starred hotels and visit chateaux, and, of course, wine producers.

It may sound expensive, but most of the places we patronize are reasonable. Nowadays, there are several in Europe that are elegant and gracious without breaking the bank. In London you can go to one of the finest restaurants and eat less expensively than at the semi-finest in Los Angeles.

It wasn't always that way. In fact, I'm amazed at the "showbiz" aspect of dining out these days in our local California restaurants. The tables are set with gold charger plates, the cutlery was formerly English sterling silver, even the rims of the wine glasses are gilded. I shouldn't be surprised, as Hollywood is just down the street from our home.

My reservations are for the frivolous glitz, not the high quality of the tableware itself. I'm especially appreciative of top-notch wine glasses. The best are the clear, unadorned Riedel stemware from Austria, where they have been produced for 300 years.

Riedel's stemware can bring out the essence of the wine, because of the way the wine and its aroma is held by the shape of the glass. There are certain kinds of wine varietals that taste best in glasses specifically designed for them.

An old friend of mine, Randall Grahm, who was known as "The Rhone Ranger" because of his love of the varietal grape from the Rhone Valley of France, founded the Bonny Doon winery in the Santa Cruz Mountains of California. He named his winery after the local hamlet of Bonny Doon. Randy was quite a character and a terrific winemaker, winning many accolades. He was proclaimed Wine and Spirits Professional of the Year in 1994 by the James Beard Foundation, and was inducted into the Vintners Hall of Fame in 2010. He wrote an award-winning anthology of his experiences as a winemaker and connoisseur.

I remember that he once decided to produce his own ice wine. That's a type of dessert wine made from grapes that have been quick frozen by a rapid change in the weather while still on the vine, harvested quickly, and hand squeezed. The process can be complicated and lengthy, from quick picking to vinifying.

Randy figured out that a faster way to produce his *"Eiswein"* was to forego the waiting period for accidental frost to arrive by throwing a truckload of grapes into a quick-freezer. The result was pretty good, but the California authorities governing the naming of wines told him he could not call it an "ice wine" because it wasn't traditionally vinified. So much for entrepreneurship!

A wise analogy I like concerns vintner Warren Winiarski, the owner of Arcadia Vineyards in Napa Valley. His Stag's Leap Wine Cellars won the Judgement of Paris blind wine tasting in 1976, setting the wine world on its back when his Cabernet Sauvignon succeeded in beating out every competitor, including the venerable French winemakers. A bottle of Warren's winning wine is on permanent display at the Smithsonian Institution's National Museum of American History in Washington, D.C.

I once asked Warren about the aging of wine, and he said that aging is not going to do the trick if the acids, fruits, and tannins are not balanced. It needs to be correct before it goes into the bottle as a young wine, then it will be great when it is opened at maturity. Each wine ages uniquely, dependent on many variables.

I will say this: both motorsports and winemaking are mixtures of science and art, and both are rich in variety and deeply complex. Both are extremely challenging! I think I have been lucky to have spent my life in both worlds.

CHAPTER 21
RAOUL BALCAEN ASSOCIATES

Heeding my friend's caution about the food business, I told my partner Eugene that we should discontinue America's Great Taste, even though we had everything ready to roll. As entrepreneurs you have to know when to pull the plug and move ahead. Which we did with no rancor on either side. Eugene could have gone further without me, but he decided not to. He wanted me there, he said, to be a partner or it wouldn't work. He was very busy himself with his regular job as a marketing director.

Looking back I regret that we gave up, but I think I got ahead of America's Great Taste too soon. I don't look back in retrospect at the specialty foods plan being a complete failure, but I was young and worrying about taking my money out of the market for the capital that would need to be poured into the venture before it made a profit.

I turned my attention more and more to the securities markets, both stocks and bonds. It was the early '80s and I was trying to maximize the use of my capital without overdoing my risk taking. "Risk Equals Reward," that is the master equation in money matters, but just as in automobile racing, too much risk can result in disaster.

That happened to me. I got screwed when Michael Milken with Drexel, Burnham and Lambert was responsible for me losing a lot of capital with his insider trading crap. He was convicted of racketeering and securities fraud. I was young, naïve, and far too trusting.

Nowadays, I invest based on what I know intimately about a company, what I research and read about it, about the industry that it is part of, and the U.S. economy as well as the global economy. I always read the British *Financial Times* and the *Economist*, both superb publications. In addition I have never forgotten billionaire Warren Buffet's advice — "Don't hire money managers. Do it yourself" — because they take a percentage of your money whether the market is up or down and they often refer to others and "divvy-up the pie."

In time I started the Raoul Balcaen Consulting business in 1985. Despite my love of the grape there was no way I could leave my devotion to anything mildly automotive. Thus I soon became known as a guru for those contemplating buying a car for investment. Whether it was a hot rod, a street car, a dragster, a truck, or a limo, people sought me out for my advice. The years I spent in the automotive industry in its many, many forms were valuable ones, as it turned out, for my new practice.

At first I'd give away my advice and information about the pros and cons of different car models. Everyone was picking my brains and I began getting heartfelt thanks for my expertise.

Here, again, my entrepreneurial nature kicked in and I realized there was another business opportunity. My knowledge and lengthy career working with all forms of automobiles and their inner workings was a valuable asset. No sense just giving it away for other people's benefit.

Many of those seeking my help were corporations that bought truck and car fleets. They wanted to make sure that their hefty purchases were cost-effective investments. Also, companies in the aftermarket and accessories industry for both cars and motorcycles sought me out for advice on how best to distribute and sell their merchandise.

Coupled with my insights as an economist and a gearhead I was in a pretty good position to put my skills to work for me financially.

I didn't simply study a manufacturer's product lines. I made a point of talking to my clients' employees, asking about their preferences, their weekday schedules, and usage of time and resources. I'd create a report on all aspects of my recommendations. I had probably the best contacts in the automotive industry from top to bottom, and was able to include their analyses and expertise as well.

I required a monthly retainer with those firms. No one objected, and before I knew it, Raoul Balcaen Consulting had ten or twelve clients signed up!

This made my seventh or eighth business that I had launched, if you count my hiring on as an engineering consultant during my days with Warren Olson, Carroll Shelby, Jim Hall, and others.

Strictly for myself, the more I learned about investing, the more I wanted to know. I already had the background, but I became seriously interested in the field. So in 1988 I took classes on the securities markets and portfolio selection.

I never handled anyone else's money, only my own. There is too much wrong advice circulating around. I never trusted money managers.

I'll make one exception: my cousin was a relatively famous one, who managed the finances of wealthy families during his entire career. He was a great source of knowledge for me.

But overall, my inclination is: never give your money to a professional unless you know everything about them. My experience has been that every time I did, and that was hardly ever, I either didn't make any money when the rest of the market did, or I lost money. I rely on my own knowledge and instincts. It has worked quite well for me.

This is not to say that all money managers are not compctent to look after your funds. There are many excellent managers but you will need to do serious research to find them.

CHAPTER 22
THE PETERSEN AUTOMOTIVE MUSEUM

H*ot Rod* magazine, the original foundation stone of what became the towering Petersen Publishing empire, has been mandatory reading for gearheads like me ever since I was a youth. Month after month, year after year, *Hot Rod* shot off newsstand shelves (or got stolen from libraries) and immediately passed from greasy hand to greasy hand in body shops and speed shops and drag strips across the United States and elsewhere around the world.

Copies used to come to my boys' club, where each new issue was awaited impatiently and eagerly read from cover to cover, many times over by several dozen of those of us in love with California's hot-rodding movement. We thirsted for news of dragsters, hot rods and modified street cars, primarily, although the magazine also covered new and classic sports cars and other automobiles from around the industry, including foreign racecars and drivers.

But in Los Angeles in the '50s, most of us young guys were interested in drag racing and hot-rod technology. We pored over photos, sketches, how-tos, test results and reports of events and exhibitions around the country. *Hot Rod* magazine was king. There was no other publication like it — though many rivals soon followed.

Robert E. Petersen was the son of an auto mechanic in Barstow, California, and grew up learning every side of that greasy business hands-on. But it wasn't just work. Bob, as I usually called him, although to many he was "Pete," was highly enthusiastic about cars and hot rods, but also many other things. A real go-getter, when he was discharged from the Army Air Corps after World War II he soon became a movie studio publicist and staff photographer, and then partnered with others to start their own publicity firm.

One of their clients was an upcoming exhibition of hot rods, which drew Bob's attention to the fact that this particular market niche was so new that it had no publication serving it specifically. Seizing the opportunity, Robert Petersen and an associate coincidently named Robert Lindsay left the publicity firm to launch — what else — *Hot Rod* magazine.

Legend has it that the two Bobs put their first issue together in Petersen's apartment, had 5000 copies printed, and personally sold them to people at the door of the 1948 Los Angeles Hot Rod Exposition, the very show they'd originally been promoting. Behind that seminal exhibition was the great Wally Parks, then with the Southern California Timing Association (SCTA) and later founder of the National Hot Rod Association (NHRA).

The first issue of *Hot Rod* actually doubled as the program for the event, cost 25 cents, and was only eight pages long. But it increased in size almost instantly as subscriptions multiplied and advertising rolled in. A year later circulation was over 50,000.

Hot Rod was to grow into a legend of its own, to be joined by Petersen's many other special-interest magazines devoted to production cars and trucks, motorcycles, off-roading, guns and hunting, photography and diverse other fields of enthusiasm.

When Robert E. "Pete" Petersen sold his company in 1996, the price was $450 million.

My idea of a real entrepreneur!

B ob and I first met during the time I was selling the NGK spark plugs for Bill Doheny and starting up IECO with my Corvair manifold. Previously in this book I described how Bob hooked me up with the editors of his magazines, who publicized me with stories they wrote and ads that I placed. That showed me the power of advertising. Business took off.

Fast forward 30 years into the '90s, when Bob, among the many other hats he wore, was on the board of directors of the Natural History Museum, Los Angeles (NHMLA). By that time the number of

Petersen magazines was enormous, and he needed more editorial office space. While looking around he came across a building that was on the market, formerly one of a chain of department stores called Ohrbach's.

He decided it wasn't what he needed for offices, partly because it had no windows, but it looked like an ideal location for another ambition of his. He approached the NHMLA and proposed a new museum, this one catering to the automobile industry that had been so instrumental in developing Los Angeles and Southern California.

The Ohrbach's property encompassed an entire city block and included a multi-story covered parking structure, as well as a capacious underground garage ideal for storing and servicing many of the exhibit cars.

The location was ideal, was right on prestigious Wilshire Boulevard at the corner with Fairfax, part of the famous "Miracle Mile." In addition to many well-known and prosperous commercial businesses along there, the Los Angeles County Museum of Art was down the street, as were the La Brea Tar Pits and Museum, the Craft and Folk Art Museum and, farther along, would be today's Academy Museum of Motion Pictures. Nowadays that stretch of Wilshire is called "Museum Row."

Petersen's vision was to establish the first major automotive museum in California, with the mission to tell the story of the automobile and its historic importance to the area, how it permeated society and played a major role in the evolution of Los Angeles. An important part of the story would be how the hot-rod culture created here moved from the West Coast to the East.

"I think culture everywhere has been changed by the automobile," said Bob, a quote which we later used in a brochure that I put together for him. "My objective is to relate the automobile to everyday life. You look at the classic designs, and even if you are not a car buff you have to be affected by the beautiful lines. We must bring to the general public the role the automobile has played in defining our past and present... as well as shaping our future and not just exotic and expensive collector cars."

Officials at the NHMLA were receptive to the idea. They already had an automotive branch, which housed donated vehicles that were stored in another building in downtown L.A. With the many, many more offered by Bob Petersen himself — his personal collection was very impressive — and other wealthy car people around the city, it was a golden opportunity to create one of the finest auto museums in the world.

The NHMLA jumped at Bob's offer to buy the old department store building on behalf of the car museum. Bob and his wife Margie, who was a wonderful partner to him, put up a lot of the money themselves, but also began to cast around for donors.

Petersen's quest for funds could have been considered a kind of conflict of interest, because the museum had its own fund-raising foundation year-round. It might appear that Bob was going to encroach upon their donors, so he had to tread lightly.

He called me and asked if I could offer my services as a consultant to the director of the NHMLA. Bob thought I could help him get together with the automotive industry, including the aftermarket and the racing community.

Nothing could have suited my background and skills better. I interviewed with the director, expressed my ideas, discussed concepts, and was quickly hired.

I asked Dean Batchelor to come on board to help me with research and other matters. I'd known Dean, a quiet, unassuming gentleman with a wealth of knowledge of the industry, since my days with Warren Olson when I was a teenager.

Dean always had my greatest respect. Another teenage hot rodder like me, during World War II he was a B-17 gunner/radio operator, and spent time as a POW after his plane was shot down over Stuttgart. After the war he modified and raced his own dry lakes 1932 roadster, then set a Bonneville speed record in a streamliner that he designed and built with Alex Xydias of the famous SoCal Speed Shop.

From racing, Dean moved into journalism — at one point he chronicled the building of the Scarab racecar, I remember — and also wrote a number of authoritative books on both hot rods and sports cars. Dean was known as a Ferrari expert, but his last book took him back to his roots for an excellent account of the beginnings and growth of the SoCal hot rod scene, *Dry Lakes and Drag Strips, The American Hot Rod.*

To the wider world, I suppose Dean Batchelor was best known for his long role as editor of the prestigious *Road & Track* magazine. All in all, he was one of the most revered and most distinguished experts in automotive reporting. His stature is reflected by the Dean Batchelor Award for Excellence in Automotive Journalism from the L.A.-based Motor Press Guild.

Needless to say, it was a great honor when Dean cordially agreed to work with me on the auto museum project.

A quality publication was needed, which we would leave with potential donors so they could think over our proposal and read how we planned to accomplish it. I created several pages of substantial literature that urged those in the industry to become a part of motorsports history, getting in on the ground floor of the new automobile museum, so to speak.

Production of this publication was delayed for a while as it went through changes mandated by the officials at the museum, but I made sure the ambitious booklet was filled with 16 brightly colored pages setting out Bob Petersen's vision and detailed descriptions of the museum's mission. The photos and text reflected the various galleries and special exhibition areas that were planned, after I worked with the NMHLA historian to narrow down which autos and eras we should highlight.

We also commissioned a scaled-down model of the future automotive museum to display prominently inside the NHMLA headquarters.

Armed with some idea of what the Petersens and the board expected from me, I initiated our fund-raising effort. We realized that building the museum was to be a massive and expensive undertaking. Major donations from the auto industry, wealthy donors, and sponsors were my targets.

Bob Petersen set me up with contacts at most of his top advertising clients and others in the racing world. The major automotive producers both domestically and internationally were added to our growing lists.

I attended every museum board meeting pertaining to Petersen's vision. Recently I donated the extensive notes I made at that time, three huge boxes, to the archives.

To complement the collections already housed in the Natural History Museum Los Angeles, we based our concept on the heritage of the automobile in Los Angeles and California, including racing, Hollywood movie stars' exotic cars, and how they all affected the rest of the nation. We also focused on automotive art, experience, and culture.

We explained to the staff how Bob's museum would be a new community center and also considered "world class" if done properly.

I figured it would be a great idea to take the new director and the museum team with us back to Detroit to help make the all-important sales pitches to potential sponsors. They agreed, so I made phone calls and set up appointments.

Unfortunately, bureaucracy raised its irritating head and I found myself stopped in my tracks. During our very first meeting with automakers' executives, right off the bat, unimportant little details best left until later were turned into monstrous discussions. I could see from our hosts' faces that they were turned off. Our talks were being dragged down with minutiae.

I talked enthusiastically about the magnificent opportunity being presented, but I could sense resistance.

Despite my assurances that the new museum would be dedicated to the preservation and interpretation of the important role of the automobile and its technology in shaping American culture, we met blank stares.

I tried giving a grand overview of how auto manufacturers could employ the magnificent new museum facility to stage new model introductions, present special exhibits, host gala receptions, and put on charity fundraisers with their local dealers. Charity is always a good persuader, and I explained how deeply Bob and Margie Petersen were involved with various charities, including one of their most important, the children's mental health unit at the non-profit Cedars-Sinai Medical Center, the hospital of choice of most of Hollywood's celebrities.

All to no avail.

A major issue, I could see clearly, was that the officials from the NHMLA were asking for far greater financial support than was reasonable, many multiple millions of dollars. And they were asking with an arrogance that some academics often display. That's not how to win over top executives of giant corporations.

We left Detroit empty-handed and disappointed. It was apparent that the museum staff and I weren't on the same wavelength. They were the authority and I was just functioning as a consultant, so I had to be careful, which is not a good place for an entrepreneur. By our very nature we are spontaneous, eager, flexible, and able to compromise. We adjust and adapt. In this case, I wasn't sure if the museum had our best interests at heart, at least in the beginning of the project.

Trying again, I put together a second trip to The Motor City, and this time I had Ford very interested. I think Carroll Shelby had put in a good word for me, and Ford appeared willing to put up $5 million. Then, somehow or other, the academics got involved again and Ford backed off. It was tremendously discouraging and served to set me against working for charities in the future.

There are people who want to "feel important and jump in front of the camera," so to speak, and get their name on prestigious lists. Many do not want to put up any money, all they want to do is bask in the glory. After a few experiences like that I became soured on fundraising for the museum.

Fundraising is an art and a chore. Much depends on contacts and networking, and one's attitude, behavior, prior relationships, manner, and support for the entity seeking funds. The latter in particular is crucial, and can make all the difference between success and failure.

During my many years I have handled fundraising for several organizations in addition to the Petersen Automotive Museum, including the Motorsports Hall of Fame of America, the Los Angeles Opera, the Los Angeles Museum of Science and Industry, and several wine societies. One fact became clear to me early on: If you don't have the complete confidence, trust, and support of those for whom you are fundraising, then no amount of effort and time invested can succeed.

After one of these group fundraising trips to Detroit, three in all, I was accused of putting a charge on my expense sheet for watching porn movies in my hotel room. I knew who the culprit was because he boasted about the films the next morning. I denied my involvement, of course, and named the guilty party. I wasn't about to get tarred with that brush. It amazed me that a member of the museum staff would stoop to that level of distraction and have the temerity to see the charge was billed to my room!

On my own, I made a fourth and final trip to Michigan for one-on-one meetings with top executives of all the big automakers, including the Germans and the Japanese. It was 1991 and our target date for opening our new museum was October 1994. We needed to step on the gas pedal!

I set up appointments to call on every division at General Motors, Chrysler and Ford. I already had met some of these executives during my racing years, and Carroll Shelby continued to open doors for me. I talked to sales and marketing people, engineers, board members, executives, and anyone else I figured was appropriate and willing to listen. I was constantly typing letters, making phone calls, meeting with people.

Some stepped up, but when I encountered opposition I was quite stunned at the excuses I heard. How could American car people, in particular, not want to be included in a museum devoted to their products, where they would be showcased before hundreds of thousands of interested visitors?

But I didn't have much fundraising luck with our foreign colleagues either, nor with the auto aftermarket industry.

Perhaps donors were reluctant to give to an unknown entity, but I had thought that Bob Petersen's name and his hugely successful empire of dozens of motoring publications made The Petersen Museum a sure bet. Didn't these firms realize the huge publicity they would receive? I was mystified.

I cudgeled my brain for answers and finally decided that we needed to create a National Council to give our proposed museum credibility. I quickly invited famous race drivers, prestigious movers and shakers in the industry, and many personal friends, to join us. The response was overwhelming and gratifying.

The Council soon included Dan Gurney, Parnelli Jones, Lyn St. James, Paul Newman, Carroll Shelby, Phil Hill, Jim Hall, Kenny Bernstein, Otis Chandler, General William Lyon, Bruce Meyer, Peter Mullin, Donald Petersen, J. David Power III, Sanford Sigoloff, Ken Behring, and Andy Granatelli. Many are my personal friends.

We also listed the Los Angeles County Board of Supervisors, the Trustees of the Natural History Museum, and the members of the Museum Foundation Alliance Board of Directors. On the last page I was awarded a slight compliment when it was noted that the brochure was under my direction. The publication was the first vehicle, forgive the pun, for our path forward and we took copies of it everywhere.

Now I was even more highly motivated. We all loved the idea of a museum devoted to the auto industry, and I worked my tail off trying to inspire the same passion in those with the necessary money to make it happen.

Still some manufacturers refused to donate — until others had taken the plunge and the museum was finally finished and open to the public! Naturally, then they wanted to be part of it. In fact many of these carmakers and automotive aftermarket performance product makers, after previously saying to us, "Why do we want to donate to a rich man's museum?" suddenly became obsessed with having their products on display there. It had been disheartening to hear those comments from supposedly smart men in Detroit who later insisted on getting on the bandwagon after others had stepped up and shown the way was clear of risks.

Many great car museums exist around the world, and in the planning stages for ours I knew I needed to see what others were doing. I wanted to visit every major automotive museum that existed in the early '90s. So I went to Europe at my own expense for three weeks and toured every auto museum I could find.

That of course including Britain's National Motor Museum, which to my mind is one of the finest historical museums in the world for automobiles. It is in the south coast village of Beaulieu on the estate of Lord Montagu, who was a highly respected British car aficionado.

Next I went to Mulhouse, in eastern France, to tour the vast French National Museum that housed the finest Bugatti collection in the world. I photographed and documented everything. Then it was on to Germany and the Mercedes-Benz, Porsche and Volkswagen museums. At all of these places I talked to their curators and inspected the exhibits, and interviewed the owners of some of the best cars. As an entrepreneur I had the talent for such investigations, and I enjoyed the challenge of the task before me.

I returned home with valuable information and ideas, which I documented in two thick loose-leaf binders and donated to the automotive museum's early archives.

At last NHMLA acquired the old department store property, including its adjacent multi-level car parking structure, and at great expense to the County of Los Angeles reconstruction began with interior renovations. I was excited at being charged with helping to bring Bob's dream and the National History Museum's display departments into reality, although our dreaming was somewhat limited by budget restraints.

We planned for the second floor to be filled with specific themes in automotive history. It would include Hollywood exotics, movie cars, muscle cars, European classics, racecars, and interpreting their roles in shaping America's passion for speed and innovation. We planned exhibits that were both visual and auditory.

The third floor housed the work of brilliant automotive artists, illustrators, sculptors, and craftsmen. The Natural History Museum designed a program with school districts to bring students in for tours and workshops demonstrating the history of America's love of the automobile and what made a car "work" in detail.

Part of the four-story building was to be set aside for facilities to host conferences, meetings, and events such as private corporate functions, films and lectures, and opportunities to launch new cars.

Below ground, there was a vast, cavernous space where many vehicles could be stored and maintained while awaiting their turn to be rotated into public view.

NHMLA automotive artist George Bartell, my close friend since he had created the cover illustration for my old IECO catalog, had painted a portrait of the very rare and fabulously beautiful 1938 Bugatti Atlantic Type 57SC that was in the collection of fashion guru Ralph Lauren. George asked if I could pass this information on to Lauren.

A good friend offered to put me in touch with Lauren. When I phoned to describe Bartel's painting of the Atlantic, offering to send it to Mr. Lauren for viewing on behalf of the artist, I mentioned that I was fundraising for the new Petersen museum. One of Lauren's staff called back and said that, because they were on the East Coast and we were on the West Coast, they didn't see any reason to contribute. I assured them that car collecting was universal, and that they could derive many benefits from their participation.

To me that was an innocent conversation during which I naturally put on my hat as an official fundraiser for the museum.

Unfortunately, the entire story got twisted around and by the time it got back to our NHMLA Director it had turned into a major misunderstanding. He called me into his office and accused me of trying to "hustle Mr. Lauren" into buying the painting. That was totally wrong, of course, completely upside down.

I tried to explain, but this individual refused to hear my side of the situation. He told me he was going to have to let me go from my contract.

I was truly outraged at the intimation that I was doing something dishonest. My principles and values have always been of the highest order and to be accused of trying to "shake down" Ralph Lauren was appalling. Because of the false charge my reputation was at stake and I had no intention of allowing anyone to besmirch it.

Being forced to leave the museum project was a huge blow after all the work I had done, especially considering the personal contacts and promises that had been made from my end. I had, in effect, held many of the reins in my hands as to the organization of the various groups involved in the automotive museum project. Letting go and wondering if others could pick them up successfully was a heavy burden on my mind.

Privately, I was uneasy about a certain assistant to the Director, a man who followed me everywhere and would kow-tow to me, which made me kind of suspicious. I knew the man didn't have a highly paid job, yet he drove an expensive car with custom wheels. I later realized he hung around me because he knew I had Bob Petersen's ear. What was going on?

I called Bob, relayed what had happened, and told him that the Natural History Museum staffers were dragging their feet and nothing was getting done. They didn't seem to have accomplished much over the previous two years. I commented that the museum people were the biggest back-stabbers I had ever come across, and told him he needed to get over there.

He listened as I gave him my entrepreneurial advice about the situation. He was very quiet. My harsh assessment certainly disturbed him, because he wanted everyone to be happy with the project. Actually he did put his foot down and I heard things were beginning to move, although there were some financial and bond issues with the Natural History Museum from the County of Los Angeles that came up.

But at long, long last the Petersen Automotive Museum was ready to open its doors to the Los Angeles public.

Well in advance of the official Grand Opening date, Bob and his wife, Margie, asked if I could help them out with the gala event. I agreed, of course, with pleasure, and we spent weeks organizing the social ceremonies. Margie and I had "worked on" many high-society fundraising parties all over Beverly Hills, and we were familiar with the kinds of guests who attended the most glamorous events and what they expected.

My own contacts with the owners of French and California wineries proved beneficial, and Marge and I discussed which ones to approach for supplies.

On the big night the press was there in full force, and there were searchlights playing all over the place just like a movie premiere. Margie and I made sure champagne and caviar was on tap as well as premium wines and gourmet dishes. On the top floor we had a wonderful champagne and hors d'oeuvres area that cost extra to enter, as we were using the evening as a fundraiser. The banquet stations were filled with elegant dishes, and the crowd was wall-to-wall.

During the opening celebration, the Director told Bob he was retiring, but would be happy to stay on as a consultant as needed. He really had done little to make things happen, but Bob knew hardly anything of my awkward "history" with this person, and hired him. A mistake!

But the new Director was very knowledgeable in accounting, and he decided to have an audit to check how much we had received in donations and gate receipts for the opening gala. The NHMLA was included in the audit, where it was discovered that a lot of funds were "mis-directed." We had an over-subscribed event with no receipts. Many more irregularities then came to light. I had my suspicions as we tried to sort it all out and they did catch the culprit, the assistant whom I mentioned earlier. He was later jailed.

Following my direct involvement, the museum story had many twists and turns that I don't need to detail here. Through changes of ownership and management it has continued to thrive, although at times that seemed doubtful, and a recent redesign of the exterior has transformed a rather ordinary old storefront building into an architectural showpiece the rival of anything in Los Angeles, which is saying something!

The all-new façade, designed by the architectural firm KPF, is a dramatic wrapping of huge stainless-steel ribbons around the entire building. It has the general organic shape of a car, and at night red lights glimmer behind every strand. It is a jaw-dropping people-stopper.

As well as signifying exactly what lies inside, the dramatic structure presents a hint of humor in stark contrast to the suddenly old-fashioned, traditional architecture of neighboring buildings with their square lines broken by neo-classical domes and pillared arches.

Today more than 700,000 enthusiasts a year from around the world visit the Petersen to see the displays, which frequently change to keep the experience fresh. Over 300 vehicles and hundreds of engines, parts, accessories, paintings, books, photographs and videotapes are now on exhibit.

And the location can't be beat: at the beginning of Wilshire's "Museum Row," it's a spot any regional visitor center would treasure.

One thing still upsets me, though. When the Petersen Museum opened there was a large glass panel etched with tributes to Bob and Margie Petersen greeting visitors in the museum foyer. Recently, during a remodeling, it was removed. I can't understand why, because I can't imagine that the place would exist without the Petersens' relentless drive. It was this extraordinary couple's hard work, day and night, that brought the dream to life.

CHAPTER 23
TRAVELIN' MAN

O nce the Petersen Automotive Museum was open and my role there had ended, an urge came over me to get away and go traveling for a while. I had the money, there wasn't anything on my business plate that couldn't be deferred, and I was single again. I really felt like taking a few trips not just out of town, but out of the country.

A good friend with whom I had enjoyed such adventures in the past was Harry Richter, a German fellow who was the general manager of the prestigious California Club in downtown Los Angeles. Founded in 1887, this was a private, members-only club for people who appreciated social interaction along with good food and wine in elegant surroundings. Their building, now on the National Register of Historic Places, is in the style of Italian Renaissance Revival architecture.

An inveterate explorer, Harry was always suggesting we take a trip here, there, and everywhere. I knew his wife, Erika, and we had sailed with them when I was married, along with several other couples. Sometimes we rented a bare-boat and lived on it for a week or two. We all got along well.

I do love to travel, and when my former wife and I were still together we had traveled extensively in Europe, driving all over England, France, Germany, Belgium, Switzerland, and Spain. On that very enjoyable trip to Spain we stayed in *paradores*. These are luxury hotels usually located in converted historic buildings, true gems for traveling in Spain. They are so readily available that it seems to me there was barely a town or village in Spain that we missed, because we drove all the country over a six-week period.

First, we covered the southern portion, attending festivals in Cordoba and Seville, then the middle, and finally northern Spain. In Toledo there was a huge religious holiday being celebrated, the Feast of Corpus Christi. The king and queen of Spain, Juan Carlos and Sofia, were inside the cathedral, Santa Iglesia Catedra Primara de Toledo, and the choir that we could hear outside the church was unbelievable for the acoustics alone.

When Mass was ended the royal couple headed up a procession walking along the streets of the Toledo. It was a spectacular moment.

After my second divorce I realized I had caught travel fever and was eager to set off again. Harry Richter at the California Club had the same "malady." I once remarked to him about his worldwide travels, "You've done more and seen more than many of these club members despite their wealth. You are a true adventurer!"

His own desire to set off again was building, but his wife didn't always want to go along, so he asked me if I'd be interested. He started talking about all the beautiful, fascinating places we could visit together, all around the world. Every exotic name was music to my soul.

We fellow travelers first went together to India's "Golden Triangle" to enjoy three weeks of touring each and every sight available to us. Our first stop was New York, where we spent a couple of nights in the Knickerbocker Club on 2 East 62nd Street. Its code name is "Knick," and it is an exclusive men's private club. It was a very special visit.

We visited Ellis Island, where most European immigrants (including mine) first arrived in the 19th century. We also had lunch in the "Windows on the World" restaurant atop the World Trade Center's Twin Towers. The view of New York harbor and all its surroundings was truly one to be remembered. (Sadly, the Twin Towers are no more, as everyone knows.)

The following day we boarded our flight with Air India on a Boeing 747 and headed via London to New Delhi. Quite a flight it was, flying over areas where no American Flag airliner could navigate a foreign airspace. I vividly recall suddenly going from light into darkness as we rounded the globe, what an experience.

Arriving at our hotel in Delhi, there were two elegantly dressed doormen in British Raj uniforms who welcomed our group at the hotel. India is a strange and exotic country, very spiritual and with many unique cultures. The people are very friendly and many very poor. They blend various belief systems and co-exist relatively well.

After visiting new and old Delhi, we headed to Jaipur in Rajasthan to see the "Pink Palace," sometimes referred to as the "Palace of the Winds." It's very exotic, having been built in 1799 by the Maharaja Sawai Pratap Singh. A truly unique piece of 18th century architecture. Also, in Jaipur is the "Water Palace" in the middle of the Man Sagar lake, another spectacular sight.

In Jodhpur we discovered many more architectural treasures. The Fort at Mehrangarh was originally built in 1459. Today it is a museum developed by the current head of the clan, Maharaja Gaf Singh II, to share the history of his predecessors.

Shortly after, we travelled to Madhya Pradesh to see the exotic monuments of Kahjuraho. Most of these incredible temples were built by hand between 950 and 1050 by the Chandela dynasty.

We then ventured on to the highlight of the Indian journey, Agra, to view the fort and spend the day viewing the Taj Mahal. Agra is in the state Uttar Pradesh and is considered neither clean nor safe. One must be very vigilant when visiting this great historical sight.

The Taj is an immense mausoleum built from white marble between 1631 and 1648 by the Mughal emperor Shah Jahan in memory of his favorite wife, Mumtaz Mahal. It is considered the jewel of Muslim art in India, a world masterpiece and a UNESCO World Heritage site.

Varanasi is an ancient city on the banks of the River Ganges. It is one of the most sacred sites for Hindus, who believe the river pays its respects to the local Shiva by the direction it flows. It is a sacred place where the cremation fires are held by the people who can afford to have their loved ones sent to this sacred place. We viewed this before dawn from afar on a small boat. An incredible experience.

After India, we flew to Kathmandu in Nepal, the jumping-off place for mountain climbers to trek Mount Everest, which is 29,032 ft high. In the city there are lot of climbers and the ever-present sherpas. These local Nepalese people are considered elite mountaineers. Everest is part of the Annapurna mountain range. To fly over it offers most exciting views from the air.

We visited the ancient Durbar square and its many religious temples, such as the Shiva Parvati, in the center of the old city. The Kumari Devi is a little girl, believed to be the reincarnation of a living goddess. She lives in a house called Kumari Ghar in prepubescent age, until reaching puberty. She then is replaced again by the next person who is perceived an incarnate.

Traveling to the base of the Himalayan range we saw many Buddhist Stupas. The largest, located in Kathmandu, was built in the fifth century. One must spin the prayer wheels on the sides of the structure, and think your prayers.

Next we flew on to the coastal city of Mumbai on the Indian ocean and popularly known as Bombay. Sadly, there people sleep on the sidewalks beside the road. This was our last stop before flying back to London, and on to LA.

After returning from India and Nepal, a group of us decided to explore Peru's famous Machu Picchu and tour Ecuador's Galapagos Islands. After flying into Lima, Peru, we then flew on to Cuzco, an ancient city high in the Andes. The city is located at an altitude of 11,150 ft, and disembarking from the plane, the thin air was like a shock to the body. It feels like a hit to the chest and it takes a while to adjust.

The locals serve warm tea made by steeping cocoa leaves, which are derived from the same plant used for the drug cocaine. It has a very mild effect, but it helps the body with the altitude adjustment.

Traveling on by train through the Huatanay Valley of the Inca empire, I had never experienced such crisp and clean air. One could see for many miles and understand why the Incas called it their sacred valley.

Machu Picchu was discovered by the American explorer Hiram Bingham in 1911. The sight is spectacular. It requires lots of climbing and physical energy to visit. One can spend days to thoroughly explore this wondrous spot.

Back in the city of Cuzco we all enjoyed the local food of lama steak for dinner, drank Pisco Sours and listened to entertainment, which included the intriguing Andean flute music.

Traveling back to Lima, the huge capital of Peru, we viewed the famous Anthropology Museum, which is well worth a visit.

Flying through Guanaquil, Ecuador, we went then to the Galapagos islands, located some 600 miles from the mainland. There we boarded our boat, a 1911 converted Dutch motor sailor. It was a tight ship that accommodated about 20 guests plus crew.

The islands were first discovered by Fray Tomas de Berlanga, Bishop of Panama in 1535. Charles Darwin sailed there in 1835 aboard the HMS *Beagle* at the age of 26. He first discovered several species of finches that varied in their bill shape from island to island, lending significant insight toward his thinking on natural selection.

We toured the islands of Fernandina, Isabela, Santa Cruz, San Cristobal and San Salvador. Some of the giant land turtles on these islands live up to 170 years. Many of the birds are unique here, like the Red-footed and Blue-footed boobies, and there are many large albatrosses. Another unique part of the wildlife are the marine iguana lizards. Both land and sea species are on these islands. The Galapagos offers an up and close view of animals, as they don't have any predators and are not at all threatened by human closeness. A delightful experience.

Brazil was my next adventure. I flew into Sao Paolo and on to Rio de Janeiro. The Guanabara Bay and city of Rio are stunningly beautiful. Sugar Loaf mountain and the tall sculpture of Christ the Redeemer atop the mountain was one of the highlights of my visit. The beach along Copacabana is also truly beautiful.

I flew on to Recife, where the old town center dates back to the 16th century. Many wealthy Brazilians have restored old colonial Portuguese houses to be used as vacation homes.

Next I traveled north to Manaus to visit the Opera House and the lower Amazon jungles. The Opera House was built in the Renaissance Revival style by a local rubber baron in 1884. A beautiful place, which has its entry area paved with rubber to reduce noise. It sits right in the middle of the Amazon rain forest. A very spectacular edifice indeed.

We also made two interesting sailing trips. Each time we chartered a 50-foot sailing ship, which we crewed ourselves. At Tahiti, we sailed for 10 days around several of the islands, which included Bora Bora and Raiatea. The other sailing adventure was to the British Virgin Islands, visiting Tortola and Virgin Gorda. These sailing trips were work, along with a lot of thrilling adventure. A wonderful experience.

It was after returning from the South Pacific that I began to woo the lady who has become the love of my life.

My new wife Franziska joined me for a different trip to South America, this time to visit Argentina and Uruguay. Argentina is a wonderful country to explore. Buenos Aires is a very cosmopolitan city. The Plaza de Mayo is lined with stately 19th century buildings. The Opera House, Teatro Colon, was built in 1908. The Ricoleta cemetery contains graves of the most influential and important Argentinians, including Eva Peron, better known as Evita, the wife of Juan Peron, former president.

The beautiful and classic Alvear Palace is an elegant hotel, to either stay and/or dine. The Ricoleta area is also called "the Paris of South America" as it features many historic buildings from the 19th century.

As a wine connoisseur, I also needed to explore the wine region of Mendoza, located in high-altitude plains of the Eastern Andes. Vineyards are planted from 2,800 to 5,000 feet. The principal red grape that is cultivated there is the Malbec, which originally came from the French region of Cahors.

After extensive visits to wine producers in this unique region, I came away with a first-hand view of solid, in-depth winemaking.

The next part of this adventure was to visit the Iguazu Falls on the Igauzu river between Argentina and Brazil. Together they make the largest waterfall in the world, and they are indeed a spectacle worth touring. Our final outing in South America was a quick ferry ride from Buenos Aires to Montevideo, a lovely city and the capital of Uruguay.

Seeing all this with Franciska made it very special.

CHAPTER 24
FRANZISKA

My wife Franziska is the most fascinating and interesting woman I have known, a very special person.

She's from a Swiss family named Moser, who live just outside Lucerne in a small town that Franziska refers to as "a cow village!" Hers is a very large family, she's the youngest of eight children. Her father was with the Swiss railroad company, while her mother trained as a podiatrist. She ran her own little business at home — while raising eight children!

Franziska has a great interest in art and is well educated in the field. She worked for an art gallery in Lucerne before moving to America and continuing her career here. She is very adroit when it comes to contemporary art, and is really abreast of what's going on, a tough, competitive world to play in. Franziska is very generous to her clients.

When we met in Los Angeles she was working with her brother, Stefan. In 1989 he had started an orthopedic prosthetic practice called Swiss Balance in Santa Monica and developed it from scratch. Franziska came to help, and other siblings followed, but she stayed on.

Franziska appealed to me greatly, but she was dating someone so I didn't follow up. But a year later we met again, through a mutual friend.

Seeing Franziska again revived the feelings I had felt the first time. Our mutual friend suggested I ask her out. So I did, and the rest is history.

She is of exceptional intellect and a kind soul, although she corrects me and says that she is an "old soul." She enjoys opera and classical music, which pleases me greatly although she's not quite the devotee that I am. She loves jazz, blues, country... she loves music!

Also, she and her brother enjoyed riding motorcycles, one of my own favorite pastimes. I have ridden all over the country and owned several motorcycles. Franziska really enjoyed riding too, and had her own Ducati. As fellow enthusiasts we began hanging out together, having fun, and falling in love. As we got to know each other she and I discovered we had much in common and were very compatible.

With her riding pillion we began touring together. On our first trip, to Cambria on the central coastline, we rode the entire way in fog and as we traveled farther north along the Pacific the weather got colder, even though it was summertime. But we had a marvelous time. After that ride I knew she was a woman of great courage.

In Los Angeles we went to many society events together, but we also started traveling around Europe. Since I wasn't working at a daily job, but making a living as an investor in the securities market and doing charity work, I had plenty of free time. I found her to be pragmatic and very realistically oriented in her thinking. We had deep discussions about worldly affairs, and I was very interested in her viewpoint as a Swiss. She is not into politics as much as I am, but we talk about the world's people and their political direction.

She had applied for U.S. citizenship, and on one of our early dates I accompanied her to the swearing-in ceremony. I was amazed at the diversity of different nationalities around us there: Russians, Slavs, Asians, Indians, Pacific Islanders, Hispanics. The place was packed with newly minted Americans.

To "pop the question," I took her to San Francisco and the Top of the Mark, the iconic cocktail bar on the 19th floor of the elite Mark Hopkins Hotel on Nob Hill. It is one of the most romantic places on the West Coast and has a 360-degree view of the city.

My parents always loved that hotel. Back in the late '40s, after we returned from Italy, they stayed there when they traveled by train to watch the Army-Navy Veteran's football game.

But my plans for a grandiose proposal overlooking the glittering City by the Bay were thwarted. The Top of the Mark was closed for renovations! I ended up with Plan B, which was the Hilton Hotel and its large penthouse restaurant. I don't believe she was surprised when I proposed, by that time I think she sensed something was going on.

In 2003 Franziska and I were married. After she joined me in my Spanish Colonial home, she made some renovations, as women are inclined to do. They were all improvements on the bachelor pad I'd lived in comfortably, I thought, since my second divorce. Franziska's deft decorating has vastly added to the home's appearance, especially with the banishment, to our benefit, of some of my antiques. Her changes were so positive that I was, in fact, inspired to redesign our spacious back garden.

Franziska has brought so much joy into my life, I cannot imagine it without her. I have a deep, deep love for her and her caring ways. She is a superb cook, which I can really appreciate as I am something of a gourmet chef myself.

We still travel as often as we can, and usually rent a villa for the summer in Provence, a beautiful part of southern France. We also go to Switzerland, of course, every year to see my wife's family.

She is a treasure in every way. Franziska is "The One" for me.

CHAPTER 25
ON THE VINE

My Italian stepmother Toni, my father's second wife, was a fantastic cook. She was also a discerning wine expert, and many of her friends owned wineries. She made us laugh when she described herself simply as a "prune picker," but in fact she was a descendant from a prestigious family in Italy going back many generations. In Sacramento, where my father was based, she had an impressive job with the U.S. Department of Defense.

Incredibly, Toni lived to be 108 years old. Always a character of the highest order, she had a great sense of humor. She often said, "You don't get that far without a sense of humor!"

Another of her passions was the opera, and she was a founder of the Sacramento Opera company. One of Toni's good friends was the great singer Beverly Sills, whom I met at a fundraiser for the opera at the old gingerbread Victorian mansion in Sacramento where the governor had once lived. When my stepmother moved away from that city I turned my enthusiasm and my involvement toward our local opera company in Los Angeles.

What am I getting at here? Merely to point out that the three topics mentioned — superb cuisine, fine wines and magnificent music — seem to have a connection. This is certainly true for me, as I am an ardent devotee of them all.

In fact, as a gourmet who highly appreciates good food and wine along with my love of opera, I became involved, as a hobby, in philanthropic work for several prestigious food and wine societies in Los Angeles. Also, I became involved in wine auctions.

As a result, one time I happened to meet General Jimmy Doolittle, the much-decorated World War II hero famed for leading America's first response strike on Tokyo right after the Japanese attacked Pearl Harbor. Earlier, he had been an aviation pioneer who won many flying races. In 1976 I was invited to a huge celebration in his honor at the Beverly Wilshire Hotel hosted by Joseph Brummit, who was an executive with TWA for the western region.

At our dining table that night was Hernando Courtright, who owned the Beverly Wilshire Hotel. His first wife was instrumental in the building of that with him. After her passing at a young age, Hernando married a lady named Florence, a commodities trader from Chicago. Courtright always called her Fiorenza, Italian for Florence. He felt that this made her special. Before his death he sold the Beverly Wilshire to a Hong Kong investment group.

Courtright was a truly fine gentleman. Thanks to him, my interest in wine led to my being invited to join the Confrérie des Chevaliers du Tastevin, an exclusive bacchanalian fraternity of Burgundy wine enthusiasts. The society is headquartered in a 12th century French monastery, the Clos de Vougeot, and has chapters worldwide. Members include celebrities, luminaries, business tycoons, diplomats, scholars, and military leaders. They hold elaborate chapter dinners during which we discuss and enjoy the Burgundy being served and how it is enhanced by the dishes that have been chosen to pair with it.

Burgundy wine is made from two principal grape varieties, the Pinot Noir and Pinot Chardonnay. Certain regions and their different climates and soil compositions give their wines certain distinctive characteristics. The French call this "terroir."

I remember an old friend, a theoretical physicist at California State University, Riverside, who loved wine. He very definitely had what we call "a knowledgeable palate." He collected extremely rare wines, and offered them to fellow connoisseurs during splendid, three-day programs of wine-tasting dinners for as much as $3,000 per person — and that was many years ago. His palate was so precise, one evening at a prestigious blind tasting, he correctly identified all five wines of first-growth Bordeaux Châteaux from the 1966 vintage, while I only was able to identify three.

ABOVE *Here I am flanked by John Hadley (left) and Joseph Brumet, then executive vice president of TWA Western region, at the Beverly Wilshire Hotel in 1976 during my induction into the Order of Chevaliers du Tastevin.*

ABOVE *A special banquet of the Chevaliers du Tastevin at the Beverly Wilshire Hotel honoring Ronald Reagan's presidency. He was a member of the group, but unable to attend. He sent a 10-minute video clip that was aired. Bob and Margie Petersen are at the table, with Father Charles Depierre to the left, and me to the right.*

-26- *Celebrity—Society*, May, 1989

CONFRERIE DES CHEVALIERS DU TASTEVIN

The Confrerie des Chevaliers du Tastevin, Los Angeles Chapitre recently held a black tie stag gourmet dinner at Chevalier Robert E. Petersen's Scandia Restaurant on the Sunset Strip. Du Tastevin, which had its origin in Nuits St. Georges, Cote d'Or, France, was acutally founded in 1703. Today, it is even more prestigious and their ceremonial dinners celebrate the habit of being pleased with best in wine and food . . . and knowing why.

Left: Lud Rennick, Chevalier (host) Robert Petersen, Commandeur Raoul Balacen III and Michael McCarty.

1st row (left to right) Mortimer Kline, Grand Officier of the Los Angeles Chapitre Grande Senechal Thomas "Tuck" Trainer. Commandeur Z. Wayne Griffin, Jr. John Hotchkis John Maher, President Great Western Savings and Loan Tom Somermeier.

ABOVE *I greatly enjoy the company of my "confreres" of the Chevaliers, including my good friend Bob Peterson (next to me in the middle), who owned the Scandia restaurant where this black-tie gourmet dinner was held. At far left is Lud Rennick, a restaurateur with fine establishments in Pasadena and Santa Monica. Michael McCarty, on the opposite end, is famed for his Michael's Restaurants in Santa Monica and New York City.*

ABOVE *Special vintage of Domaine Chandon's California sparkling wine at the Beverly Wilshire*
Hotel. From left to right are Michael McCarty, Beverly Wilshire director, first president of California
operations of Moet, John Wright, Jack Hennessey, myself, and Dan Berger of the LA Times.

ABOVE *Father Charles Depierre at the Mondavi vineyard in Napa Valley, California, blessing the grape harvest as part of an Italian tradition. From the left, Robert Mondavi, as well as his sons, Tim and Michael. A very special event.*

ABOVE *Opening of Wolfgang Puck's new (at the time) restaurant in Las Vegas in 1992. From left to right, Wolfgang Puck, William Panzer, William Tilly, and me.*

ABOVE Shelby American employee reunion held at Lime Rock, Connecticut in 2000, sanctioned at the annual Shelby American Automobile Club convention.

ABOVE My autographed memento of the Scarab Reunion at Elkhart Lake, Wisconsin in 2008.

ABOVE I had so much interest in the Scarab Formula 1 effort, because I thought we really were going to have a winner. That wasn't to be, but at least I got to enjoy this one again in 2008 during the Scarab Reunion at Elkhart Lake, Wisconsin.

RIGHT At the 2008 Scarab Reunion I was reunited with many old team-mates, including my long-time friend and mentor, Phil Remington. All the Scarab cars were there, and many ran on the track. It was a wonderful occasion.

MONTEREY HISTORIC AUTOMOBILE RACES

Nation's premier vintage racing event will grace Laguna Seca Raceway

YOU CAN hear the drone of the engines long before you see them break the horizon in a swarm. Suddenly, they cross over the rise of the hill — a pack of Jag D types passed by a Maserati 300S, which is neck and neck with a pair of Testa Rossa Ferraris.

The scene is repeated time and again, different time periods; different cars, as each racing group takes to the track. However, this is not some European racing circuit during the 1930s, 50s or 70s. Rather, it is present-day Monterey during the height of the greatest weekend in vintage racing.

The Monterey Historic Automobile Races, the nation's premier vintage racing event, marks its 20th Anniversary this year during three days of festivities Aug. 20-22 at the Laguna Seca Raceway.

A world class variety of historic race cars, some not seen on a race circuit since the 1930s, and still others with seven-figure values, come to Monterey each year to play a part in the pageantry, spectacle and fun of the event, making it the "Super Bowl of Vintage Racing."

More than 30,000 racing fans from as far away as England, Italy, Japan, Germany, the Netherlands and Australia flock to the picturesque Monterey Peninsula each year during the internationally anticipated weekend.

Spectators can mingle in the paddocks with historic and vintage vehicles, and perhaps run into some of the race car drivers who piloted them to victories. Recent participants in the weekend include Sterling Moss, Juan Manuel Fangio, Jackie Stewart, Dan Gurney, Danny Sullivan and Phil Hill, among others. Each year, marques such as Aston Martin, Bugatti, Maserati, Ferrari, Porsche, Cobra and Corvette

again race as they were meant to through the hills of the Monterey Peninsula.

During its history, the Monterey Historic Races has presented such memorable moments as the first running of a pre-war (1937) Auto Union C-Type V16 in America since the Vanderbilt Cup of the 1930s; the great German giants of racing, such as Herman Lang at the wheel of a 1937 Mercedes-Benz W125; World Champion Phil Hill driving a 1924 Alfa Romeo P2 with 3-time World Champion Jackie Stewart driving a 1932 Alfa Romeo P3 and 5-time World Champion Juan Manuel Fangio driving a 1951 Alfa Romeo 159 all on the same track at the same time; the winning 1959 Aston-Martin LeMans Team reunion; Stirling Moss driving the all-conquering 1955 Mercedes-Benz 300SLR sports

car; and Mrs. W.O. Bentley watching Phil Hill drive a 4.5-1liter Bentley and proclaiming, "I do believe that we have just seen the first international win ever for a Blower Bentley."

"There are fascinating stories behind each of those moments, and the hundreds of others we've seen over the past 20 years," states Steven J. Earle, president of the Santa Barbara-based General Racing Ltd. and founder of the races. "We could talk about each particular event for hours. Individual pictures like these — segments of racing history, really — are what the Monterey Historics are all about, and what sets this weekend apart from other vintage

See **HISTORIC RACES**, page 33

ABOVE My past comes alive again: two historic cars that I helped build returned to the track during a vintage event a few years ago at Laguna Seca Raceway, CA. That's the Jim Hall Lister at left, alongside Lance Reventlow's Scarab Mk I.

ABOVE *Old racers Phil Hill and Carroll Shelby attended a garden party at our home in 2010.*
Happy times.

ABOVE *Together again after so many years, I stand proudly alongside one of the still-beautiful*
Scarabs with my old team-mates, driver Bruce Kessler and body stylist Chuck Pelly, kneeling.

288

Developing a fine palate takes a lot of practice, much tasting and analyzing, and learning to attach words to certain characteristics. Believe it or not, it is a lot of work to develop discerning senses. Novices sometimes look askance at the spittoons we use, but you don't want to make yourself tipsy and risk ruining what is supposed to be serious business. Enjoyable, but serious.

At meetings of the Chevaliers in Beverly Hills I always thought of Hernando Courtright's favorite saying about the elegance of the French and Burgundian cultures and how it related to ours in California. "The Philistines are descending among us!"

His metaphor implied that our membership-selection process needed to be carefully monitored to keep the proper social order in the Beverly Hills chapter. I'm afraid such organizations tend to attract sycophants, persons who aren't as interested in the group itself as they are in the prestige of being seen as members of it.

When Hernando died in 1986, his funeral was a large affair at the Good Shepherd church in Beverly Hills. The line of mourners wound around the block up and down Santa Monica Boulevard. I was among the group who dressed in the robes of the Chevaliers du Tastevin, complete with ribbons, to pay our respects to a fine gentleman.

Later, his widow Florence married the 16th Chief Justice of the California Supreme Court, Malcolm Lucas. In 1970 he was the trial judge in the prosecution of Charles Manson in the Sharon Tate murder case.

Bob "Pete" Petersen, who also loved wine, was a Chevalier in our Confrérie in Beverly Hills as well as a member of the Vikings, a drinking club that met at Scandia, his fine restaurant in Hollywood. He asked me about helping him to set up a Hollywood chapter of Chaines des Rotisseurs, an old French group that held food and wine events in different cities. I have to say that Bob and I did launch a great group.

My deep interest in wine has stayed with me for as long as my passion has for auto racing — longer, in fact, for I can date it from the time I was a young child in Italy, where my father became an aficionado of the local wine vintages. Although I no longer belong to many of the wine societies and rarely attend auto races, my enjoyment of both has never diminished.

O enology has been one of my enduring hobbies. The word means the science of viniculture, and it embraces the study of the winemaking process along with the industry beyond the product, the history and the culture, everything that goes into what we aficionados sometimes romantically refer to as The Grape.

Wine has a long, incredible history, an interesting mix of an old body of scientific knowledge blended with creativity. Oenology really is an art form as well as a science.

As it happens, I have a family connection to oenologists. My stepmother Toni's sister was the private secretary to Professor Maynard Amerine, a pioneering researcher in the cultivation, fermentation, and sensory evaluation of wine at the University of California, Davis. He wrote 16 books as a wine bibliographer and collector.

I became a member of the Society of Oenologists when I was accepted as an associate. A truly special privilege.

I am often asked about my favorite wines. I reply that a true aficionado should never have a favorite wine, but be open to tastings of new offerings, and even revisit those tried previously. There is no ultimate best choice, but sometimes a gem or two will have staying power.

While some people believe that appreciating The Grape is just a matter of taste, the truth is that having educated myself on the many layers of winemaking, I find that drinking it is all the more pleasurable when I have an appreciation for the several stages it has gone through just to be in your glass. I find that the more you know about something, the more you will enjoy it.

Learning about the various techniques that make a wine unique, that's particularly interesting to me. From the growing and harvesting of the grapes, the various critically important soils and climates in which they grew, the selection, crushing and pressing, and on through fermentation and aging and bottling, my inner child always wants to know how, why, where and when.

Why does one winemaker bottle his wine right away, while another prefers to leave it in the oak barrels or stainless-steel tanks longer? How does a winemaker choose which grapes to grow in given conditions of climate and soil? Just as I asked myself questions about why certain racecar engine parts perform the way they did when I was building engines, so did I wonder about the six stages of wine production, and seek answers.

I'm entirely serious when I say that the world of wine is deep and complex.

In addition to those cerebral aspects, sharing an interest in wine brings together different people from different walks of life. I enjoy socializing with such interesting individuals.

Of course, the entrepreneur in me got involved, and I speculated in many high-level wines for profit. I once bought a case of 1982 Petrus, gambling on its future worth, and it did become really valuable. Château Petrus at the Jean-François Moueix wine estate in France produces only one wine, a very fine Bordeaux, which is regarded as the most outstanding of its appellation. A single bottle can cost more than $5,500, while a case can go for $66,000. So my investment was somewhat large, but I reassured myself that it would be highly profitable. Until my second wife wanted a motorcycle.

She was an avid Harley Davidson rider, and loved to wear those black leathers and all the glitz. I had bought her a small Harley, the Sportster, but she wanted a big one, a real "HOG!" Needless to say, I sold my case of Petrus wine for a mere $16,000 and bought my wife the Harley of her dreams.

My old auto racing life played a role in that transaction. I'd put the word out to all my contacts that I was looking for a good used HD. Pretty soon Chuck Daigh called and said he met a guy who had one. I went down to his shop and bought it on the spot. Happy wife, happy life.

Being an oenologist has taken me on many travels. Among my favorite trips to other countries were those to Mexico, where at the invitation of the owner and fellow Chevalier Tito Brockmann we visited his family estate at a massive ranch. He also took us to the ranch of a friend who bred fighting bulls for the bullfights that are so much a part of Hispanic cultural history.

Tito's grandfather was a German mining engineer who emigrated to Mexico after the American Civil War. The family owned a large hotel chain in Mexico and were close friends of Hernando Courtright, my longtime friend.

One time at Tito's invitation I put together an outing for 40 people from our Beverly Hills wine society, Chevalier du Tastevin. Each person carried a six-pack of fine French wines, which I carefully selected. We flew into Guadalajara airport and rode in vans to an estate just north of the city, where we were royally entertained by dancers and singers during a luncheon at "Tequila Town." There we learned about the cactus plant that was used to make that potent drink, and how it was made. While touring the tequila factories we were offered plenty of it.

For the grand dinners we had scheduled to pair our own wines from home with carefully selected complementary foods. What memorable meals they were, all set off by our enjoyment of our host's beautiful estate and perfect hospitality. A true delight in gracious living.

My knowledge of oenology became quite well-known, and frequently I was invited to handle the choice of wines for opening nights and parties.

Wine itself has never been a business for me, but rather a life-long hobby — except for a brief while when I joined my friend Warner Henry as a consultant.

Warner wanted to start a wine-distribution business alongside the large coatings company that he owned, which produced materials for preserving roofs and adhering carpeting. That took up the bulk of his time, of course, so he made me president of his wine-distribution business at the beginning. He named it Vintage House. Most of the labels he carried were from vineyards in Napa Valley and Sonoma, plus he imported French and Italian wines.

I began my relationship with Warner by setting up a public relations campaign to develop a good image for the wine company. I had a ton of ideas that were right up my alley due to my background and education. Not only did I figure out how Vintage House could best present itself, I also calculated how Warner could build his wine business with healthy margins and get a good profit from sales.

To me, this always translated into buying the unique product, boutique wines that produced the most net return on investment and specializing in being expert at selling. At the same time Warner and I were concerned to present the company as one of the most prestigious in the wine industry, although we didn't always agree on the path to get there.

I also thought it helpful if Vintage House customers were knowledge-oriented, so I would spend a day in the field with each sales rep and go around to their accounts and talk to them. They were usually surprised and pleased to see one of the top executives of the company making personal calls.

Warner didn't go out himself, but he agreed with my strategy. He was still running the Henry Company, his coatings and adhesives firm. After a while, though, Warner and I parted company to go our separate ways. Two entrepreneurs with different ideas as to strategy. Vintage House later became the Henry Wine Group, consolidated under all of his companies.

In 1987 Warner sent me a letter that I have kept as one of my treasures. It reads in part:

> Raoul's substantial contributions to our organizational structure, the operational systems he has set up, his marketing efforts and programs, and his overall sense of guidance have been of very significant value for us over the past eighteen months. Fortunately, he has agreed to remain as a resource, in a consulting and advisory role, and will be helping us to form a board of directors. I am grateful beyond words for the contribution and the class you have brought to this enterprise. Thank you.

In turn, I applaud Warner Henry and his wife, Carol, for founding the Los Angeles Opera Company. This became another of my hobbies, and I worked very hard at fundraising for them, working on wine auctions and other events. The L.A. Opera is a great success, attracting the best talent in the world. One of their former general directors was the great tenor Placido Domingo, often called "The King of Opera."

Consulting on wines became a natural addition to my business portfolio, putting my experiences and lessons learned from the America's Great Taste venture to good use for others.

As a consultant I gave advice to clients wanting to know the best wines to buy, and my opinions on the most prestigious wineries, domestic and international, with which to do business. I enjoyed pairing food with the appropriate wine for clients.

For large dinners I was very careful to test everything a day or two beforehand. Carroll Shelby knew of my wine expertise and whenever he planned to throw a party he'd call me up and ask me to choose and arrange the delivery of the wines. I'd buy cases wholesale for him and not mark them up, which he appreciated. Thus, I had one foot in wine and the other foot in automotive consulting.

In California, the name of the "vineyard" plays a big part in sales, and there is often too much glitz that goes along with it because of specialized promotion techniques. I'd like to see a broader selection of wines than those that have become popular because of some celebrity owner of the vineyard.

For instance, if you are blind-tasting California chardonnays from Sonoma 2016 vintage, they should all be represented instead of only the best-known favorites. You can educate your palate well this way.

Of course, my passion for fine wines abroad brought me to many wonderful experiences around Europe. One of my friends in Belgium, the nation of my ancestry, was a Catholic monsignor, Charles Depierre. His family had a huge, very historic wine cellar at their home in Bruges. That's quite common in Belgium, by the way. Many dedicated wine enthusiasts there have very nice, beautifully appointed private cellars that I would say surpass the typical ones I've visited in France or the U.S.

The Belgians are big collectors of Burgundy wines in particular. That interest dates back centuries, to the time that the region was a part of France's Dukedom of Burgundy, or Bourgogne in French. In Bruges there is a fabulous canal-side restaurant named Duc du Bourgogne. Whenever we dined there with my friend's family we were treated to some marvelous, very old vintages of Burgundy wine. Along with scrumptious cuisine, of course.

Incidentally, my friend Charles's brother, Albert Depierre, was an amateur historian. He generously took on the task of tracing my Balcaen family's genealogy back through the ages; that's how we know the history that I put into the beginning of this book.

In Germany we enjoyed the Rieslings, from both the Mosel and Rhine areas. Some Americans think Riesling is too sweet and too low in alcohol, as it is grown in a cold climate, but I cordially disagree. Riesling is one of the world's finest grapes.

Grape vines can be over a hundred years old, depending on how they've been nurtured. The theory behind it is that the roots and the tiny root hairs of older vines burrow deep into the soil and thus can absorb more of the trace minerals characteristic of the particular location, which add to the complexity and depth of flavors of vintages from there.

At a tasting, one of the characteristics we look for is minerality. Others include viscosity, opacity, aroma, sediment (if tasting a red wine), and, of course, taste.

Oenologists often ask each other when we meet: How's your palate today? Some people have an extraordinary reputation for having a great palate one day and not the next.

My hobby has proven to be a great way to meet people here at home and abroad although I have noticed that some businessmen, accountants and lawyers join in these to find new clients and not to truly enjoy the sensual pleasure of tasting differences in the various products.

With all my wine traveling I never know when I might find myself in the midst of an adventure. One time when I was visiting Italy the terrorist organization, the Red Brigade, was dominating the country. I was at the Folonari winery in Brescia, famous for its Pinot Grigio and Chianti wines, awaiting the arrival of Signor Folonari, the proprietor.

A well-armored jeep roared up similar to those used by the terrorists. We all stopped talking and stared. Then out stepped the smiling Signor. He drove the special jeep because he was afraid of being kidnapped or shot at. The jeep could easily have been mistaken for a Red Brigade vehicle and thus free from being stopped and captured.

With my time now mine to command, in 1978 I began to devote more of it to charitable institutions and found myself moving up in the social world. One episode was for the California Science and Industry Museum (CSI) located at Coliseum Park in downtown Los Angeles, to help with a proposed exhibit honoring the state's prized wine industry.

I became involved through a gentleman named John Bowles, the president of Rexall Drugs at the time, and Jack Hennessy, a director of Domaine Chandon in Napa. That of course is the US home of Moët & Chandon, the world's largest producer of champagne. Its chairman of the time, Fred Chandon, was another of my like-minded friends who enjoyed socializing and sharing our interest in The Grape. "Fred" was a shortened version of his full name, Count Frédéric Paul Hervé Chandon de Briailles. His son was a racecar driver.

John Bowles introduced me to a group called California Wine Patrons, of which I later became president. Our mission was to raise funds to implement the CSI's plan for a special wine museum.

Accordingly I spearheaded banquets and parties at many venues in the Los Angeles area, including the Science and Industry Museum's own Rose Garden. To draw up plans for exhibits, we commissioned a famous New York industrial designer, Louis Nelson. He had created the Mural Wall for the Korean War Veterans Memorial in Washington, D.C., and was married to Judy Collins, the singer.

These efforts paid off, and thanks to a lot of great donors who were mostly from old Los Angeles society, we did manage to create the wine museum on a lower floor in the Science and Industry Museum.

Unfortunately, the city-owned CSI board was filled with bureaucrats who, as is the wont of such people, never seemed to get anything done. Worse, hardly had we installed the exhibits than the devastating Northridge earthquake struck Southern California. This caused consternation and it was decided to safeguard our exhibits by relocating them to the CSI basement.

To my mind, that was not the greatest venue. A "basement" is not a "cave" (in the French vintner's sense of the word).

Then the bureaucrats in Sacramento, the state capitol, decided that the wine museum was installed in a building that was still unsafe. I wasn't told, but the building sustained enough damage that it had been condemned.

Ignorant of that fact, I held a fundraising banquet at the Beverly Wilshire Hotel as president of the California Wine Patrons. We raised a goodly sum — which wound up going with our museum and all its beautiful displays, lock, stock, and wine barrels, 400 miles north to a new location at Yountville in Napa Valley.

Napa, of course, is acknowledged as the center of California wine production, although many other worthy vintners now thrive in other areas of the state. But it was two Napa Valley vineyards who, in 1976, won top honors against France's best vintners in a blind tasting in Paris. I shall always cherish the memory of learning that Château Montelena's 1973 Chardonnay and the 1973 Cabernet Sauvignon from Stag's Leap Wine Cellars were named best wines in the world. A bottle of each is at the Smithsonian's National Museum of American History.

This result was, naturally, a shocker in the wine world and a major turning point for the American wine industry, which blossomed into vineyards in other states including Oregon, Washington, Virginia, New York and elsewhere.

Thus, in my comparatively short lifetime I have had the pleasure of seeing American vintners rise in stature from unknowns to being recognized as world class.

CHAPTER 26
GIVING BACK

M y life has been about far more than motorsports, naturally, but everything I have achieved has been inspired, shaped and guided by the boyish excitement I felt that night so long ago when my mother inadvertently introduced me to hot rod street racing.

My drive to excel had found its road. Everything I did from then on, all the lessons I learned, all the success I earned, whatever wisdom I may now be able to offer, I owe it all to the loud, colorful, intensely demanding sport of speed.

So now it's only right that I try to pay it forward.

Two of today's top-flight racing organizations with which I am very pleased to be involved are the Motorsports Hall of Fame of America (MHOFA), and the Road Racing Drivers Club (RRDC).

T he Motorsports Hall of Fame is racing's equivalent to Baseball's Hall of Fame in Upstate New York. Originally founded in Novi, Michigan by the late attorney and former city mayor Ron Watson, who directed its growth for many years, MHOFA is now based at NASCAR's Daytona International Speedway on the eastern coast of Florida. Its sparkling new headquarters include a capacious museum literally alongside the famous Super Speedway. More than 100,000 race fans a year visit the multitude of fascinating displays.

MHOFA's new president and CEO is my friend George Levy, whose stellar career in motorsports includes being a race reporter and then editor of *AutoWeek*, a later career in automotive advertising for many prestigious clients, and more recently authoring books on Can-Am and Formula 1 racing.

I am honored to be on the museum's Board of Trustees — my name is listed alphabetically, meaning I'm just under Mario Andretti! My title is Development Ambassador, and in that role I do my best to bring my fundraising skills to the fore to support the organization and its goals and preserve its heritage. One result I'm proud of is the $2 million that I helped bring for constructing the museum's theatre, named for the great publisher Bob "Pete" Peterson who did so much to grow the sport.

MHOFA's main mission is to celebrate and instill the American core values of leadership, creatively, originality, teamwork and the spirit of competition, all of which are so richly embodied in motorsports. As declared on the organization's website, this is "A place to immortalize the immortals."

The MHOFA encompasses the full range of American motorsports, including cars and motorcycles of very kind, off-road vehicles, powerboats and racing airplanes. Each year we induct seven outstanding drivers and other key personalities from all across the broad spectrum of the sport.

Just to name a few of the most famous inductees to date, the long honor roll includes some I had the fortune to work with closely, including Ed Donovan, Ed Pink, Ed Winfield, Jim Hall, Robert Petersen and, of course, Carroll Shelby.

As a Trustee I am always invited to attend the annual award ceremonies. In 2019, its 31st annual event, I was pleased to see my late hero and top craftsman Phil Remington on the induction list along with Augie Duesenberg, Dario Franchitti, Don Schumacher, motorcycle champion Kevin Schwantz, and Tony Stewart. As a plus, everyone's favorite "race queen" Linda Vaughan joined the ranks. For decades Linda's always-vivacious personality and spectacular beauty have graced every great racing event from NHRA to NASCAR to Indy, where she has represented sponsors under the titles of Miss Hurst Shifter and Miss Stock Car Racing. She is a real joy!

The Road Racing Drivers Club is a lively, enthusiastic organization of many of America's and Europe's most successful racing drivers.

One of the most prestigious groups to bring together those who share a passion for the sport, members include not only drivers but also those in the industry, race officials, and motorsports journalists who have made significant contributions to auto racing.

I felt honored and elated when my old boss and longtime friend Jim Hall nominated me for membership several years ago. Since joining as an Associate, I have endeavored to be an active contributor to its mission, drawing from my experience in fundraising as well as my love for the sport.

Founded way back in 1952, initially by prominent American sports car racers, the RRDC focused upon a significantly much-needed single concept at the time: to give drivers a voice, especially when it came to safety.

In those years there still were very few rules concerning safety, both at the tracks and in the shops. Many races were held at the only feasible venues in their areas, if not in ordinary town streets then on borrowed airport runways. Hazards lurked everywhere, with little but stacks of hay bales between drivers and disaster. Spectators were "protected" only by holding them back behind flimsy temporary barriers, such as lengths of unrolled wooden snow fencing.

As for the speeding cars themselves, before the safety movement began one never saw roll-over bars to guard against flips, in a crash an entire tank of high-octane gasoline was free to spray everywhere because fuel bladders were known only in aviation, and if driving suits were worn at all, the material was ordinary cotton soaked in some solution that was supposed to retard fire. No wonder most drivers rebelled against strapping themselves down with lap belts. They'd rather try to jump out of the car before impact, or hope to be flung out before it caught fire.

"Hope is not a strategy," as the wise old saying goes.

As the sport became more popular it was obvious that a professional structure should be established to address not only driver safety, but also driver training, equipment standards, and other issues pertinent to the sport. The result has been a tremendous advance in numerous areas of racing safety, including specially engineered and situated trackside barriers, racecars built to be "survival cells," and cadres of well-trained and equipped safety personnel.

Over time the formerly horrific safety issue has come under very good control, although nobody would declare the work is done, so the emphasis of such organizations as the RRDC is more on recognizing, promoting, and mentoring aspiring American drivers.

Under the strong, savvy, energetic leadership of famed former driver Bobby Rahal, club activities include a scholarship program, motorsports symposiums on subjects such as marketing and business skills, and the annual awarding of trophies in the names of Phil Hill, Bob Akin, and Mark Donohue.

CHAPTER 27
GOLDEN AGE BIRTHDAY

By May 2006 my age had nudged up into my seventh decade. To celebrate the special occasion my wife, Franziska, invited friends and colleagues to send us memories and photos from our past. The response was unbelievable!

Many people related reminiscences of our friendships, of our work together, and the great times we had, many funny, some sad. In addition to personal friends, most who participated, of course, were friends from the Golden Era of Racing.

Jim and Sandy Hall wrote from Midland, Texas, saying they remembered when I blushed, as a teenager, at any mention of the opposite sex! They added, "We always think of you as an outstanding person in our lives. We're so happy for all you have accomplished. If anyone ever deserved success, it's you."

Jim went on to remark that he recalls me as "enthusiastic, diligent, earnest, innovative, and lovable!" He said that he remembered a street-smart California boy with a lot of talent and ability with mechanical equipment. "He was tough, but he also had an artistic flair. He was a self-starter and, for a young man, he could accomplish a lot with very little supervision."

He also mentioned the Lister Chevrolet that I put together for him, as well as the Lotus 11. "They were both beautifully turned out. Nobody had better-looking cars at the track. I was sure proud of them," he wrote.

"We really had fun, a couple of young guys out there competing against more experience and funding."

Gigi Carleton wrote of the time I went to the Pebble Beach Concours d'Elegance with my red Ferrari 308 GTB, where I met up with Gigi and her husband, Bob. He'd never been in a Ferrari, so I invited him for a ride on our way to dinner in Carmel. Despite being a big guy at 6' 2" and around 220 lbs., he got into my low-slung car just fine.

However, it was another matter when it came time to get out. The Ferrari was so close to the pavement that he couldn't get purchase for his long legs. Gigi had followed us along to the restaurant in her own car and wondered why Bob and I were still sitting in the car. The truth was, Bob tried every which way to get himself out. He was shouting with frustration and Gigi was breaking up with laughter. Finally, Bob crawled out on his hands onto the street, inching his way along.

Gigi wrote to me much later, after Bob has passed away, that the incident was a happy memory she will always treasure.

I received dozens of photos depicting happy days in Acapulco, Paris, Monterey, Long Beach, and many racing venues. Bob and Margie Petersen sent me notes from the Petersen Automotive Museum Council. I particularly appreciated this one:

> Dear Sonny,
> You were there at the beginning and thanks for all your hard work in helping to make mine and Margie's dream come true with the Petersen Automotive Museum. We sure have had fun along the way starting long ago with our friend Lance Reventlow and his Scarab racing days. It's been a great ride with wonderful memories. So glad you and I have been there to share it.
> Happy Birthday!

Bob's words just about sum up my feelings, too.

AFTERWORD
A SUMMATION
OF VALUES

Looking back over all the varied careers I have carved out for myself, thinking about the many geniuses I have known in different fields, remembering my global travels, and always mindful of my heritage, I see how everything came together to help build my character.

It includes my experiences and interactions with other human beings, each one unique in his or her own way; blending teamwork with my insistence on independence; giving rein to self-reliance while acknowledging when it was time to delegate; and the protocols learned as part of a military family.

When I reflect on lessons from my father and my own service in the U.S. Army, I think, perhaps subconsciously, that both gave me the discipline to stay the course and the ability to use my own judgement. My time in the Army reinforced my determination to always reach for freedom, and to work towards everything to ensure that I kept that freedom. As a recruit it was all taken away from me and I felt bound and helpless, although I knew it would come to an end. Even so, it's a scary thing to have freedom denied you.

All these things combined to form the person who is Raoul F. Balcaen, III, aka "Sonny."

However, the one, single trait that I believe carried me through the roller-coaster of my life, especially during the Golden Age of Racing, was the pursuit of perseverance. It could even be called my motivation, which was to go beyond the state of the art in all my endeavors.

Perseverance can produce unexpected results. My constant urge to go beyond a goal has frequently led to greater results than I'd ever been able to imagine. And a few downfalls. I always felt, and wanted to feel, that I was building something. I built an enterprise, IECO, that Chuck Daigh expressed a desire to emulate after he left racing. He succeeded, building powerboats and becoming famous for them. I was friends with Chuck until he passed away in 2008.

Another trait I had was my compulsive determination to ensure that everything I did was correct, or as correct as possible. This often led to my decision to go my own way.

Other times, of course, it was necessary to delegate tasks to others. I learned that from publishing pioneer Bob Petersen. Because of the very nature of his enterprises, he delegated all the time, which is the secret to good growth with a large institution such as he created. I encompassed Bob's ideas into my first business venture, IECO but delegating was initially not in the cards as I could only afford part-time employees!

Frankly, I must admit that I often had a hard time delegating in the early days because I am a control freak. It's a typical failing of entrepreneurs. We don't trust anyone to do the job as well as we think we can handle it ourselves. People like me felt a need to control everything. Eventually I managed to master my doubts about associates but it was an effort.

Underlying it all has been my natural curiosity, which somehow complemented a good grounding in scientific methods, of cause and effect. I always wanted to know how the world worked. I still do.

I was never afraid to ask questions. I was especially interested in statistics and probabilities, and these I learned from lectures, scientists, books, and from the times I accompanied my logistician father to his office in Italy. I didn't have a math-oriented brain like my Dad until much later in life; when I became an economist, I discovered that I probably had indeed inherited some of his talent in that respect.

Figuring out how to handle the many ups and the several downs over the years as I struggled to make sense of some parts of my life has given me an enriched understanding of what it takes to stick to our dreams, to insist on excellence and insightful preparation, to be a risk-taker, and to carry on despite the odds. I have always sensed, even as a child, that I would be able to mold my life, that I was my own responsible architect and that the decisions I made would affect my life in the future.

That was one of the reasons why I never got involved in drugs, although there was plenty of opportunity when I was part of our young group of entertainers in West Hollywood and Beverly Hills. Instead, I was motivated by my passion toward racing and other projects I took up, and stoking that passion through fitness of the mind, body, and spirit. I always believed in the ancient Greek philosophy of "A sound mind in a sound body!"

I also believe in giving someone else a chance to present their ideas. We should listen to what motivates their suggestions for improvements and changes. I have often wanted to hear race team owners and drivers give credit for victories to their behind-the-scenes crews of mechanics, designers, and builders who comprise the hundreds of oft-unsung heroes. Too often they remain unheralded when all the fanfare is on the driver. Today the driver is considered as close to a god.

Although I don't consider myself a trailblazer in giving fellow mechanics a voice, I have always made it a point to spread a little praise around when it is warranted. In short, it is not necessarily who is behind the wheel but who is behind the team, the car and the engine.

I shall never enjoy the honor of being awarded the Borg-Warner trophy for winning the Indy 500, nor hold the 24 Hours of Le Mans trophy in my hands, but there were always times when I celebrated our drivers' wins just as much as if I had been behind the wheel myself.

I am a firm believer in the saying "Association does not causation make." I knew the contributions I had made as a gearhead to provide a performance car that took men and women to victory. My "Pirelli Suit," the coverall that mechanics wear at the track, was not the stylish rig covered in wealthy sponsor patches that champion drivers wore, but I was just as proud of the dirt on my hands as the wreath adorning the guy on the podium accepting his accolades.

How do you get into racing, I'm often asked? These days, unfortunately, it takes money to become a successful driver — either money of your own, or that of someone with significant wealth who is willing to take a chance on backing you. In the old days we'd borrow our parent's car, as I did, or beg a friend to let you have a go in his hot rod, or just get to work and build our own car.

Today, it is entirely different. Many Millennials feel privileged and expect to get onto a NASCAR or other race team without putting in the time and the underlying work. They need to do their research and not expect to be picked up without establishing a racing history and reputation on the lower circuits. As for becoming a professional race team member, you need a good background in hands-on mechanical engineering as well as a passion for cars and engines.

I have always wanted to know how the world works. I have finally figured out how some of it works, and how much of society works, but I am still learning.

One entrepreneur who impresses me is billionaire Peter Thiel, a young American who was born in Germany and founded PayPal, Palantir Technologies, and Founders Fund. He is also a philosopher with really good ideas, believing that, in this day and age, we don't have our future defined. He said we don't look to the future at all and therefore we're not focusing on it, so we're not moving in the right direction.

Another saying I live by is "Sycophants are opportunists who pander to power."

Dad always told me that if I needed to talk to someone or go somewhere, just go do it and eventually I'd get an answer. I guess he applied the Five Degrees of Separation theory without realizing it. This is the theory that anyone can be connected to any other person through a chain of acquaintances that has no more than five or six links, or intermediaries. On the other hand, he always followed orders while realizing that within a bureaucracy, which comprised his entire world, you learned how to work out problems with whom you knew and who pulled the strings of power. I grasped that myself early on in my career, taking the trouble to find out who was the boss, observing behavior, and trusting my intuition to argue my point when I believed in it strongly enough. Carroll Shelby once said to me, "Sonny, you know when not to take no for answer."

When I am in a reminiscing or analytic mood, I think back to other moments that shaped me. One, early in my career as a mechanic for Reventlow's Scarab, was after the dyno test described in the Prologue of this book. I didn't recognize back then how important teamwork was, what a combined effort was needed to build racecars. We'd throw pieces into the pie, bench racing, and someone would make a suggestion, have an idea, and someone else would embellish it, and before you knew it, a solution to a problem would surface. It was creativity at its finest, something that I learned to trust as I became more educated, an intellectual, and a serious thinker. I have always got along with people who knew what they're doing or had the potential to learn. But people who haven't a clue and refuse to listen, I consider them to be frauds, especially sycophants. They're best ignored.

At my ripe old age of 85 I can, most of the time, spot a phony thanks to my psychological interest and training. I listen to people talk, observe how they behave, and I look for patterns. I am also a fan of cognitive dissonance, a phrase coined by psychologist Leon Festinger who came up with the theory of holding two or more conflicting beliefs or ideas. It is amazing how many people have this "condition," with the result they don't know whom or what to believe when the beliefs contradict each other. Their uncertainty causes dissonance, a mental discomfort, leading to an alteration in one of the attitudes, beliefs, or behaviors to reduce the discomfort and restore balance. In auto racing a name springs to mind of someone who at times might have experienced this condition — the brilliant British driver, James Hunt. His nickname was Hunt the Shunt because he was often doing unplanned, surprising, and weird things on the track that could have been considered contradictory but they were usually successful. On the other hand, in my opinion, was Fangio and Phil Hill. They were very methodical and practical and would plan everything out in advance.

One racer I admired tremendously because he competed against unimaginable odds was Scottish-born British Formula 1 and sports car driver Archie Scott Brown. Discovered by Brian Lister, whose cars he drove with amazing speed, Scott Brown overcame birth defects that harmed his legs and severely withered his right hand.

At one point, after he won a major sports car race in England, one of his defeated competitors complained to officials about Archie's unformed hand. His license was revoked, but a few months later the president of the British Racing Drivers Club headed up an appeal and the license was restored.

He certainly didn't drive like someone with a handicap. In his short career he scored a total of 71 race victories, 15 during tough international competition. In 1957 he won 13 races with Lister's big Jaguar-powered car, setting four new lap records. In 1958 he was racing for the lead of a furious race around Belgium's ultra-fast Spa circuit when he crashed and died at just 31. Too many died too young back then.

Archie once came around to visit our Scarab shop (as practically everybody in racing seemed to find excuses to do) and I thought he was a very interesting fellow.

In the '60s Carroll Shelby sent me to London to consult with Ford of Britain on his behalf, and I lived in an apartment in Chelsea for several months. Chelsea was in the midst of the Swinging Sixties, as they were called in London, the heydays of the Beatles. King's Road that wound through Chelsea was the center of the action. I'd see John Lennon shopping there years before he was knighted. He wore a three-quarter-length coat designed in Baroque-style fabrics and drove a Rolls-Royce Silver Cloud painted in psychedelic colors.

The UK is awash with historical statues and sites, and one custom I found charming was to attach a "Blue Plaque" to a building if a person of fame over the centuries had lived there. In London alone these total nearly 1000 by now.

Among those I passed while walking to and from my Chelsea flat was a plaque on a building stating that British poet and playwright Oscar Wilde had once made it his abode. Others around the city include "the usual suspects" from the greats of art, music and literature, but several commemorate famous figures in auto racing, such as world champion Graham Hill, and speed record setters Sir Malcolm and Donald Campbell. There's even one noting the former Cooper Car Works.

Up in Cambridge, the university town where Brian Lister ran his racecar factory, on Hills Road a plaque proudly calls attention to Archie Scott Brown's house.

As racers the world over are a friendly bunch, one of the many Brits I knew well was Sir John Whitmore. He very kindly invited me to stay at his manor house in Epping for a couple of weeks. Whitmore's career as a racing driver brought him a British championship in "saloon cars" (sedans to you and me) and a European Touring Car Championship. He also raced with the great Jim Clark at Le Mans and was a member of the Ford GT40 factory team.

After retiring from the cockpit he became the pioneer of what is called "business coaching," and co-founded the phenomenally successful Global Performance Consultants International. Plus, he wrote five books.

I was impressed with one of his many aphorisms about the psychology of doing business: "Self-belief is the lifeblood of performance at work." Fortunately, I came to that realization naturally myself very early in life. It has stood me well.

London is a very cosmopolitan place, but I was often surprised by who I'd bump into. One day I was walking past the entrance to the Marble Arch tube station and up the steps emerged Dr. and Mrs. Furness, the parents of my former girlfriend, Stephanie! What an extraordinary coincidence!

As we talked they asked where I was living, and I told them about being a guest of Sir John Whitmore.

"Ah. An aristocrat with many stories," remarked Dr. Furness.

What were the odds of that meeting? Yet, that has often been the story of my life, people coming into my sphere, others leaving it, and every one of them having a reason, it seems to me, for our paths to cross.

One such was when Alma Hill, Phil Hill's widow and a good friend to my wife and me, introduced us to Charles March, the 11th Duke of Richmond and Gordon. Lord March is best known to the racing community for the marvelous historic car race meetings he puts on at the old Goodwood Motor Circuit on his family's historic estate near Chichester, West Sussex.

After we chatted awhile about racing, the Duke invited us to attend the Goodwood Revival, a very special weekend of classic car racing. The Revival is one of the largest historic motorsports events in the world, and is distinguished by the requirement that all participants dress in period clothing styles, to best present the feeling of the era in which the vintage cars originally raced.

Franziska was stunning in a long skirt. I wore a pretty fancy vest, or waistcoat, as they are called over there. I was delighted to chat with many of my friends, drivers, and exhibitors who were competing, including Sir Stirling Moss in a Ferrari, and Sir Jackie Stewart who led the parade. He was chosen as a tribute to his phenomenal racing career.

My old friend and partner Pete Brock was there too, driving a Corvette Sting Ray, the very model this multi-talented man helped design before his work with Carroll Shelby's Cobra.

All of the cars at the Goodwood Revival were pre-1966 and brought back many memories, as did the World War II uniforms people were wearing. The event also celebrated 100 years of the Royal Air Force and several vintage planes were on display.

Friday was practice and qualifying for grid positions, followed by the Kinrara Trophy for closed-cockpit GT cars pre-1963. Saturday races included the Fordwater and Goodwood Trophies. There were also races for motorcycles and touring cars. The most prestigious car race of the weekend was the Royal Automobile Club Tourist Trophy Celebration on Sunday, which featured classic Aston Martins, Jaguars, and Ferrari automobiles that took part in past TT races.

At the wrap-up ceremonies the prizes and medals were handed out by the Duke. After Franziska and I returned home we received a letter in his own handwriting on the official Goodwood letterhead:

> Dear Mr. and Mrs. Balcaen,
> Thank you very much for your letter of 11th October and for sending the Amanda Ross-Ho artifact. A very interesting and intriguing concept, which has been a conversation piece since arriving in my office. Thank you.
> I am so pleased that you enjoyed your visit to the Revival in September — always nice to hear, and that year we were blessed with such wonderful weather.
> Yours sincerely,
> Charles

I should explain his reference to an "artifact." Ross-Ho is an American artist whose creative mind once produced a giant "DO NOT DISTURB" sign, like those we put on hotel room doors only this one was three feet high. Franziska and I thought it might tickle Charles March, who has a light-hearted sense of humor.

As I look back at how many wonderful young drivers met premature deaths pouring their heart and soul into racing, I think about my days in my dragster and my sports car. It hadn't taken me long to decide to focus on being the best engineer I could be. Sure, I loved to race but there's something about creating and inventing products and watching them make a difference that you can see and hear that turns my wheels. My gift of being able to perceive and figure out how engine parts could be improved and then going ahead and proving the theory gave me as big a thrill as any winning driver. I was ecstatic each time "my" engine or car won a race and had such great success. The satisfaction, the knowledge of one's contributions, often left me grinning ear to ear.

Like many people I have had plenty of disappointments as well as exhilarating moments both in racing, in business, and in my personal life, and I have always had the attitude that I would move forward despite setbacks. In this way I was always rewarded in my mind with the situation that came about as a result of what I decided to do. I never dwelt on my errors to analyze them. I just kept going. And, I feel fulfilled with all of my different occupations and life focus.

Reading occupies quite a lot of my time. Not fiction but books and articles about real-life issues and those that teach me something although I continue to think for myself regardless of an author's opinions. My areas of interest are finance, economics, and politics. I am an avid reader of the *Financial Times* of London and *The Economist*. The latter publication had a terrific impact on my life and still does. I study its articles, many written by the most brilliant and knowledgeable experts, and especially its editor-in-chief, Zanny Minton Beddoes, with whom I am extremely impressed.

Advice? I always tell people that they should never fear failure. It's also important to give credit where it is due. For instance some journalists credit Frank Iacono for the dragster I built. It was my pride and joy and building it was as much of a thrill to me as driving and winning in it. He bought the car from me yet there are plenty of stories that give him credit for building the car as if he created it from scratch. After many years it needed some upgrading but not basic changes in its design or geometry. It is considered the oldest continuous dragster!

Another area where I'd have liked to have gotten a little credit was when I brought a lot of donors to help Bob Petersen finance and build his automotive museum in Los Angeles but the current archives have no record of my contributions. I admit this can be a common practice not only in racing but in many other industries where the right people fail to be given credit for their work. I feel an entrepreneur can best out-perform the corporate executive because they don't have to be part of the hierarchy. People need to be honest instead of bragging about something they didn't create or build. Of course, many brash designs and "raisons d'etre" change over time. But the base concept is only somewhat enhanced.

One person I admire for his astute and realistic clarity is billionaire philanthropist Charlie Munger. He has had an extraordinarily successful career in finance and has been a director of many large conglomerates, including Berkshire Hathaway with Warren Buffet. Not only have I had the honor to personally meet Charlie, I have listened to him and his lectures for many, many years. He has long since become my guru as one of the most brilliant and philosophic investors in the world. His talks on YouTube enthrall me for hours.

Although at this writing Charlie is 98 years old, he still has the tack-sharp mind to draw on all those decades of wisdom, and share it to all who are willing to listen. He is nothing but a man of values, that is basically all he cares about. He says that he doesn't invest, but buys businesses, or pieces of them, when the price is right. In other words, he doesn't look at an investment like a gambler or as a trader, but as an owner. One of his quotes has helped to guide me at times:

"Opportunity comes, but it doesn't come often, so seize it when it does come."

This again is the ability to recognize luck. I knew during most of my life that I had more to offer and I was able to recognize those moments when opportunity raised its heartening head.

I am also great admirer of Dr. Robert Cialdini, Regents' Professor Emeritus of Psychology and Marketing at several universities and the author of *Influence: The Psychology of Persuasion*. I have always taken his six rules to heart:

- Reciprocity: people feel obliged to return favors.
- Authority: people look to experts to show them the way.
- Scarcity: the less available the resources, the more people want it.
- Liking: the more people like others, the more they want to say "yes" to them.
- Consistency: people want to act consistently with their values.
- Social Proof: people look to what others do in order to guide their own behavior.

Finally, from me, a few words of advice from a lengthy career in the Golden Age of Racing, from my work as an entrepreneur, as an oenologist, and as an economist:

"Keep moving forward whatever the endeavor."

Much as I was impassioned with racing, I didn't allow it to define me as a person, as proven by my later activities and as pointed out by my friend and neighbor, top businessman Jim Ellison.

Work with those who know what they are doing; if they don't, then part ways. But if you see they have potential, be there to help. You will be doing them a favor.

Develop knowledge all of your life. Be constantly learning. Look at your management style and that of companies you plan to invest in. Look at their service record. Keep abreast of what is going on in the world. Remain skeptical about the news you read and watch on TV. Be true to yourself, and always be curious!

INDEX